Praise for *Talking on Eggshells*

"Sam Horn is the real deal. Her brilliance has personally impacted and upleveled my life. Her stories and insights are thought-provoking and will intrigue and inspire you."
— **Lisa Nichols**, founder of Motivating the Masses

"Sam Horn's relationship principles can help you be more successful in your career and with clients, coworkers, and even your kids."
— **Jack Canfield**, coauthor of the Chicken Soup for the Soul® series and *The Success Principles*™

"Want happy relationships? Read *Talking on Eggshells*. You'll love Sam Horn's innovative ways to make peace with the people in your life."
— **Ken Honda**, bestselling author of *Happy Money*

"Getting along well with others is an art and a goal that requires a step-by-step strategy. *Talking on Eggshells* shows how to do it."
— **Heidi Zuckerman**, CEO and director of the Orange County Museum of Art and host of the *About Art* podcast

"Sam Horn is a master connector. Whether you're networking, hosting a meeting, or negotiating a deal, Sam's techniques can help you communicate and cooperate in a way that's a win for all involved."
— **Dr. Ivan Misner**, *New York Times* bestselling author and founder of BNI

"A. Must. Read. Now. Practical and effective ways to best approach both difficult situations and difficult people — a special invitation for leaders to invest in your people and build a high-performing team to achieve more, together."

— **Jennifer Treglia**, senior director with Johnson & Johnson

"Having hard conversations is … hard. What do you say? What *shouldn't* you say? How do you avoid being taken advantage of in the heat of the moment? Sam Horn addresses all this and more in her new book, *Talking on Eggshells*. From dealing with sensitive, stressful situations to learning how to handle someone who just doesn't seem to care what you think, you'll discover valuable tools you can use to apply what Sam calls 'Tongue Fu!' I really think it is valuable to read this book so that no matter what happens in the moment, you can come out the other side of relational conflict in a better, more connected place."

— **Joe Polish**, founder of Genius Network

"Sam Horn has been on my *Brave Table* podcast, and her energy and insights resonated with listeners. She is an incredibly inspiring communicator."

— **Dr. Neeta Bhushan**, cofounder of the Global Grit Institute

"Anyone who runs a small business or is in sales or marketing (and aren't we all?) will benefit from this book. Sam Horn's techniques can help make every customer a return customer."

— **John Jantsch**, founder of Duct Tape Marketing

"If we are to create a livable long-term future for humanity, we each need to set an example of integrity and treat others with compassion and respect. *Talking on Eggshells* shows how to do that — even in stressful situations when we're tempted to do otherwise. Sam Horn is a brilliant writer, and her style and narrative will captivate you. You will learn more than you can imagine from reading this amazing book."

— **Lynne Twist**, author of *The Soul of Money* and *Living a Committed Life*, founder and president of the Soul of Money Institute, and cofounder of the Pachamama Alliance

"Ever wish you knew what to say — when you don't know what to say? Sam Horn will show the way."

— **JJ Virgin**, CNS, *New York Times* bestselling author of *The Virgin Diet*

"The course-correct for today's cancel culture."

— **John Mackey**, founder of Whole Foods

"*Talking on Eggshells* is a must-read! No more struggling to figure out what to say (and not say) in sticky, stressful, sensitive situations. This treasure is packed with word-for-word scripts rooted in clarity, compassion, and timeless wisdom."

— **Marie Forleo**, author of the #1 *New York Times* bestseller *Everything Is Figureoutable*

"A master class in how to create receptivity, rapport, and respect at work, at home, online, and in public."

— **Ajit Nawalkha**, cofounder of Evercoach

TALKING

— ON —

EGGSHELLS

Also by Sam Horn

ConZentrate: Get Focused and Pay Attention — When Life Is Filled with Pressures, Distractions, and Multiple Priorities

Got Your Attention?
How to Create Intrigue and Connect with Anyone

Never Be Bullied Again: Prevent Haters, Trolls,
and Toxic People from Poisoning Your Life

Pop! Create the Perfect Pitch, Title, and Tagline for Anything

Someday Is Not a Day in the Week: 10 Hacks to Make
the Rest of Your Life the Best of Your Life

Take the Bully by the Horns: Stop Unethical, Uncooperative,
or Unpleasant People from Running and Ruining Your Life

Tongue Fu! Deflect, Disarm, and Defuse Any Verbal Conflict

Tongue Fu! at School: 30 Ways to Get Along with Teachers,
Principals, Students, and Parents

What's Holding You Back? 30 Days to Having the Courage
and Confidence to Do What You Want,
Meet Whom You Want, and Go Where You Want

TALKING
— ON —
EGGSHELLS

SOFT SKILLS FOR
HARD CONVERSATIONS

SAM HORN

CEO OF THE TONGUE FU! TRAINING INSTITUTE

New World Library
Novato, California

New World Library
14 Pamaron Way
Novato, California 94949

Text design by Tona Pearce Myers

Library of Congress Cataloging-in-Publication data is available.

First printing, June 2023
ISBN 978-1-60868-849-4
Ebook ISBN 978-1-60868-850-0
Printed in Canada on 100% postconsumer-waste recycled paper

New World Library is proud to be a Gold Certified Environmentally Responsible Publisher. Publisher certification awarded by Green Press Initiative.

10   9   8   7   6   5   4   3   2   1

As Henry Adams said, "A teacher affects eternity; he can never tell where his influence stops." I am so grateful to my many teachers for the enduring influence they've had on me and countless others. May this book continue their legacy by teaching people the skills that help us communicate collaboratively, graciously, and proactively.

— CONTENTS —

Part III: Manage Your Expectations, Emotions, and Mindset

What Can I Say and Do If I...

Part IV: What to Do If Someone Doesn't Care What's Fair

What Can I Say and Do If...

— INTRODUCTION —

When I was a little girl, my parents were embroiled in a cold war. Dad was emotionally distant. Mom was emotionally wounded. They didn't yell or fight. Quite the opposite. They were honorable people who taught us kids to do the right thing. They just didn't know what to say to heal years of hurt feelings and missed connections, so they didn't say anything. As you can imagine, that approach "trickled down," and my siblings and I tended to shy away from uncomfortable conversations, too.

Later, I was in a relationship with a bully. I didn't know he was a bully going into it. On paper, he looked like a Renaissance man. When he planned every detail of our dates, I thought, *Cool.* I didn't know it was a warning sign of his need for control that would turn into jealousy and character assassination. I tiptoed around him, as I never knew what would trigger an attack.

Without realizing it at the time, I learned to "talk on eggshells" in two of the major relationships in my life. I know what it feels like. And it doesn't feel good. It's exhausting constantly being on edge because you're trying to say the right thing and worrying you'll say the wrong thing.

Those relationships were filled with regrets. That is why I'm on a mission when it comes to this topic. I believe that if we see a problem and think, *Somebody ought to do something about that!* we should act, because we're as much a somebody as anybody. My thinking was, *There has to be a better way to communicate with people in good times and bad.* A way to:

- have honest conversations instead of ignoring what's happening.
- think on our feet and say what we mean in the moment.
- hold people accountable for treating us with the respect we deserve.

If any of that resonates with you, you're in the right place.

Are You Talking on Eggshells?

"My silences had not protected me.
Your silence will not protect you."
— CIVIL RIGHTS ACTIVIST AUDRE LORDE

Does it feel like you're talking on eggshells these days? Are you:

- dealing with someone who complains, shames, and blames?
- working or living with people who take their frustration out on you?
- at odds with someone who has polar opposite beliefs?
- being targeted by a bully, controller, or manipulator?
- in a relationship with someone who's aloof, distant, or unavailable?
- feeling increased stress, anxiety, or burnout due to divisiveness?

If so, you're not alone.

A 2021 report from management consulting firm McKinsey reveals, "Rudeness is on the rise, incivility is getting worse." The irony is, we're not taught what to say when people are unfair or unkind. We often don't say anything — or say the first thing that comes to mind — which often makes matters worse.

What if there were ways to confidently handle challenging situations in the moment — instead of thinking of the perfect response on the way home? That's not an impossible dream. That's what you're about to learn in this book.

What Is *Tongue Fu!*?

"The world is full of good people. If you can't find one, be one."
— ACTIVIST AND NUN MOTHER TERESA

In case you're curious about this work's backstory, it's based on a communication process I developed more than twenty years ago called *Tongue Fu!*

When the book of that name was originally published, I had an opportunity to go on a media tour. I was flying to my first stop and needed to check a quote to make sure I had it right for an interview. I pulled out a copy of the book from my purse. A woman seated across from me glanced at the cover, *yanked* the book out of my hands, and said, "That looks interesting. Tell me what it's about."

I said, "Well, it's about how to deal with difficult people without becoming one yourself."

She said, "Ohhh, I wish I'd had your book on the plane I was on before this one. I was seated next to the most obnoxious man. I could have used your book. *I would have hit him with it.*"

That is not what *Tongue Fu!* was about, and it's not what this book is about. If someone's being inappropriate, it's not about hitting back, getting mad, or getting even. It's not about putting people in their place. It's about putting *ourselves* in people's places so we can respond with compassion instead of react with contempt. It's about how to be the quality person we want to be — even when other people aren't.

How do we do that?

Recently, I was listening to the always-intriguing Guy Kawasaki podcast *Remarkable People* while on the treadmill. He was interviewing negotiation expert Barry Nalebuff, who said something so profound, I jumped off the treadmill to write it down. He said the goal, in tough situations, is to *fight fire with water.*

That is the purpose of *this book* in four words. If someone picks a fight with us, we don't *fight* back, we *flow* back. If someone is ranting, raging, resenting, or resisting, we keep our cool. We continue to treat them with respect and use positive, proactive responses to create rapport so (most of the time) they're motivated to respond in kind.

That said, please use the material in this book in a safe and logical manner. It is best to seek independent professional counseling and legal advice if you're dealing with a challenging individual to ensure the suggestions you receive are tailored for your specific circumstances.

The Purpose of This Book Is to Teach How to Be a Force for Good

"What you do makes a difference, and you have to decide what kind of difference you're going to make."
— PRIMATOLOGIST AND ANTHROPOLOGIST JANE GOODALL

You're about to learn what to say — and not say — in character-building situations you face almost every day. You're about to learn the social skills we all wish we'd been taught in school along with math, science, and history.

In our increasingly divisive world, someone's got to set an example of decency and diplomacy. Why not us? As the beloved actress Betty White said, "I just made it my business to get along with people, so I can have fun. It's that simple."

Did I mention fun? I also hope you have fun reading this book, that you share it with family members and coworkers, and that it catalyzes meaningful discussions on how to get along better with just about anyone, anytime, anywhere.

How to Get the Most Value from This Book

"Getting along well with other people is still the world's most needed skill. With it ... there is no limit to what a person can do."
— PERSONAL DEVELOPMENT PIONEER EARL NIGHTINGALE

I know you're busy, so I've done my best to make this book real-world relatable. Each chapter of parts II, III, and IV features a question about a sensitive situation you might face and a variety of constructive ways to respond (instead of react) in that situation. I hope you find them valuable.

You're welcome to read the book sequentially. If you've got an urgent issue, though, feel free to check the index, find where that situation is addressed, and then jump ahead to those pages. I've intentionally kept the chapters short so you can dip in and derive value even if you only have a few minutes. Want to go deeper into a topic? Check out the notes section in the back of the book for podcasts, TED talks, support groups, and books referenced throughout this book.

I Hope You'll Use These Insights Daily

*"If you've made a decision and haven't taken action,
you really haven't made a decision."*
— SELF-HELP EXPERT AND AUTHOR TONY ROBBINS

You'll notice each chapter ends with a *Words to Lose* — *Words to Use* reminder card that summarizes what to do, and not do, in that situation. Many people tell me they take pictures of these "CliffsNotes" and keep images of them on their phone so they're in sight, in mind.

In fact, I returned to a medical center as a patient several years after doing a training there. The receptionist saw me walk in, beckoned me over, and pointed to a printed reminder card still taped to her desk. She said, "Sam, I never understood why people were rude to me when I was nice to them. Then I took your workshop and realized I was using what you call *fighting phrases*. No wonder people got upset with me. They thought I was arguing with them."

She pointed at her card. "This has made such a difference. It helps me *catch* and *correct*. If I'm about to tell someone what they *should* do, I stop midsentence and change that *command* into a *courteous request*. I enjoy coming to work now because these *friendly phrases* have made this a much friendlier place."

When you finish the book, don't put it away; keep it close by so you can access it in trying times. You may even want to start your day by turning to a page, any page. With more than two hundred quotes on how to be a good person, chances are you'll discover an insight that is just what you need to recommit to setting an example of grace under pressure.

Ready? Turn the page. Let's go.

PART I

GET COMFORTABLE
WITH CONFLICT

"When things go wrong, don't go with them."
— SINGER ELVIS PRESLEY

Chapter 1

WHY DO WE TALK ON EGGSHELLS?

"Civility isn't an optional value. It is the key to civilization."

— NEWS COMMENTATOR VAN JONES

"I'm conflict-averse. My parents fought all the time when I was a teen. I would hide in my room with my pillow over my ears, silently begging them to stop. I know this still affects me. I head the other direction at the first sign of incivility. Help!"

First, if you identify with this scenario, kudos to you for recognizing this tendency in yourself. You're right. If our childhood years were full of unresolved, angry conflict, or if we've had unpleasant confrontations in the past, we may be reluctant to bring that back into our life now. The thing is, ignoring incivility doesn't make it go away; it makes it worse. In a moment, I'll show how to change a "conflict-averse" label, because it perpetuates an unnecessary and unhealthy fear of conflict.

Let's start by identifying some of the reasons we tiptoe around sensitive situations, even when we're smart, talented adults who otherwise have our act together.

I had an opportunity to ask Parisa Khosravi, former senior vice president in charge of global relations for CNN Worldwide, why she thinks we tend to avoid difficult conversations. She said, "I think we're taught to. One of the reasons our family came to the U.S. from Iran was because it's a country with 'free speech,' yet many of us are self-censoring these days. I remember my uncle telling me, 'There are only two things you can't talk about in the U.S. Never ask someone how much money they make. And never ask people how old they are.'"

She continued, "That was interesting because in Iran, those were points of pride, but here they're 'off-limits.' Now, there is so much off-limits. Religion. Politics. Democracy. Vaccinations.

"Even with family members, I don't 'go there' with them on these topics, because I know if I do, we'll end up not talking to each other."

Does that sound familiar? What's a situation in your life where you may be talking on eggshells or avoiding "off-limits" topics with someone? Ask yourself if any of the following rationales might be causing you to "self-censor" or be reluctant to speak up.

Why Are We Reluctant to Speak Up?

"The mistake many of us make in our crucial conversations is we believe that we have to choose between telling the truth and keeping a friend."
— AUTHOR KERRY PATTERSON

- I don't want to say something I might regret.
- I don't want to make things worse.
- I don't want to hurt someone's feelings.

- I don't want to annoy, offend, or anger.
- I don't want to rock the boat.
- I'm afraid of repercussions.

Do you relate to any of these motives for self-censorship? Do you believe that telling the truth will ruin a relationship? Did you notice that *all* these reasons are fear-based projections of things going *wrong*?

What if, instead of projecting *worst*-case scenarios, we project *best*-case scenarios? What if, instead of assuming that truth telling will result in losing a friend, we understand that *compassionate* truth telling can be the key to *keeping* a friend?

What if we could learn how to clearly and respectfully express how we feel and what we want so people aren't annoyed, offended, or angered? What if, when emotions are running high, we know how to use words and phrases that prevent resentment and produce receptivity? What if our ability to initiate honest conversations results in people thanking us for having the courage to broach something that's been bothering them, too?

If we could do all that (and that's what you're about to learn how to do), then we can stop talking on eggshells and start talking authentically.

Stop Talking on Eggshells, Start Talking Authentically

"Hold the vision, not the circumstances."
— author Mary Morrissey

Let me share an example of what can happen when you choose to hold the vision of what you want, instead of letting circumstances rule the day. Then you'll have a chance to identify your habitual communication style to determine whether it's been helping or hurting you.

A friend's twenty-year-old granddaughter — let's call her Brittany — always thought of herself as shy and conflict-averse, yet she summoned the courage to talk to her boss about something that went wrong at work. Brittany works at a Salvation Army store. She has developmental challenges, and this is her first job in customer service. She prides herself on doing her best to take good care of everyone who comes in the store and was excited when her boss told her she was up for a promotion. The very next day, though, her boss told Brittany she was in danger of losing her job.

Brittany was devastated. Before, she probably would have dissolved in tears, gone home, and spiraled into depression. This time, though, she used an approach her therapist taught her.

She went to her boss's office, asked for five minutes of her time, and said, "*Please help me understand* how I could be up for a promotion yesterday, and you're threatening to fire me today."

The manager explained that a customer had accused Brittany of being incredibly rude and thought she should be reprimanded for her poor service. Brittany remembered the incident the manager was referring to. She explained that the customer wanted to return a used mattress for a refund. Their store policy is not to accept returned mattresses if the protective plastic cover has been opened. Brittany said she had politely explained this, and the customer became irate.

Aahhh. Now that the manager had the full story, she ended up apologizing and thanked Brittany for enforcing their store policy even though it hadn't been easy. As a result, Brittany is still working at the store and got the promotion she'd been promised.

Let's put this in perspective. That promotion wouldn't have happened if Brittany had avoided the hard conversation and not asked the manager why she'd reversed her decision. Those six words, *Could you please help me understand*, turned what could have been an *uncomfortable confrontation* into a *clarifying conversation*.

Let's Lose the Word *Confront*

*"Whoever battles with monsters better see
that it does not turn him into a monster."*
— PHILOSOPHER FRIEDRICH NIETZSCHE

Did you know the word *confront* is defined as "to face, especially in challenge; to oppose an enemy"? No wonder we're reluctant to confront others. Such an aggressive, warlike word makes us feel like we're going into battle. It has a connotation of violence and intimidation.

Look what happens when we change the word *confront* to something less aggressive, like *clarify*. Imagine how it would feel if, instead of *challenging* someone's decision, we asked if they could *please help us understand* the rationale behind their decision.

Asking is the opposite of attacking. It is open-ended and seeks to gather information instead of assuming the other person made an inexcusable decision. It helps us feel more comfortable bringing up issues that are bothering us, because we are not opposing others or challenging them. We are simply, as author Stephen Covey suggested, "seeking to understand."

How about you? Did someone recently make a decision that hurt you or that didn't make any sense? What did you do? Did you stuff down your feelings and walk away, yet you're still simmering about it? Did you tell that person exactly how you felt ... *in your head*?

It may not be too late to approach that person again and say, "Could you please help me understand..." Who knows, something might have gone on behind the scenes that explains or justifies what happened. Discussing this with them could lead to a mutual "aha" that heals the hurt. If nothing else, the other person gets to hear your point of view instead of making a one-sided decision based on limited or inaccurate information.

Perhaps most importantly, when you take responsibility for addressing what happened instead of ignoring your feelings and continuing to feel unfairly treated, you have a chance to correct the situation. Staying silent only perpetuates a situation.

Let's Replace Negative Labels

"Labels are for clothing. Labels are not for people."
— TENNIS PLAYER MARTINA NAVRATILOVA

There are several lessons to be learned from Brittany's example. First, by asking for clarification instead of ignoring the issue, she was able to explain the facts of the situation to her boss, rather than potentially losing her job.

Equally important, she chose to put her "conflict-averse" label in the past. If Brittany told herself she was afraid of conflict, that's how she would continue to be. That label would have defined and defeated her and relegated her to avoiding conflict at all costs.

Now, she sees herself as someone who asks for *clarification*. She models Stanford psychologist Carol Dweck's theory that we either have a *fixed* mindset or a *growth* mindset.

A *fixed* mindset essentially says, "I am who I am, and I can't change that. My talents, intelligence, and abilities are set in stone, and there's nothing I can do about them."

A *growth* mindset says, "I believe I have the agency to evolve and get better. With effort, drive, and perseverance, I can develop my abilities and improve my situation."

Have *you* called yourself conflict-averse? If so, it's time to up-date that label. One way to put labels in the past (and, by the way, this applies to *any* label, whether it's "I'm shy," "I'm lazy," "I'm a procrastinator," "I'm a klutz," or ...) is to say, "*I used to ...*, *and now I ...*" For example:

- "*I used to* be conflict-averse, *and now I* know things only get better if I address them, not avoid them."
- "*I used to* procrastinate, *and now I* act on what's important, so I create results, not regrets."
- "*I used to* get angry when people mistreated me, *and now I* ask for clarification to find out what's behind their decision."
- "*I used to* rehash what people did to me and tell others about it, *and now I* bring it up with the person responsi-ble so we have a chance to have a fresh start."

Another way to put labels in the past and feel more comfort-able speaking up for yourself is to figure out what your habitual communication/conflict style is.

The Four Communication/Conflict Styles

"Peace is not the absence of conflict.
It is the ability to handle conflict by peaceful means."
— U.S. PRESIDENT RONALD REAGAN

Most of us default to a habitual style when things go wrong, which is usually based on what was modeled by others during our child-hood. However, there's an interesting twist. We've either *internal-ized* and followed the example that was set or — and this is a big *or* — we have consciously chosen to do the *opposite* of what was modeled for us.

For example, a young man told me he'd grown up in a verbally abusive family. Instead of using it as an *excuse* to berate others, he used it as an *incentive* to never raise his voice and to speak calmly even during an argument.

I've named the four communication/conflict styles starting with the letter *A* so they're easier to remember. Review them and consider: Which is your normal style? What was modeled in your home while you were growing up? Have you followed what was modeled, or have you chosen to do things differently?

Avoid: We steer clear of a challenging person or situation and try not to think about them or it. We live in a river of denial and do our best not to ponder what's wrong, because we don't want to — or don't know how to — deal with it. We hope it will go away or somehow get better.

Accommodate: We give in and go along to get along. We try to keep the peace so we don't challenge people; we do it their way and acquiesce to their belief or way of thinking. People pleasers who seek approval from others often fall in this category.

Anger: We vent how we feel and take our frustration out on others. Either we get mad in indignation or righteousness or we use anger as a tool of intensity to get other people to back down. We grow loud and intense when things go wrong. We use intensity to win or to get our way.

Assert: We approach the other person and seek a win-win resolution or try to navigate a better path forward for the situation or relationship. We understand that people can't read our mind, and it's up to us to speak up when we're not getting what we want or being treated the way we want.

Which style is your default? Be honest. Is your go-to style supporting your success or sabotaging it? Is it contributing to quality relationships or compromising them?

From now on, be like Brittany. Accept that things don't get better by themselves. Update your label and choose to *address* conflict instead of *avoid* it, *accommodate* it, or get *angered* by it. Rather than seeing conflict as a *confrontation*, see it as asking for *clarification*. By doing this, you evolve your ability to address whatever comes up, instead of playing ostrich, burying your head (and feelings), and wishing it would somehow, magically, improve on its own.

A woman raised her virtual hand during a webinar I was presenting and said, "I saw a TV interview with the playwright Wendy Wasserstein recently, and she said, 'I really worked at becoming more assertive, and now none of my friends will talk to me.' She may have intended that to be tongue-in-cheek witty. The thing is, she expressed my secret fear."

I told the woman, "I'm glad you brought that up. I don't mean to infer that assertiveness happens overnight and works perfectly every time. Being comfortable with conflict is a mindset and a skill; it takes time to develop. The good news is, there are specific ways to be *gracious* instead of *grating* when you assert yourself, so people are more receptive to what you say."

In the next chapter, I'll reveal the six steps to ISA — Interpersonal Situational Awareness — that I shared with her. Developing these abilities can help you "read the room" so you can anticipate and respond to what's happening — appropriately, confidently, and collaboratively.

Reminder Card of What to Do
When Talking on Eggshells

Imagine you have a colleague whose norm is to be confrontational. He grew up in a culture where getting intense and loud is how you win your point and get your way. Interacting with him makes you want to run away. What do you do instead?

Words to Lose	Words to Use
Avoid, accommodate, anger *"I'm not going to say anything lest I set him off."*	**Assert** *"Please lower your voice and speak to me with respect."*
Be afraid of confrontation *"I'll just give in so he stops shouting at me."*	**Ask for clarification** *"Can you please help me understand why you made that decision?"*
Project worst-case scenario *"If I say anything, he'll get really angry, and then I'll be sorry."*	**Project best-case scenario** *"This is an opportunity to set the record straight, and I welcome it."*
Accept label of "conflict-averse" *"This is why I hate arguing and avoid it at all costs."*	**Adopt label of "conflict-comfortable"** *"This is important to me. I will speak up for what I feel and want."*

Chapter 2

DEVELOP INTERPERSONAL SITUATIONAL AWARENESS

"No man (or woman) in a hurry is quite civilized."

— STATESMAN WILL DURANT

"Many of our new hires are smart and talented, yet some are a bit clueless when it comes to social skills. How can we teach them to get along well with others?"

This question was posed by an HR director of a Fortune 500 company. She didn't stop there, continuing: "You've heard the saying 'You're not a prophet in your own land'? We try to teach people skills in our customer service and leadership development programs; the training doesn't always 'stick.' Is it too late to motivate employees to be more caring and considerate in their communications?"

I told her, "It's only too late if you don't start now."

"Is there a secret sauce to social skills?"

"Great question. I think *situational awareness* is at the heart of *social skills*."

"What do you mean?"

I replied, "Let me tell a story about myself to show what it means. I was in a checkout line at the store yesterday. An older woman in front of me was chatting with the cashier while slowly taking items out of her cart and placing them one by one on the conveyor belt.

"I was in a hurry and was impatient with her for taking so long. I'm embarrassed to admit, my thoughts toward her were not civil. Thankfully, a few mindfulness tips from my *Talking on Eggshells* course kicked in. I stepped outside my self-absorption and realized I was getting uptight with someone for taking an extra couple of minutes. What a complete lack of empathy and compassion.

"Instead of standing behind her doing a slow burn, I put things in perspective and offered to help out. Once I stopped focusing solely on my agenda, I realized this lady was someone's grandmother. Who knows, she could've been moving slowly because she had arthritis or wasn't feeling well. An excursion to the store might be her only opportunity that week for socializing.

"Or, she could have been a master teacher there to remind me that hurrying and impatience are a misuse of our mind and time."

Author Vern McLellan said, "Ambition is a get-ahead-ache." I had been so caught up in my rush to get ahead, I hadn't noticed what a kind person she was. And social skills are all about *noticing*.

Why Situational Awareness Is at the Heart of Social Skills

*"There is little we can change until we notice
how failing to notice shapes our thoughts and deeds."*
— EMOTIONAL INTELLIGENCE PIONEER DANIEL GOLEMAN

A failure to notice what's happening around us doesn't just shape our thoughts and deeds; it relegates us to showing up in a constant state of selfishness. What is selfishness but focusing solely on what *we* want, need, think, and feel?

When we don't pay attention to our surroundings, when we say and do whatever we want without considering our impact on others, we embody what is called … *cluelessness.*

I will always be grateful to Glenda, owner of our local preschool, for delivering a master class in socialization. I went to pick up my sons Tom and Andrew one afternoon and was chatting with Glenda as the kids played a boisterous game of pretend baseball.

A potential new client had brought her four-year-old to check out the premises. He marched over to the group, grabbed the plastic bat out of my son's hands, and started whacking him with it. Glenda took the bat out of his hands, said a firm *"No!"* and placed the bat in an out-of-reach toy chest. The boy promptly threw himself on the floor and started wailing and kicking in a major tantrum.

The mom pleaded, "Please give him the bat back! He's too young to know what he did was wrong."

Glenda smiled serenely and said, *"He knows now."*

Situational Awareness Is about Doing What's Right

"Being considerate of others will
take your children further in life than any college degree."
— SOCIAL ACTIVIST MARIAN WRIGHT EDELMAN

Ideally, growing up, we had some Glendas in our life who "socialized" us and taught us to behave responsibly in public. Hopefully, we had caring adults (and siblings?) who modeled how to be considerate and *take turns*, instead of thinking only of what *we* want.

Who served that role for you? Who taught you to transcend

your own needs, notice what's going on around you, and act in thoughtful, informed ways that serve the greater good?

That's the goal of socialization — to learn to behave appropriately when dealing with others. This ability to act in conscious and conscientious ways — what I call *Interpersonal Situational Awareness* — is a deal maker or deal breaker for our personal and professional success. ISA is the beating heart of soft skills, and the key to handling hard conversations (*any* conversation) with diplomacy, maturity, and accountability.

The rest of the book provides practical suggestions for how you can use ISA in just about any situation. Let's kick-start that process by sharing six ways you can practice ISA starting... right *now*. As you read these ISA practices, please be thinking about whether they are already part of who you are and how you show up. If you'll be walking into a challenging situation soon (live or virtually), ask yourself how you can use these six practices to increase the likelihood that it goes well.

Six Ways to Practice ISA...Starting *Now*

"Initiative is doing the right thing without being told."
— WRITER VICTOR HUGO

1. **Set the precedent.** Thank you, Victor Hugo, for introducing a key ingredient of ISA. *Initiative.* Our goal is to take the *initiative* to be a considerate person, which means showing care and concern for the rights and feelings of others. Don't wait for people to model this or for someone to ask you to do this. Go first. Be thoughtful — instead of thoughtless — because everyone wins when people practice ISA in service of the greater good.

2. **Project potential regrets.** Imagine someone does something inappropriate. *Before* saying what's on the tip of your tongue, take a few seconds to ask yourself, *Will I be sorry I said this?* If so, practice *Tongue Glue!* Imagining how you'll feel about what you said or did in the heat of the moment is the key to being *mindful* instead of *myopic*.

3. **Replace *my* agenda with *our* agenda.** Emotional compulsion (urgently feeling you *must* say something *right now*) is often driven by *your* priorities, not the group's. Instead of succumbing to impulsivity, ask, *What are their priorities? Shall I put a sock in it and hear what other people think instead of vehemently expressing what I think? Instead of going to the mat over an issue and alienating everyone, is it wiser to onboard other perspectives and explore how we can work together to create a win-win solution?* You'll discover how to do this in chapter 19.

4. **Surface the subtext.** *What isn't being said?* There's a West African saying, "For news of the heart, ask the face." Skilled ISA practitioners know that body language tells the *real* story. Is someone agreeing, yet their clenched jaw shows they're resistant? Are they saying they understand and have no questions, but they're frowning and slouched in their chair with their arms tightly crossed? Unvoiced dissent derails success. Gently probe with Socratic questions until the truth, the whole truth, and nothing but the truth comes out. You'll learn how to do this in chapter 10.

5. **Honor your intuition.** Persian poet Rumi said, "There is a voice that doesn't use words. Listen." Security consultant for high-profile individuals Gavin de Becker debriefs clients who have been assaulted and asks, "Did you have any warning?" Guess what they all say? "I *knew*

something was wrong." Yet their intellect overruled their instincts. They looked around and thought, *I'm in an armored car. No one's around. I'm being silly.* If something feels off, it probably is. Honor the instincts that alert you to dissonance. Your sixth sense has your best interests at heart and warns you of potential physical or psychological danger. You'll learn how to act in alignment with your instincts in chapter 25.

6. **Try to light a spark, not make a mark.** Making a mark is about proving how smart, talented, and skilled you are. That's ego. Lighting a spark is about showcasing and leveraging the smarts, talents, and skills of others to create a "rising tide" community. That's grace. Novelist Toni Morrison said, "Make a difference about something other than yourself." Think of ISA as a way to be a servant leader who uplevels every situation you're in.

An Example of Why It's So Important to Practice Mindful ISA

"In influencing others, example is not the main thing.
It's the only thing."
— PHYSICIAN AND HUMANITARIAN ALBERT SCHWEITZER

In every workshop, I ask participants to share a time they *did* practice mindful ISA and a time they *didn't.* These incredible stories provide all the evidence people need in order to understand the pivotal role mindful ISA plays in producing wanted or unwanted results.

A divorced dad told our group, "I picked my kids up from their mom's house yesterday and was in a rush to get home. Traffic was lined up, and I waited for what seemed like forever to cut across the highway to go the other direction. I finally got fed up, wheeled our van across the intersection, and just missed getting hit by a semitruck. The kids screamed, 'Dad, you almost killed us!'

"I was so stressed-out (and scared), I yelled back at them. They both started crying, and I felt like a jerk. I wasn't thinking about their safety or how much I loved them. I wasn't thinking about anything except how frustrated I was.

"From now on, I will drive responsibly. I don't care how 'late' we are; I will pay attention to what's around us and keep my kids' safety, well-being, and trust top of mind. And even if I'm stressed, I won't yell at them, because I know that makes them scared of me and that's the last thing I want."

This father's story was a metaphor waiting to happen. ISA is a form of "defensive driving" and "driving responsibly" when dealing with others. As he pointed out, it's keeping who and what is important front and center and acting in alignment with those goals and values, even in — especially in — stressful times.

Your Career Success Is Directly Proportional to Your ISA

"There are two types of people — those who walk into a room and say, 'Here I am' and those who walk into a room and say, 'Ah, there you are.'"
— ADVICE COLUMNIST ANN LANDERS

In case you're wondering how ISA affects your career, I'll tell another story about myself. My first major job out of college was running tennis champion Rod Laver's Hilton Head Island pro shop and representing his facility at our resort board meetings.

I was young, eager, brimming with ideas. In retrospect, a bit *too* full of ideas. After several meetings, one of the board members pulled me aside and gently suggested I *sit on my hands*. I wasn't familiar with the expression and asked what he meant.

He said, "Sam, you're not honoring the seniority in the room. All these executives have more experience than you. It would be wise to do more listening than talking until you earn your wings."

Yikes. I had been so excited about these business development opportunities that I hadn't asked myself if my ideas were welcome and whether this was the right time and place to introduce them. I hadn't been sensitive to the group dynamics and was taking up a disproportionate amount of meeting time.

I'll always be grateful to Dale Schuette, GM of the Palmetto Dunes Hyatt, for his diplomatic intervention that taught me to stop being a "Here I am" person and more of a "There you are" person.

How about you? Do you ever find yourself enthusiastically sharing ideas without considering whether they're appropriate or welcome? Do *you* sometimes take up a disproportionate amount of meeting time? Might it be smarter to "sit on your hands," listen, and speak up only when you're sure your comments will contribute to the balanced flow of conversation, instead of interrupt or disrupt it?

ISA Is a Way to Think Upstream

"We've got to stop just pulling people out of the river.
We need to go upstream and find out why they're falling in."
— ARCHBISHOP DESMOND TUTU

Kudos to Desmond Tutu for that wonderful explanation of what ISA is — at its best. He's right. Interpersonal Situational Awareness is not just seeing what's in front of us and responding to that. It's "going upriver" and determining what might be causing a problem so we can fix it at its source.

Jennifer Treglia, senior director with Johnson & Johnson, told me that this definition of ISA really resonated with her, as it is the number one job skill she tries to pass along to mentees. "To me, ISA is being entrepreneurial. It means *going above and beyond the obvious*. Instead of just answering a question, it's getting creative and introducing something that exceeds expectations. It's asking, *How can I be* additive *and pleasantly surprise people instead of just 'doing my job'?*"

She added, "I guarantee, doing this is a competitive edge for anyone's career. Everyone you deal with will admire this about you and become your champion, because this high-level ISA is so rare and welcome. If you get good at delivering *nuance*, everyone will want you on their team."

Well said. Do you make it a point to be additive? Do you go above and beyond to pleasantly surprise people? Are you sensitive to nuance, adapting what you say and do accordingly?

If so, good for you. If ... not so much, rest assured — the coming chapters show a variety of ways to exercise ISA in just about every situation imaginable.

In case you want another example of someone who demonstrated excellent ISA, consider Edie, an office manager who was long overdue for a raise. She told me her contractor boss was notoriously "budget conscious," so she did her homework. She documented the money she had made and saved for the company by reducing costs, streamlining procedures, and systemizing their client records. She even collected testimonials from VIP clients, who all vouched for the fact that she was a bottom-line asset.

Her boss agreed to meet with her Friday afternoon. As soon as she walked in his office, though, she immediately noticed how flustered he was. He plopped down in his chair. "I just found out the water pipes burst on one of our properties and flooded the entire building. It's a real mess."

Edie realized this was not a good time to ask for a raise. It didn't matter whether she deserved the raise; what mattered was her boss was not in a mood to grant it.

She said, "Want to reschedule this for next week so you can take care of that property?" He was enormously relieved and thanked her for her thoughtfulness.

That's ISA in action. Edie ended up getting her well-deserved raise because she had the *presence of mind* to read the writing on the wall and reschedule to a time her boss was more likely to say yes.

Can you think of a time you set aside your agenda when you realized it wouldn't carry the day? A time when, even though what you were requesting or recommending was justified, you anticipated it would get rejected? Anticipating consequences and adapting your agenda accordingly is yet another form of ISA.

ISA Quiz

As mentioned, I ask program participants to share times they did and didn't practice ISA. I also distribute a quiz to kick-start their reflection on the many impacts ISA has had on their life. It can be enlightening to identify who's influenced you (for better or for worse) and gain clarity on how ISA has affected your personal and professional success. You might want to copy this quiz and take it and a friend to lunch so you can gain additional insight from each other's answers.

1. *What* does Interpersonal Situational Awareness mean to you? How would you define it?
2. *Who* do you know who's good at ISA? Describe a time you witnessed their ISA in action.
3. *Who* is someone who is *not* good at ISA? Describe a time you witnessed their lack of ISA.
4. *When* is a time you demonstrated good ISA — a time

you were attentive to what was happening and acted in appropriate, positive, proactive, visionary, strategic ways?

5. *When* is a time you did *not* demonstrate thoughtful ISA — a time you didn't read the room or surface the subtext, and you said or did something you regretted?

6. *Why* is it important to practice mindful ISA? How does it benefit you and those around you?

7. *Why* don't we sometimes practice considerate ISA? Are we self-absorbed? Busy? Distracted? Convinced we're right? Laser-focused on our agenda? Or do we simply not care?

8. *What* is your best tip for how to practice mindful ISA? What advice would you give on how we can improve our ability to think upstream and read and lead a room?

This quiz is useful for more than self-reflection. A lawyer asked for permission to pose these questions when hiring. She said, "Sam, job candidates always say they have good social skills, but that doesn't mean it's true. These questions help me determine whether it's just a buzzword they've been told to include on their résumé or a meaningful part of who they are and how they show up."

Anyone Can Learn Social Skills at Any Age...and It's Worth It

"The more people you know, who know you in a positive way, the more successful you will be at anything you attempt."
— SELF-DEVELOPMENT AUTHOR BRIAN TRACY

Let's adapt what Brian Tracy said. The more people who know you in a good way because you practice mindful ISA, the more successful you will be in just about anything you do.

The HR director who asked the question at the beginning of

this chapter said, "I'm glad it's not too late for people to learn ISA and they can get better at social skills at any age. I have some executives who are, shall we say, set in their ways. They have a *This is just the way I am — you can't teach an old dog new tricks* mindset. I try to tell them, no matter how senior you are or how technically skilled you are, if you don't have good soft skills, you're hitting your head on the ceiling of your career."

She's right. As former Chrysler CEO Lee Iacocca said, "If you can't get along with people, you don't belong in this business because that's all we have around here." Regardless of your age and stage, it's worth learning how to get along better with people, because it makes your life — and the lives of people you care about — better.

Our next chapter takes ISA to another level by showing exactly what to say — and not say — when things go wrong.

Reminder Card for Developing Interpersonal Situational Awareness

Imagine you're a teacher. You deal with the often-conflicting priorities of the principal, parents, school board, and staff, all while having eyes in the back of your head trying to educate your energetic students. A parent has complained that her child is being teased.

Words to Lose	Words to Use
Focus on selfish considerations *"Do you know I don't even have a teacher assistant this year?"*	**Serve the greater good** *"I'm glad you told me about this so we can resolve it."*
Ignore the room *"I didn't even notice that Rob was bothering Aaron."*	**Read and lead the room** *"I'm going to separate them so they're no longer sitting next to each other."*
Be myopic *"It's unrealistic to think I can watch them every minute."*	**Be mindful** *"Aaron is a sensitive child and deserves to feel safe in class."*
Follow *my* agenda *"I'll do the best I can, but you need to remember I have twenty-five kids."*	**Craft *our* agenda** *"What are your suggestions on how to encourage Aaron to stand up for himself?"*
Ignore intuition *"Something seemed off with him, but he said he was fine."*	**Act on intuition** *"I'm going to talk with Rob about his behavior and hold him accountable."*
Think only of the moment *"I'm glad we had this talk."*	**Think upstream** *"I'm going to show a film in class about teasing so we get ahead of this."*

Chapter 3

SET AN EXAMPLE OF PROACTIVE GRACE

"Be soft. Do not let the world make you hard. Do not let pain make you hate. Do not let the bitterness steal your sweetness. Take pride that even though the rest of the world may disagree, you still believe it to be a beautiful place."

— WRITER AND NEW MEDIA ARTIST IAIN THOMAS

"I get discouraged watching the news, with example after example of man's inhumanity to man. It seems these days rudeness is all the rage, so to speak. Any suggestions as to why I should treat people with respect when they're not treating me with respect?"

Does it sometimes feel like the world is trying to make you hard or hateful? Are you wondering what to do if people take their frustration out on you and you're tempted to take your frustration out on them? Are you asking yourself why you should be diplomatic when other people aren't?

You may have heard this parable (attributed to the minister Billy Graham) about an elder teaching his grandson how to win the battle of emotions.

A grandfather was teaching his grandson about life. He told his grandson:

"A fight is going on inside me. It is a terrible fight between two wolves. One is evil — anger, envy, ego. The other is good — love, kindness, compassion. The same fight is going on inside every person."

The boy asked, "Which wolf will win?"

The grandfather answered, "The one you feed."

In tense situations, it can be tempting to feed the wolf of anger and impatience. It is in our best interests to choose instead to feed the wolf of empathy and compassion.

In the short term and in the long run, how we treat people is our legacy. We have a daily responsibility to stay conscious of that and to show up in ways we can be proud of.

You may be thinking, *I agree with that, although sometimes it's easier said than done.* You're right, which is why I'm sharing the following example of what can happen when we choose to be compassionate, even if it sometimes seems as if the people we're dealing with don't deserve it.

My eighty-four-year-old aunt Kay drives to her local hospital five days a week to volunteer. During the most difficult days of the Covid pandemic, she worked at the information desk. When I asked what it was like working under those stressful conditions, she said, "It took everything in me to stay calm and compassionate and try to be helpful, no matter how people were treating me. Our policy was either 'No visitors' or 'One visitor per day' for patients who were not quarantined. As you can imagine, family members were distraught that they couldn't be with their loved one. Some took their anger out on me, as I was the first point of contact."

"What do you do if someone yells at you?"

Kay said, "That just happened yesterday. A woman came rushing up to my desk, frantically held her phone up, and said,

'My daughter just texted me! She's been in an accident, and she's here in the ER! I've got to see her right away!'

"I told her, 'Let me contact them to see what's happening.' I called the ER. The on-duty nurse told me someone was already with the daughter, so she couldn't allow the mom in. When I told the mother that, she lost it and started sobbing and screaming at me all at the same time.

"I don't like being screamed at, but I put myself in her place and thought, *How would I feel if my daughter was in the ER, and I couldn't get in to see her?*

"That gave me the incentive to get creative. Instead of telling her, 'It's our policy; *there's nothing I can do,*' I said, '*Let me see if there's something I can do.*' I called the ER back and asked, 'Who is with the daughter?' The nurse checked and found out it was the Uber driver who had brought the young woman in. I asked to speak to him, explained the situation, and thanked him for helping out. He left, and the mom was able to be with her daughter."

What a powerful example of proactive grace. Instead of just shrugging her shoulders and saying, "Don't get mad at me. It's not my fault," Aunt Kay got creative to see if there was some way she could help. Instead of taking umbrage at being screamed at, she had the empathy to see past that behavior and empathize with the person's experience.

The Power of Proactive Grace

"Being negative only makes a difficult journey more difficult. You may be given a cactus, but you don't have to sit on it."
— MINISTER JOYCE MEYER

When life gives us a cactus, as it did in that situation with Aunt Kay, we have a choice. We can react, or we can get resourceful and turn things around for everyone's benefit.

A premise of this book is that choosing to "get off the cactus" and get resourceful is a plus for all of us. We can't always choose how people treat us; we *can* choose how we treat them. When we choose to be kind, most people choose to respond in *kind*. If for some reason they don't, at least we did our half. At the end of each day and at the end of our life, we'll be able to look back and know we were *additive*. That's what we can control, and it matters.

Let me define what I mean by the term *proactive grace*, starting by contrasting it with the word *reactive*.

Reactive means "responding with hostility, opposition, or a contrary course of action, often as a result of stress or emotional upset."

Proactive means "creating or controlling a situation by *causing* something to happen."

In other words, *reactive* is when we say or do the first thing that occurs to us — without considering the consequences. *Proactive* is having the ISA to anticipate consequences *before* we act and opting to behave in ways that make things better, not worse.

Grace, to me, means, "going out of our way to set an example of integrity, empathy, and goodwill — even if people don't appreciate it or return the favor."

Please note the phrases *going out of our way* and *even if people don't appreciate it or return the favor*.

Grace is not based on reciprocity. It is not something we do only when it is noticed and returned. That would make grace conditional. Our goal is to extend grace unconditionally. It is a life choice. People like Mother Teresa, Nelson Mandela, Desmond Tutu, Malala Yousafzai, and the Dalai Lama are not the only ones who can embody and gift grace. Each of us can strive to live like them and like Gandhi, who said, "My life is my message."

What do you want to be known for? Being a bridge builder? A peacemaker? An example of integrity? A model of proactive grace? Clarifying that, right now, can serve as a saving grace and an emotional North Star that carries you through the most trying times.

Proactive Grace Can Be a Saving Grace

"In a world where you can be anything, be kind."
— JOURNALIST CONNIE SCHULTZ

Here are a couple of phrases that can ground you in proactive grace if you're in the middle of a patience-testing situation. The first is, *How would I feel?*

"*How would I feel* if this was happening to me? *How would I feel* if I was in this person's shoes? *How would I feel* if I was on the receiving end of what just happened?"

Remember what Aunt Kay did when that mom was screaming at her? She asked herself, *How would I feel if my daughter was in the ER, and I couldn't get in to see her?* Those four words transformed her impatience into empathy and motivated her to *want* to help.

Another phrase Aunt Kay uses is *I'm trying to help, if you'll let me.* This often brings people who have lost control to their "senses." They realize that you are not the enemy — you are their ally — and (hopefully) they stop taking their stress out on you.

Compassion Is at the Heart of Proactive Grace

"Guard well within yourself that treasure, kindness."
— NOVELIST GEORGE SAND

Another way to fast-forward through frustration and return to kindness is to take a moment to ask, *How will what I'm about to say make* them *feel?*

I'm speaking about this from experience. I'm on my book deadline right now, and time is precious. A client had referred a colleague, who wanted to give a TEDx talk, to me. I agreed to a thirty-minute free "strategy call" as a favor. The time for our appointment came and went. She finally called twenty minutes late, discombobulated and full of excuses. She claimed she "couldn't find" my number (even though it was on the confirmation email) and launched into an all-over-the-map monologue about her recent weeks.

Full confession. I usually have the "patience of Job" (as the biblical saying goes). Not this time. I was frustrated that she had forgotten our call, irritated that she didn't seem to appreciate the fact that I was giving her free consulting, and a bit annoyed that she kept talking about her problems (a recent divorce, health challenge) without asking any questions. Then I realized it was time to return to integrity and practice what I teach.

Annoyance often comes from ego. Annoyance is based on *Don't you understand how busy I am? Don't you realize I've taken time out of my day for you?* Frustration is a clear sign we're focusing solely on how *we* feel, not on how *they* feel.

If I had continued to focus only on how I felt, things would not have ended well. Instead, I observed, "Sounds like you're going through some challenging times."

She burst into tears and said, "I am! Thank you so much for understanding!"

I realized I was hearing a woman who was hurting. A woman whose unexpected divorce was hijacking her productivity and peace of mind. Seeing things from her point of view inspired me to wonder, *How can I uplift her? How can I say something to move her forward and make her feel a bit better about herself and her life?*

I said, "We have a few minutes left. Would you like some practical tips about how to clarify your message and build your platform to position yourself for a TEDx talk?"

She gave a heartfelt sigh. "That would mean so much to me."

So, I shared some tips. At the end of our call, she said, "You'll never know how much your kindness means to me."

A Five-Second "Turn Contempt into Compassion" Switch

"Contempt is the weapon of the weak and a defense against one's despised and unwanted feelings."
— PSYCHOLOGIST AND AUTHOR ALICE MILLER

I admit that when I started that strategy call, I hadn't been feeling kind; I had been feeling, well ... let's call it what it was ... *contempt*.

Contempt is a strong word. Dictionary website Oxford Languages defines it as "the feeling that a person or a thing is beneath consideration, worthless, or deserving scorn." Interestingly, it also defines contempt as "disregard for something that should be taken into account."

Impatience is low-grade contempt. When we are impatient, we are disregarding something about a person that deserves to be taken into consideration. I had not taken into account the fact that this woman was going through a particularly rough time. This was probably not how she normally rolled. Recognizing the distress beneath her words helped me connect with our shared human condition and shift from contempt to compassion.

We can do this by asking, *What could this person be going through that could be causing them to act this way?* That simple question can help us see that this might be circumstantial, an exception to their norm. What they're doing might be a result of angst, grief, or personal trauma. When we see beyond the behavior to what might be causing it, we get where someone's coming from. *That* is when we begin to care for (instead of feel contempt for) our fellow/sister human beings. That's when we're motivated to treat them with the decency they deserve.

Who Do You Feel Contempt For?

"Contempt, simply put, says, 'I'm better than you.
And you are lesser than me.'"
— PSYCHOLOGIST JOHN GOTTMAN

John Gottman has found, after decades of pioneering research, that *contempt* is the most important sign that a relationship is in trouble. In an interview with Anderson Cooper on CNN, he said, "It's virtually impossible to resolve a problem if someone is getting the message that you're disgusted with them and condescending and acting as their superior."

On top of that, Gottman's research found that couples who are contemptuous of each other are more likely to suffer from infectious illness (colds, flu, and so on) than couples who are not contemptuous. He said, "Contempt is the most poisonous of all relationship killers. We cannot emphasize that enough. Contempt destroys psychological, emotional, and physical health."

Is there someone in your life you're feeling contempt for? You've heard the phrase "Familiarity breeds contempt"? Could it be you've been around this person for a long time, you've formed a negative judgment of them, and you're no longer seeing things from their point of view? That is a prescription for antipathy. Here are six questions that have the power to transform contempt into compassion:

1. *What could be responsible for them behaving this way?*
2. *Am I somehow feeling I'm "better" than* — or superior to — this person?

3. *How would I feel if* I were them?
4. *How will I make them feel* if I continue treating them with contempt?
5. *How can I give myself peace of mind* by treating them with proactive grace?
6. *How can I treat them more compassionately* so we're on the same side instead of facing off?

Ask, "What Could Be Responsible for Them Acting This Way?" to Turn Antipathy into Empathy

"Treat people as if they were what they ought to be,
and you help them become what they're capable of being."
— WRITER JOHANN WOLFGANG VON GOETHE

Another example of how to turn impatience into empathy comes from a man whose mother had been in a rest home for three years. He used to dread driving out to see her every Saturday because all she ever did was complain. She complained about her roommate, that no one ever came to see her, and about her aches and pains.

He explained how he overcame his feelings of dread. "I asked myself, *How would I feel if I were in bed eighteen hours a day, seven days a week? How would I feel if the person in the next bed played the TV so loud that I could hardly hear myself think? How would I feel if every morning I hurt, and I couldn't see a day when that wasn't going to be the case?*

"Those four words, *How would I feel*, got me right out of my frustration. When I considered what my mom's days are like, and when I stopped to think of all she's done for me, I realized it's the least I can do to spend time with her every Saturday and be more supportive.

"Then I asked myself, *Why does Mom complain all the time?*

I realized *she didn't have anything else to talk about.* So I took a photo album with me the next time I visited. One photo of a crazy uncle had us laughing so hard we couldn't stop. One picture of our mountain cabin brought back a whole hour of memories. Now, every Saturday, I take a 'prop' to give us something to talk about."

I told him, "Kudos. Queen Elizabeth said, 'Good memories are our second chance at happiness.' You're really helping her re-find happiness every Saturday."

Set Up a Ripple Effect of Respect

*"If you change the way you look at things,
the things you look at change."*
— SELF-HELP AUTHOR WAYNE DYER

Please note, proactive grace transcends *not being rude.* It is being *resourceful* on behalf of a situation and taking the initiative to en-vision and introduce a new dynamic that creates a better outcome that benefits all involved. This is the core of this book.

Asking *How can I be a* force for good *in this situation?* gives us the incentive and impetus to get creative. This is the quintes-sence of proactive grace. We don't just *read* the room; we *lead* the room. We don't just *reflect* the mood; we *direct* the mood. We don't *passively accept* harmful norms; we *proactively create* health-ier norms.

I had an opportunity to speak at the Asian Leadership Con-ference in Seoul about *Tongue Fu!* (which was the #3 ranked book in Korea at the time). One of the participants in my session raised her hand and said, "Koreans have a name for what you're talking about; it's called *nunchi.* We are taught it from an early age — it means the art of and ability to gauge people's moods and act ac-cordingly."

The good news is, when you model nunchi, it boomerangs back to you. As the ABBA lyric goes, "Every feeling you're showing is a boomerang you're throwing." If you're ready to learn specific ways to set in motion a ripple effect of nunchi that comes back to you, keep reading to discover how to P.L.A.N. for challenging conversations.

Reminder Card for Setting an Example of Proactive Grace

Imagine you're the catering manager for a community center. A local club was scheduled to have their annual fundraiser from 6 to 9 p.m. A power outage in the area has created snafus. Servers and attendees are arriving late, and the chefs are behind schedule in preparing the dinner. The club president is in your face complaining about the debacle. What do you do?

Words to Lose	Words to Use
Reactive "*This is a catastrophe.*"	**Proactive** "*Let's get this food ready and served as soon as possible.*"
Grumpy "*We're as stressed-out as you are.*"	**Gracious** "*Our team is doing everything we can to get this event back on track.*"
Impatient "*I've told you three times already that complaining doesn't help.*"	**Empathetic** "*I'm putting myself in your shoes and imagining how you feel.*"
Contempt "*I've lost all respect for you for the very unpleasant way you're showing up.*"	**Compassion** "*I know you put a lot of time and effort into this and wanted it to go perfectly.*"
Resentful and no nunchi "*I don't get paid enough to get treated like this.*"	**Respectful and full nunchi** "*Sir, thank you for giving grace to our team, who are doing their best to make this right.*"

Chapter 4

P.L.A.N. FOR CHALLENGING CONVERSATIONS

"Don't leave it to chance, plan in advance."

— SAM HORN

"My sister's son is living with us to save on expenses while he goes to college. The thing is, he plays his music loud, has friends over without our permission, and regularly raids the refrigerator. I know I need to have 'the conversation' with him, but he's very independent and I don't think he's going to take it well. Help!"

Situations like this can be stressful for any of us. I felt immediate compassion when I heard this from a new acquaintance. These situations rarely get better on their own, and I knew it was up to the aunt to set and enforce expectations. Here are some ways that I taught her to prepare for this challenging conversation to increase the likelihood it would go well.

The Four-Step P.L.A.N. Process to Prepare for Challenging Conversations

"If you fail to plan, you plan to fail."

— AUTOMOTIVE PIONEER AND INDUSTRIALIST HENRY FORD

Before reading these steps, bring to mind a situation where you need to have a difficult conversation. It could be with a coworker, family member, neighbor, or vendor. You might want to jot some thoughts down as you form what you want to say. This can ensure that what you say is clear and actionable instead of being INFObesity (blah-blah-blah) that goes in one ear, out the other.

P — **Put Your Purpose in One Sentence:** It's hard to stay on purpose if we don't know what our purpose is. What's your end goal? What do you hope will happen? Distill that into one succinct sentence so it's easy to remember and achieve. Be sure to articulate what you *do* want instead of what you don't. If you say, "I hope I don't get tongue-tied and forget what I want to say," guess what will happen? Instead, say "I will stay focused and keep my cool, no matter what."

L — **Learn Their P.I.N.:** Do your homework to clarify the other person's *priorities*, *interests*, and *needs*. What can you say out of the gate to let them know *you* know what *they* value? Mention their priorities, interests, and needs up front so they know it will be worth paying attention.

A — **Anticipate Resistance and Make It Moot:** Why will they take exception to your proposal? If you don't voice that, they won't be listening; they'll be waiting for you to stop talking so they can tell you why this won't work and why they won't do it. The way to win over a naysayer is to anticipate and address their objections and then show why they may be a nonissue.

N — **Name a New Next Direction:** Steve Piersanti, former CEO of Berrett-Koehler, told me, "Want to know my number one criterion for publishing a book? *What's the shift?*" He's right. Informing people how we feel can be a dead end unless we introduce how we'll improve the situation. Simply explaining why we think a situation is dissatisfactory gives the impression there's nowhere to go with it. How will you suggest a new, better way this can be handled? What action do you want the other person to take? What change do you want them to make — in their mind and their behavior? How will you meet them halfway?

The woman who was hosting her nephew got back in touch to say, "Success! I used your suggestion and started my conversation by saying my husband and I were glad our nephew could save money on rent by living with us, and we're happy to support him. Then I said, 'It's my fault we didn't establish ground rules from the beginning to make sure this arrangement continues to be a win for all of us.'

"We explored how he could contribute as a member of our household so we would all get along. He agreed to wear his earbuds so he can listen to his music but we don't have to. He agreed to follow the same rules our sons did when they were home, mainly that you ask before bringing friends over to make sure it's a good time and that you only eat food you've bought instead of finishing off everything in the refrigerator. Planning that conversation made all the difference as far as him being open to this, instead of thinking, *You're not the boss of me.*"

Talk Yourself *Into* Rather Than *Out of* Success

"Argue for your limitations, and sure enough, they're yours."
— AUTHOR RICHARD BACH

A woman named Anne told me she's been concerned about her elderly mother and was dreading having "the" conversation about her moving out of her home into a retirement community. Anne explained, "My mom is a fiercely independent woman. I'd been putting off this conversation for months because I didn't want her to shut me out. I realized I was only imagining worst-case scenarios. Instead, I used your P.L.A.N. method to picture best-case scenarios. I booked an appointment with a therapist who helps clients navigate this delicate transition. She suggested that instead of 'expressing my concerns' and telling Mom why I think it's time to do this for her 'own good,' I *ask* what she wants.

"I couldn't have been more surprised at what unfolded. Mom admitted she had fallen several times in the past few months and hadn't told me because she was afraid I'd worry. She also confessed that, as much as she loves her home of thirty years, she's been lonely. She said she's embarrassed about the clutter that has accumulated and has no idea how she's supposed to downsize all her stuff into a one-room apartment.

"It was probably the most honest conversation we've ever had. I listened more than talked and realized she saw this as the end of her freedom, and I understood how scared she is of what it signaled.

"At the end of her pouring out what's been on her heart, I volunteered to stay for an extra week so we could work our way through her house, cleaning it room by room, deciding what to keep, what to give to friends and family members, what to trash, and what to donate.

"I hired a professional organizer, June, who had done this for many families, to help us make the tough decisions. June held us accountable with 'Yes, I know that cost a lot. The question is, *Do you love it? Do you need it? Will you use it?*' We put on Frank Sinatra songs and spent the next seven days swapping stories and going down memory lane. Before I left, Mom and I had a virtual call with the therapist, who had researched retirement communities that had my mom's priorities: a swimming pool and a book club."

Anne said, "I'm a big proponent of your P.L.A.N. method because it helped turn what I had feared might cause a rift into a coming-together that was better for all of us."

Turn F.U.D. into a Positive Story

"Your greatest work of art is the story you tell about yourself."
— AUTHOR TARA CONKLIN

My son Tom is an aeronautical engineer who works for NASA. He introduced me to the term *F.U.D.*: fears, uncertainty, doubts. His first few months of training at Johnson Space Center's Mission Control consisted of going through one simulation after another of what could go wrong on the ISS (International Space Station). That way he, and the other flight controllers, could respond quickly and effectively if something actually went wrong, instead of freezing with F.U.D.

One night he couldn't sleep, so he decided he might as well go in to work early. No sooner did Tom arrive than the console he was near lit up like a Christmas tree with cascading malfunctions. Tom didn't even have time to alert the flight director (the senior person in Mission Control); he just took off his badge, threw it at the guy next to him to get his attention, and began analyzing what could be contributing to this crisis. When the flight director arrived a moment later, guess what Tom's first words to him were?

"I've done the sim." He had studied this particular scenario, had already practiced the steps needed to fix it, and was already on it.

There are some *talking on eggshells* (T.O.E.) situations that blindside us, and we need to think on our feet and respond right then. There are also T.O.E. situations we know about in advance. In those situations, it's smart to take a page out of the NASA training manual and do *simulations*.

Design a Plan So You Don't Fall into Someone Else's Plan

"If you don't design your own life plan, chances are you'll fall into someone else's plan. And guess what they have planned for you? Not much."
— SELF-HELP EXPERT AND MOTIVATIONAL SPEAKER JIM ROHN

What is a situation you're dealing with that is not what you want or need it to be? Is this a partner who is preoccupied and not giving you their full attention? A boss who criticized you in front of your coworkers? A neighbor whose dog is barking nonstop?

Picture when and where you'll bring this up. See the other person responding positively. Mentally *simulate* what might happen when you bring this up. How will you address their priorities, interests, and needs so they're motivated to give you a chance? What might they say? How will you respond calmly and succinctly? How will you propose a solution that serves both of you?

From now on, instead of winging it, invest the time to P.L.A.N. how you'd like this interaction to unfold. Things may not turn out exactly as you hoped, but they'll turn out better than if you didn't take the time to envision how to turn your intentions into improved results.

Reminder Card to P.L.A.N. for Challenging Conversations

Imagine your elderly father is in the early stages of dementia. He has gotten lost twice driving home recently and has moments of disorientation. He loves his independence, yet you think it's time — for his safety and the safety of others — to take away his car keys.

Words to Lose	Words to Use
Leave it to chance *"I'm dreading this conversation, but here goes."*	**P.L.A.N. it in advance** *"I'm going to talk with a therapist to get suggestions on how to handle this in such a way that Dad can hear it."*
Focus on your priorities, interests, and needs (P.I.N.) *"Dad, I'm worried about your driving."*	**Focus on their P.I.N.** *"Dad, I understand how much you value your freedom and ability to drive where you want, when you want."*
INFObesity *"I've done my research, and I've got statistics that show you're at an increased risk of a car accident."*	**New next direction** *"With Uber and Lyft, you can still go where you want to go when you want to go."*
F.U.D. story *"My dad is never going to forgive me for this."*	**Faith story** *"I believe I have a responsibility to address this, and if I do so compassionately, Dad will understand."*

PART II

KEEP YOUR COOL IN THE HEAT OF THE MOMENT

"Don't let people pull you into their storm, pull them into your peace."

— BUDDHIST NUN AND AUTHOR
PEMA CHÖDRÖN

What Can I Say and Do If People Are ...

Chapter 5

— RUDE? —

"Don't look at me in that tone of voice."

— SATIRIST DOROTHY PARKER

"Is it just me, or is rudeness getting worse? I work remotely, which means I'm on video calls all day. In many of our meetings, we can't even see faces because people don't have their cameras on. It seems this gives some people permission to behave badly. Any suggestions?"

It's not just you. An April 2018 cover story by Joe Dawson in the Association for Psychological Science *Observer* confirms the suspicion that anonymity can result in people behaving antisocially. Dawson reports that "anonymity may make it easy for people to act antagonistically, unprofessionally, or unethically." He cites research by Stanford University's Philip Zimbardo "showing a link between anonymity and abusive behavior. Scientists have found a tendency for many people to act rudely, aggressively, or illegally when their faces and names are hidden."

53

Perhaps when people aren't face-to-face, they don't feel that human connection that helps hold them accountable for decency. When they can't see the hurt expressions or offended looks, they don't consider the consequences of their microaggressions.

The question is what to do about it.

How can we create human connection in virtual settings so people are motivated to be civil? In chapter 19, I give specific suggestions on how to establish and enforce rules that help us host remote (and in-person) meetings that are positive and productive. For now, let's focus on specific ways to transform rudeness into respect.

You've heard the expression "It's nothing personal. It's just business." *All* business is personal. Even when we're on opposite sides of the planet and listening to disembodied voices on a computer with cameras off, it's wise to remember we're dealing with human beings. The more we keep that in mind and choose to imbue our interactions with human warmth, the more likely we are to get along with others and enjoy our interactions with them.

Here are six suggestions that can help set the stage for rapport and respect. They're not "perfect"; they are a head start.

How to Transform Rudeness into Respect

*"We all require and want respect, man or woman,
black or white. It's our basic human right."*
— SINGER ARETHA FRANKLIN

Understand why people are rude. In today's rush-rush world, people are time pressured. It's tempting to take their impatience out on you online because it doesn't seem like they're interacting with a human being. They're just typing words on a screen, dashing off a text, answering emails. They don't consider how their words might make you *feel*. In a way, you're not *real*. They're communicating through their computer or phone — an inanimate object with no feelings. That's not an excuse; it's simply an explanation of why some people don't treat others with the dignity and decency they deserve.

Give yourself peace of mind instead of giving people a piece of your mind. In other words, as Buddhist nun Pema Chödrön suggests, "Be the sky, not the weather." Rather than letting someone's bad mood or outrageous behavior affect your day — in other words, letting them pull you into their storm — pull them into your peace. One way to do that is to have a mantra you repeat to yourself so you focus on that instead of whatever mud they're slinging at you. My friend Dr. Ivan Misner, founder of networking organization BNI, told me a wonderful story he shares in his "Who's in Your Room?" workshops about someone who used to throw "verbal grenades" into conversations to "stir things up." A therapist suggested that family members respond with a neutral "Hmmm" and then go back to what they were saying. The therapist told them, "Remember, she's doing this to be the center of attention. Do not argue. Do not object. And whatever you do, do not react, because that will reward her and she'll keep saying outrageous things because she knows it works." Ivan said, "Sure enough, the next get-together, she started making outlandish claims. The other family members just said, 'Hmmm,' and then continued the conversation. It took a while, but the contentious family member finally quit her attempts to rile everyone up, because *it wasn't working.*"

Eliminate fighting phrases that rile people up. Certain words set up an adversarial tone that unintentionally reinforces rudeness. Later in the chapter you'll get a sample list of fighting phrases to avoid lest you unnecessarily inflame emotions (yours and others').

Introduce friendly phrases that establish a tone of civility. You can make it difficult for people to be difficult by using words like *please, thank you, appreciate, you're welcome, grateful, look forward,* and *fortunate.*

Gently call people on their inappropriate behavior. If someone persists in being dismissive or disrespectful, politely bring it to their attention. You can do that by saying, "Did you mean to say that?" or "I'm trying to help, if you'll let me," or "Please speak to me with respect," or "I understand you're upset by what happened. Please put yourself in my shoes and imagine how that email made me feel."

Understand that rudeness is contagious — and so is respect. A 2015 University of Florida study found, "Rudeness in the workplace isn't just unpleasant: it's also contagious. Encountering rude behavior makes people more likely to be impolite in return, spreading rudeness like a virus." This may not be comforting; however, it can put things in perspective to remember that when someone is rude to us, chances are someone was rude to them earlier that day and they're just "passing it along." The good news is, *you* can be the compassionate person who turns around their day. You can set in motion a ripple effect of respect that positively affects them, and everyone they deal with, from that moment on.

Counteract Rudeness and Set in Motion a Ripple Effect of Respect

"I alone cannot change the world, but I can cast a stone across the water to create many ripples."
— ACTIVIST AND NUN MOTHER TERESA

My sister and business manager Cheri Grimm is exhibit A of how treating people with respect sets up an ongoing ripple effect.

When I show up at speaking engagements, the first thing my contact often says is "Can you please clone Cheri?" They tell me what a joy she is to deal with. My consulting clients say the same thing. They often email me praising her warm professionalism and expressing how they wish they had someone like her working with them.

Cheri always takes an extra minute to add something personal. It could be following up to ask about a client's father who was rushed to the hospital. It could be to ask how they enjoyed their vacation or to send best wishes on their birthday.

You know the famous quote attributed to Gandhi, "Be the change you wish to see"? Cheri is a walking, talking example of how to "be the *tone* you wish to receive."

Oxford Languages defines *tone* as "(a) the attitude of a writer toward a subject or audience conveyed through word choice and style of writing; (b) the overall feeling, or atmosphere, of a text often created by the author's use of imagery and word choice."

Notice that *tone* consists of word choice, attitude, atmosphere, and feeling. Our goal, when dealing with negative behavior, is to use words that create a prevailing tone, attitude, atmosphere, and feeling of respect so people are motivated to follow our example.

Replace Fighting Phrases with Friendly Phrases

"Precision of communication is more important than ever, when a misunderstood word may create as much disaster as a sudden thoughtless act."
— WRITER JAMES THURBER

Here are just a few fighting phrases that can lead to unintended conflict — and their more positive, proactive counterparts that can lead to cooperation and collaboration.

Fighting Phrase #1: *Can't ... because.* "You *can't* play with your friends *because* you haven't finished your home-work," or "You *can't* watch TV *because* your chores aren't done." The words *can't ... because* are like slamming a ver-bal door in someone's face. People perceive we're reject-ing their request, and they'll resent us because this comes across as a negative ultimatum.

Friendly Phrase #1: *Can ... as soon as.* "Yes, you *can* play out-side *as soon as* you finish your homework," or "Yes, you *can* watch TV *right after* your chores are done." Feel the difference? A mom told me, "My kids used to see me as a 'meanie' because I always told them no. I've realized they often *can* do what they want, *as soon as* they take care of their responsibilities. This puts *them* in charge of getting what they want, instead of seeing *me* as blocking them from what they want. This switch transcends semantics. It changes the whole dynamic of our relationship."

Fighting Phrase #2: *You have to.* "*You have to* call your mom and tell her we can't come this weekend," or "*You need to* get gas in the car on the way home." These are orders. People are thinking, *You're not the boss of me.*

Friendly Phrase #2: *Could you please.* "*Could you please* call your mom and let her know we can't make it this weekend?" or "*Can you please* get gas on the way home?" Turning commands into courteous requests is more likely to elicit willing cooperation versus reluctant com-pliance. A man told me, "Now I know why the affection is gone from our marriage. We were ordering each other around like children. My wife and I have agreed to rein-troduce common courtesy into our relationship. We like each other again, and it's because we're asking instead of ordering."

New Language Can Open Up New Worlds

"We spend so much time being afraid of failure, being afraid of rejection. But regret is the thing we should fear most."
— POLITICAL COMMENTATOR AND COMEDIAN TREVOR NOAH

I hope you're seeing a trend. When we use friendly phrases instead of fighting phrases, we take the shackles off our language, open new worlds of receptivity, and prevent rejection and regret.

Fighting Phrases #3: *Problem* and *No problem.* "I don't have a *problem* with that," "No *problem*," "Any other *problems* we need to discuss?" or "What's your *problem*?" For most people, the word *problem* means something is *wrong*. Many of us use the word habitually without realizing we're imprinting the perception that something is wrong with them or with us.

Friendly Phrases #3: Any words that don't mean something's *wrong*. "Sure, you're welcome to do that" or "Happy to. It was my pleasure," or "Anything else you want to discuss?" Learning this, a man slapped his hand to his forehead during a webinar and said, "Ohh, wish I'd known this on Saturday. My son called from college and said, 'Can I talk to you, Dad?' Guess what I said? 'Sure, son, what's the problem?' I don't want to give the impression the only reason to call home is when something's wrong. Next time, I'll say, 'Sure, son, good to hear from you. What's on your mind?'"

Fighting Phrase #4: *There's nothing...* "*There's nothing* I can do," or "*There's no way* I can change this." These "dead end" words make people feel we're shrugging them off and don't care.

Friendly Phrase #4: *There's something*..."*There's something* you can do." People are less likely to kill the messenger when we have to give bad news if we show empathy. Instead of explaining it's not our fault, we can often get creative and suggest possible next steps. An oncologist told me this has changed the way he delivers diagnoses: "Instead of telling a patient, 'We caught it too late; there's nothing we can do,'" I say, '*I wish* there was more we could do. *There is something* I can suggest. Here's the phone number of a support group...' I may not be able to change the diagnosis. At least I can show them I care."

Fighting Phrases #5: *Always. Everyone. Never. No one.* "You're *always* late," "*Everyone* is upset that you didn't show up," "You *never* listen to me," or "*No one* appreciates the healthy meal I made. I *hate* it when that happens." Extreme, "all or nothing" words create extreme emotions. People will protest, because generalizations and exaggerations are often untrue.

Friendly Phrases #5: Words that are specific instead of sweeping. "You've been late twice this week. What's up?" "Could you please put your phone down and give me five minutes of your attention?" "I made an effort to fix a healthy meal. It'd mean a lot if you let me know what you think of it." Sweeping generalizations are destructive. It's more constructive to ask for clarification or for desired feedback. A woman in a workshop smiled and said, "You may have just saved my marriage. I've gotten in the habit of using those all-or-nothing words: 'You never help out around the house,' or 'We always do what you want on weekends.' From now on, I'm going to ask for what I *do* want instead of accusing him of doing what I don't want."

Fighting Phrase #6: *Unfortunately.* "*Unfortunately*, I can't be
at your soccer game this weekend," or "*Unfortunately*, we
can't afford that." This word will *pop* out of an email or
conversation and be the only thing people focus on.

Friendly Phrase #6: *Fortunately.* "I'll be out of town this
weekend. *Fortunately*, I'll be back in time to be at your
soccer game next Saturday," or "That's out of our budget.
Fortunately, we get to swim in the lake, which is free."
Although this may seem like an insignificant switch, it
can motivate people to focus on what's right instead of
what's wrong.

Imagine being on the receiving end of those fighting phrases.
They don't feel very good, do they? The good news is, friendly
phrases have the power to advance conversations instead of anchor them in arguments.

Words Are Deal Makers or Deal Breakers

*"The happiness of your life depends
on the quality of your thoughts."*
— EMPEROR MARCUS AURELIUS

To riff on Aurelius, "The happiness of our relationships depends
on the quality of our words." I'm not the only one who thinks that.
An hour into a daylong training, we took a break so people could
get up and stretch their legs. A woman came up to me and said,
"Sam, if I had to go home right now, this workshop would have
been worth it. I use every single one of those fighting phrases. No
wonder my kids and husband and I are always at odds. I can see
this will make a difference, but how am I supposed to remember
all this?"

I told her, "Good question. People sometimes ask how my brain works. I tell them, 'I juxtapose everything, because I think it's the quickest way to make complex ideas crystal clear.'"

What do I mean by *juxtapose*? Draw a vertical line down the center of a piece of paper. Put *What Doesn't Work* on top of the left column and *What Does Work* on top of the right.

Whenever you're discussing a topic, put the beliefs and behaviors that sabotage or undermine effectiveness in the left column. Then put the beliefs and behaviors that support or increase effectiveness in the right-hand column. Put the *don'ts* on the left — the *dos* on the right.

Voilà, you've just condensed your insights about what compromises success and what contributes to success into a visually organized page with contrasting columns that *show the shift*. It's a strategic way to summarize what's been said and make ideas easy to remember. I have featured these *Show the Shift* frameworks in most of my books. I think it's one reason they've become evergreens that still sell years after they've been published.

I often turn the *Words to Lose* and *Words to Use* frameworks into magnets and give them out during my presentations. A mom told me, "I put your magnet up in my kitchen to hold myself accountable for using positive words with my kids. What I didn't anticipate is that they have started using them, too. What an unexpected and welcome bonus!"

That is one of the many benefits of shifting your language. People around you will notice and often voluntarily adopt these cooperation-building phrases. That's a win for everyone.

— Reminder Card of What to Do If People Are Being Rude —

Imagine you're a flight attendant. Today's travel had weather delays and cancellations. A number of passengers on your flight are tired and cranky and are taking it out on you. What do you do?

Words to Lose	Words to Use
Can't ... because *"No, you can't have a drink, because drinks aren't served until a half hour into the flight."*	**Can ... as soon as** *"Yes, you can order a drink as soon as we're a half hour in the air."*
You have to *"You have to wait your turn."*	**Could you please** *"Sir, could you please wait until I finish delivering these? Then it will be your turn."*
Problem/no problem *"So, you have a problem with your TV?"*	**Any words that don't mean something is wrong** *"Let me see if we can get your TV working."*
There's nothing ... *"There's nothing we can do. We're out of snack boxes."*	**There's something ...** *"Let me see if we have any peanuts or pretzels up front."*
Extreme words *"No one appreciates how hard we work."*	**Words that are specific instead of sweeping** *"I'm grateful to the woman on the previous flight who went out of her way to thank us."*
Unfortunately *"Unfortunately, we have to sit on the tarmac until the tower clears us."*	**Fortunately** *"Fortunately, we can wait on the tarmac and don't have to return to the gate."*

Chapter 6

— ARGUING AND DISAGREEING? —

"I will not take 'but' for an answer."

— POET LANGSTON HUGHES

"I am dreading going home for the holidays. My brother and dad are quite vocal about their political beliefs. Last year's gathering turned into a shouting match. My brother stormed out and vowed never to return. He and my dad are back on speaking terms, but barely. How can I keep this year's get-together from deteriorating into another debacle?"

Talk about a timely question. We live in a polarized world. People not only have *strong* views; they also often have polar-*opposite* views.

Kudos to Supreme Court Justice Ruth Bader Ginsburg for showing we don't have to be contentious when we disagree. I saw her interviewed on my favorite TV show, *CBS Sunday Morning*. The journalist asked if her nickname the Notorious RBG, a riff off the rap star the Notorious BIG, was a "weird connection."

Ginsburg smiled. "Why would that be surprising? We have a lot in common. We were both born and bred in Brooklyn, New York."

When asked how she and Justice Antonin Scalia (from a different political party) could attend opera together, she shared this six-word anthem for our times: "*We are different. We are one.*" What a wonderful example showing that differences don't have to be divisive, as long as we focus on what we have in common instead of on what we have in conflict.

The Word *But* Is a Wedge, the Word *And* Is a Bridge

"Just because I disagree with you doesn't mean I hate you.
We need to relearn that in our society."
— ACTOR MORGAN FREEMAN

You may be thinking, *Easy to say. Tough to do.*

You're right. I'm grateful to my college philosophy instructor for using an innovative way to show us how to embrace this dichotomy. On the first day of class, he wrote on the board $7 + 2 = 9$. $6 + 3 = 9$. He then said, "The way *you* do things is not the *only* way to do things." He said the "rules of engagement" for his course were to have a "healthy debate." That meant honoring people's opinions even if you didn't agree with them. Especially if you didn't agree with them.

One way he held us accountable for that was to ban the word *but*. He called it "the bad-news but" and felt it was at the center of most disagreement. Read these sentences and imagine being on the receiving end:

"I hear what you're saying, but ..."
"You did a good job on that test, but ..."
"I'd like to help you, but ..."

"I know it's important to you, but ..."
"I'm sorry, but ..."

Do you feel that the speaker really doesn't hear what you're saying, you didn't do a good job, they don't want to help, they don't understand how important this is, and they're not truly sorry?

That's because the word *but* cancels out what was said before it. That little three-letter word creates an either/or, right/wrong dynamic that pits us as adversaries. It actually escalates conflict because it seems we're taking exception to what the other person is saying.

So, how to fix this? It's simple. Replace the word *but* with the word *and*.

"I hear what you're saying, *and* can you tell me how you've come to that conclusion?"
"You did a good job on that test, *and* you missed a question on the back of the page."
"I'd like to help you, *and* let me finish with this customer and you're next."
"I understand this is important to you, *and* do you have ideas on how to implement this?"
"I'm sorry that happened, *and* let me put you in touch with your account manager."

See how the word *and* makes what came *before* and *after* it both true? See how it *bridges* what's being said instead of *blocks* it?

I've come to believe this simple shift — replacing *but* with *and* — is the single best thing we can do to prevent conflict and produce cooperation. I know that's a rather grandiose claim. It's just that hundreds of people, over the years, have told me dramatic stories of how making this shift improved their relationship with just about everyone.

Differences Don't Have to Be Divisive

*"Our maturity will be judged by how well we are able
to agree to disagree and yet continue to care for one another,
and seek the greater good of the other."*
— ARCHBISHOP DESMOND TUTU

The bridge-building power of the word *and* came in handy when I discovered a longtime friend had a belief that shocked me. We've had monthly phone calls for years. I deeply admire what a generous servant leader she is. So, my mouth literally fell open when she stated, during one of our calls, that a certain politician was "the best president our country has ever had."

I really didn't know what to say, because I thought just the opposite. After our call, I wasn't sure we'd ever speak again because this schism created a crisis of conscience. How could someone I respect admire someone who I felt was an unconscionable bully? After thinking it through, we both decided that what mattered more than our different beliefs was our twenty-five-year friendship. Here's how we navigated our differences.

Identify Diametrically Opposed Beliefs
and Steer Clear of Them

"Quicksand conversations are easy to get into, hard to get out of."
— SAM HORN

We decided that for us, politics is a *quicksand conversation*.

A what?! Here's what I mean by that term.

I grew up riding horses in dry riverbeds in our small Southern California town. We had to keep our eyes out for quicksand. In case you're not familiar with quicksand, it is a mushy mix of sand and water that can't support weight. It's deceptively easy to wander into and really hard to extricate yourself from. In fact, the more you struggle, the deeper you get sucked in.

The question is, did we stop riding because we knew there was quicksand out there? No, we kept riding; we just kept our antennae up for telltale signs of quicksand and steered clear of it. I imagine you already see the analogy. My friend and I decided we wanted to keep talking (riding), as there are plenty of other things for us to discuss, including many values and experiences we share, instead of this one thing we don't.

How about you? Do you and a friend or family member have radically different views? Are you going to sever ties with that person and never see them again? Will you engage in a shouting match — or focus on what you have in common instead of what you have in conflict?

If you'll be seeing them at a gathering, you might want to ask these questions in advance and identify quicksand topics to avoid.

Seven Questions to Determine Whether to Speak — or Not to Speak

"We meet aliens every day who have something to give us. They come in the form of people with different opinions."
— ACTOR WILLIAM SHATNER

1. Will people at this gathering have polar-opposite beliefs about an issue?
2. Are we open to listening to each other and having a constructive conversation about this issue?
3. Is it possible we might change each other's beliefs about this issue? Could *they* change my mind? Could *I* change theirs?

4. Will discussing this serve any good purpose, or could it ruin this event or relationship?
5. Do we value this gathering and want to continue it? Do we appreciate this relationship and want to keep it?
6. If so, is it wise to focus on what we have in common instead of what we have in conflict?
7. Shall we agree, for the common good, to steer clear of this quicksand topic so we can honor this event and preserve our relationship?

In the past few years, a discouraging number of people have told me they have cut ties with a friend or family member because they kept getting into ugly arguments.

Hmm. Stop seeing someone altogether because we disagree about a certain issue? Is that the only option? Instead of abandoning that relationship, would it be wiser to declare a toxic topic off-limits? Could you say, "It's clear we have different points of view about this, and I value our friendship too much to jeopardize it by having a knockdown, drag-out fight that puts that at risk. Let's talk about other things, shall we?"

Differences Don't Have to End a Relationship

"You don't want someone who can't tell the difference between having a different opinion and dismissing your opinion."
— ADVICE COLUMNIST CAROLYN HAX

CBS Sunday Morning showcased another example of how people from different backgrounds can transcend their differences and be friends. On the surface, this was implausible because they are so opposite. One is Black. The other is white. One is from Hawaii. The other is from New Jersey. One is a politician. The other is a musician. Yet they both see themselves as renegades, and growing up with absentee dads, both felt invisible and like outsiders and wanted to find where they belonged.

Who are these two individuals? Barack Obama and Bruce Springsteen. They found their "both" by focusing on their similarities versus their dissimilarities and have reaped the rewards of a rich relationship.

Think about a family member or friend you're disagreeing with. Odds are you have far more shared good times and mutually meaningful experiences than you do contentious ones.

Could you choose to fast-forward to the end of your life and ask yourself what will be more important? If you permanently part with this person over this rift, will you regret it and wish you could have a do-over? It is not sacrificing your integrity to stay in a relationship with someone you disagree with. As long as there's more in the credit column than the debit column, it could be a worthwhile investment.

I had an opportunity to talk with Dan Pink, the author of *The Power of Regret*. After reviewing thousands of responses to his worldwide survey, he discovered there are basically four types of regrets:

- **Foundation Regrets:** "If only I had done the work."
- **Boldness Regrets:** "If only I had taken that chance."
- **Moral Regrets:** "If only I had done the right thing."
- **Connection Regrets:** "If only I had reached out."

What does this mean for you? It means that fast-forwarding to how you'll feel about abandoning a relationship can motivate you to figure out how to repair it instead of walk away from it. Perhaps you can work with an impartial mediator to discuss divisive issues so you both feel heard? Perhaps you can use the P.L.A.N. approach to address this and come to a "Let's agree to disagree" reconciliation?

As *Outlander* author Diana Gabaldon says, "No two people read the same book." Agreed. We don't have to be on the same page to enjoy the same book, as long as we both like the book.

Keep Your Options Open

"To affect the quality of the day, that is the art of life."
— POET, ESSAYIST, AND PHILOSOPHER RALPH WALDO EMERSON

A manager pushed back: "This idea of quicksand topics may work with family. It doesn't with customers. Even if we don't agree with them, we still have to deal with them."

Got it. Customers can be challenging, and you often don't know someone's quicksand topics on first meeting. I have a friend, Rebecca, who's a big fan of improv, and she gave me a tool that might work in these settings.

Rebecca decided to see if she had what it took to be a stand-up comedian. At the first meeting of a class on this topic, the instructor explained the *Yes, and...* principle. He said, "No matter what idea the audience presents to you, you've got to *riff off* it and *run with* it. Just as musicians riff off chords to make new music, your job is to riff off ideas to create new options."

Rebecca said, "This mindset really teaches you to accept an idea even if you don't like it. It's amazing. The more accustomed you get to responding to *anything* people say with *and*, the more options it opens up, because you're focusing on how it can work instead of why it won't."

What an eloquent explanation of why the word *and* is so crucial when dealing with diametrically opposed beliefs. It sets up a "We're in this together" frame of mind. Instead of seeing each other as enemies and *dissing* what the other person says, we see them as allies and *expand* on what they say.

As for that manager who said we can't have quicksand, "off-limits" topics with customers? Here's what to say: "Mr. Tyler, I can see we have different points of view about that. Let's focus on what we have in common so we can work together to get this finished." Or "Ms. Smith, we could go back and forth on that all day and we're not going to change each other's minds. Instead, let's agree to disagree on that aspect of this, and turn our attention to our shared interests."

Anthropologist Ruth Benedict remarked, "The purpose of anthropology is to make the world safe for human differences."

Well said. The purpose of proactive grace is to make interactions safe for human differences. The ability to get along with others doesn't mean there's an absence of differences; it means we are able to discuss differences without butting heads. The word *and* is the fulcrum for doing that.

Get Off Your *But* in Virtual Communications

"The test of a first-rate intelligence is the ability
to hold two opposed ideas in the mind at the same time."
— AUTHOR F. SCOTT FITZGERALD

I love F. Scott Fitzgerald's quote because it encompasses what we're talking about. The word *and* is a way two opposing ideas can be held in our mind without canceling each other out.

The word takes on an even more important role in communications when we can't see the other person's facial expressions or body language. As a result, we have no context to intuit their intent. If we start off a phone call with "I know I was supposed to call you back, *but...*" or send an email with "We agreed to that price, *but...*" we have just crossed verbal swords.

That's why it's so important to proofread emails, texts, social media posts, and digital reports before sending them. If you want people to keep reading, versus *get upset* by what they're reading, the couple of extra minutes it will take to do this will pay off in terms of reduced misunderstandings.

The Four Stages of Habit Change

*"We can do anything we want as long as
we stick to it long enough."*
— ACTIVIST HELEN KELLER

A retiree said, "You've heard 'You can't teach an old dog new tricks'? You're making sense, but I'm a creature of habit. I use the word *but* all the time *without thinking.* How am I supposed to change this habit when I'm not even aware I'm using the word?"

Good question. Here's how. Stick with the four As of habit change and you can get to the stage where your default is to use *and* instead of *but.*

A = Aware: Congrats. You just became *aware* you're doing something you *don't* want to do and discovered there's something you *do* want to do. That's the first step of changing anything.

A = Awkward: Doing things differently can initially feel un-comfortable. Remember the first time you played golf? You probably didn't play very well. Instead of quitting, you said, "Of course I'm not very good. This is new; I haven't done it before. I want to play, so I'll keep prac-ticing."

A = Applying: At this stage, you keep applying the tech-niques you've been taught and get improved results. You work on using your driver, woods, irons, and putter. You understand the mechanics and capacity of the different clubs and keep honing your skills. You're not perfect, but you're enjoying your rounds and getting better because you're playing consistently.

A = Automatic: At this point, the new skill comes naturally. You drive the ball down the middle of the fairway. You loft your irons and think *In the hole* with your putter. You don't focus on the mechanics anymore (knees, shoulders, hips, club speed) because they're a grooved part of you. As runner Jim Ryun said, "Motivation is what gets you started. Habit is what keeps you going."

I told this retiree, "If relationships are important to you, promise to be more mindful about the word *and*. You can overcome years of habit if you're motivated to make this shift. Don't just do it for yourself; do it for everyone you interact with."

Author Marshall Goldsmith says, "If you want people to change, give them a chance to watch you change." In our next chapter, we'll discuss more ways to change your language so other people are motivated to change theirs. Together, you can cocreate better outcomes.

Reminder Card of What to Do When People Are Disagreeing

Imagine your mother-in-law is very free with her advice. You understand she raised a fine son (your husband), yet you don't agree with some of her suggestions, particularly regarding how you raise her grandchild. You don't want to ruin the relationship; nor do you want to have a disagreement every time she comes to your house.

Words to Lose	Words to Use
Say *but* *"I know you believe in gluten-free foods, but I think that's extreme."*	**Say *and*** *"I know you believe in gluten-free foods, and I think it's OK if he has a snack at soccer."*
Act as adversaries *"I know you mean well, but I'm tired of you telling me what to do."*	**Become allies** *"I know you mean well, and I'm glad you care about your grandson. So do I."*
Quit the relationship *"I've had it. You're not welcome in our home anymore."*	**Avoid quicksand conversations** *"Can you please respect our right to handle this in a way that feels right for us?"*
Decide you can't change the *but* habit *"I know you think you're right, but you don't have any idea…"*	**Catch and correct the habit** *"See the but sign on our fridge? It's our reminder to ban that word."*

Chapter 7

— BLAMING AND SHAMING? —

"What you're thinking is what you're becoming."

— BOXER MUHAMMAD ALI

"We were packing swag bags for a conference and discovered the team left out two items from our sponsors, and we'd have to start over. I asked how this happened, and the blaming began. What can we do if everyone's pointing fingers at someone else as to whose fault it is?"

Muhammad Ali was right. What you're *saying* is what you're becoming, too. And when people are blaming and shaming, they are becoming enemies. One of the first things you can do to become allies instead of adversaries is to stop asking, "How did this happen?!" That actually encourages people to find fault. Instead, say, "*We're here to find solutions, not fault.* The question is, what can we do about this now?"

You can also say, "Getting upset with each other won't undo

what happened. Instead, let's figure out how we can work together as a team to get these bags repacked ASAP."

Or say, "*Let's not do this.* Throwing each other under the bus is taking valuable time away from solving the issue. *A better use of our time* is for us to pitch in and get these ready for tomorrow."

Or say, "*Blaming each other won't help.* Instead, let's ..."

Those phrases — *We're here to find solutions, not fault; Let's not do this; A better use of our time; Blaming each other won't help* — are all *verbal pattern interrupts.* They help switch attention from blaming and shaming to working together to solve a problem instead of belaboring it.

The Power of a Pattern Interrupt to Change Behavior

"If you don't use your power for positive change,
you are part of the problem."
— CIVIL RIGHTS LEADER CORETTA SCOTT KING

What is something that recently went wrong? Did people go back and forth faultfinding and finger-pointing? From now on, if that happens, do a verbal pattern interrupt.

A pattern interrupt is something designed to jolt people out of their current emotional or physical state and compel them to think and act differently and nonhabitually. Anyone who knows me knows I like to use the pattern-interrupt phrase *The good news is...* Those four words have a tangible ability to shift me (and whoever I'm talking with) from focusing on what we don't like to what we might.

A project manager I work with has picked up this habit. Her computer crashed while she was working on a project. She said, "Sam, the bad news is, it will take a few days for this to be repaired.

The good news is, this gives me time to make those hand edits we were discussing." Well done.

Notice that the key to an effective pattern interrupt is to give people something to *start*, not just to *stop*. The phrase *Instead, let's...* is a way to shift attention away from destructive behavior (without condemning it) and toward a more constructive course of action that shapes it.

In fact, when done well, a *verbal pattern interrupt* is a *language* form of an *intervention*.

Intervention is defined by *Cambridge Dictionary* as "the action of becoming intentionally involved in a difficult situation, to improve it or prevent it from getting worse," and as "an occasion when someone's friends or family speak to them about a problem or situation because the person's behavior is unreasonable or harmful."

Blaming and shaming is a problem behavior that is "unreasonable" and "harmful." Someone needs to *intervene* to "improve" this difficult situation and "prevent it from getting worse." The recommended *Words to Use* in this chapter (and in all the chapters) are a way to act on behalf of the greater good.

A colleague told me, "My parents and I held an intervention for my brother, who had become addicted to opioids. He had back surgery after an accident and was prescribed pain medication following the operation. The problem was, he became dependent on it and became someone we didn't even recognize. He had huge mood swings, ranging from depression to raging tantrums. He was angry at us for intervening, but he's in treatment now and will hopefully be able to free himself of this addiction.

"I knew about those types of major interventions in substance-abuse issues. I never realized we can do these on a 'minor' level when people are blaming. You're right, getting mad at people who are doing this doesn't change their behavior, because it's a form of blaming itself."

Well said. Proactive pattern interrupts are intended to *guide* people, not *guilt* them.

Combine Verbal and Physical Pattern Interrupts to Increase Effectiveness

"If you do not change direction,
you might end up where you are heading."
— ANCIENT PHILOSOPHER LAO-TZU

Want another way to redirect blamers and shamers who are headed for disaster?

Use this hand gesture to get their attention. (No, not that one!) Hold your hand up like a traffic cop would. This is a universally understood signal to cease and desist. In fact, it's more effective to combine words *and* gestures when intervening.

Why? If people are blaming and shaming and you try to talk over them, what will happen? They'll talk louder. The voice of reason will get drowned out in the commotion because you're doing the same thing they are, just at a different volume.

If people are getting into it, hold up your hand palm out to cause a pause and say, *"We're here to fix the course for the future, not assign blame for the past.* Let's focus on how to move this forward."

A workshop participant said, "I'm a coach for my son's basketball team. There's another way to do a verbal/physical pattern interrupt if people need to break it up." He formed his hands into a *T*, like a referee, and called, *"Time-out!"*

Excellent idea. The visual *T* combined with the word *time-out* is sure to get people's attention. If people are getting into it, hold up your *T* and say loudly so everyone can hear, *"Time-out!* Throwing each other under the bus won't help. Instead, let's …"

We Can Bellyache, or We Can Get Busy

"You don't make progress by standing on the sidelines, whimpering and complaining. You make progress by implementing ideas."
— U.S. CONGRESSWOMAN SHIRLEY CHISHOLM

I'm grateful to my parents for teaching my brother and sister and me that standing on the sidelines was not an option. Their motto was "You can bellyache or get busy." As I mentioned, we lived in a small Southern California town, more horses than people. When I was twelve, we moved to a ranch a few miles out of town. Mom and Dad thought it was a perfect opportunity for us to learn responsibility and to raise our 4-H and FFA animals on our own land.

When you live on a ranch, things go wrong. The windmill breaks, and you have to truck into town to haul water back for the livestock. Your pigs decide to root in your just-planted garden. Lambs get stuck in cattle guards. You run into a rattlesnake in the henhouse. Your horses get into the grain shed, and you have to walk them (for hours) so they don't get colic. Yes, all this actually happened.

One time we got a call in the middle of the night from a neighbor telling us our cattle had gotten out of their pasture and were roaming the county road. Dad rousted us out of bed to help. The bellyaching began.

I whimpered, "It's 2 a.m.!"

My brother turned on me and said, "*You're* the one who left the gate open."

I started crying. "It wasn't me. *You* were the last one in the barn."

Back and forth we went. Dad interrupted: "Bellyaching won't get our cattle back. Let's get busy rounding them up, find out where they got out, and fix the fence. Tomorrow we'll sit down and figure out how to keep this from happening again." Thanks, Dad, for teaching us to fix what goes wrong instead of fight about it.

Don't Fight, Fix

"You could write a song about some kind of emotional problem you're having, but it would not be a good song, in my eyes, until it went through a period of sensitivity to a moment of clarity. Without that moment of clarity, it's just complaining."
— SINGER-SONGWRITER JONI MITCHELL

What a profound insight from Joni Mitchell. She is right. The goal of a proactive pattern interrupt (for ourselves and others) is to clarify how we can contribute, instead of complain.

The CEO of an ad agency told me this technique helped him during a meeting to "get to the bottom" of why a VIP client had canceled his account. The CEO asked, "What happened?" and the blaming began. Brian, the account manager, defended himself by saying he called in sick the morning of a meeting and had asked the receptionist to ask Joe, the creative director, to cover for him. The receptionist said it wasn't her fault, because Brian should have talked directly to Joe. Joe said he was blameless because he never got the message.

In the middle of this, the CEO remembered the "don't fight, fix" approach. He held up his hand to cause a pause and said, "We could spend the rest of the day going back and forth about who dropped the ball on this, and it won't get that client back. Instead, let's reach out, apologize for what happened, reassure him it won't happen again, and offer to go to his office tomorrow to make this right so he chooses to continue to work with us."

Sometime in the near future, something will go wrong, and

the blaming will begin. Instead of passively allowing it to continue, intervene with a pattern interrupt to switch people from pointing fingers to planning what they can do about it, now and in the future.

Poet Adrienne Rich says, "The moment of change is the only poem." When used well, pattern interrupts are a poetic way of changing people's behavior — for good.

Reminder Card of What to Do When People Are Blaming and Shaming

Imagine you're a server. Just as you come out of the kitchen with a tray full of food, a busser coming the other way bumps into you with a tub full of dirty dishes. Everything goes flying. The blaming begins.

Words to Lose	Words to Use
Find fault *"You weren't looking where you were going!"*	**Find solutions** *"Let's clean this up ASAP before anyone trips over these dishes."*
Bellyache *"Oh no! I have to ask the chef to start that order from scratch!"*	**Get busy** *"Chef, I'm sorry to have to ask this, and can you please prepare this order for table 3?"*
Fix the blame in the past *"Why didn't they label these kitchen doors In and Out?!"*	**Fix the course of the future** *"I'm going to ask the manager today to label these doors In and Out."*
Point fingers *"I am not the one who ran into you; you are the one who ..."*	**Pattern interrupt** *"Blaming each other won't help; let's both pitch in to take care of this so we can get back to work."*

Chapter 8

— MAKING MISTAKES? —

"Your best teacher is your last mistake."

— CONSUMER PROTECTION ATTORNEY RALPH NADER

"I train all our volunteers for our nonprofit. People are so sensitive these days, they take offense at the least little thing. How can I give feedback without them getting mad at me?"

Great question. How can we help people perform *better* without making them feel *bad*?

A shout-out to Rod Laver for teaching me the secret sauce to giving *constructive* (versus *destructive*) feedback. As mentioned previously, I had the privilege of working for him. The day after our national tennis camp, Rod asked if I'd like to "hit for a bit," which was his way of rewarding me for weeks of hard work. Would I like to hit with the G.O.A.T. — one of the greatest tennis players to ever play the game? The answer to that was an immediate, heartfelt "Yes!"

Rocket (his nickname) made me work for every point, running me side to side. Finally, he (intentionally?) hit a weak lob, which set me up for an easy overhead. In my eagerness, I committed a cardinal sin and looked where I was going to *put* the ball instead of keeping my eyes *on* the ball.

Well, I didn't just mishit the ball — I took a mighty whiff and *missed* it entirely. It was so embarrassing, I started *should*-ing all over myself: "I *should* have kept my head up. I know better than that! What a stupid mistake."

Rod, known for his sportsmanship, called me over and said something so profound, I remember it to this day: "Sam, champions never use the word *should*. If they make a mistake, they immediately switch their attention to how to get it back and get it right the next time."

Thank you, Rocket. A true gentleman on and off the court. He's right. The word *should* serves no good purpose, because in this context it pertains to the past. Do you know anyone who can undo the past?

Which is why, when someone makes a mistake (and that includes you), it's best to follow Rocket's advice and focus on how to get it back and get it right *next time*. That's the way to be a *coach* instead of a *critic*. And that's the way to *shape* behavior instead of *shame* it.

The Word *Should* Is a Form of Disrespect

"Before you criticize someone, you should walk a mile
in their shoes. That way, after you criticize them,
you're a mile away, and you have their shoes."
— COMEDIAN JACK HANDEY

Thought we could all use some humor about now. Jack Handey has a point, though. Next time we're tempted to criticize someone, maybe we should take a hike.

Especially if we're giving feedback to someone who's tackling a new task. Almost by definition, they'll get it wrong, because they haven't done it before! Their ego will be fragile, because who likes making mistakes?

If we criticize what they did wrong, they'll resent us, even if what we're saying is right. They'll either get defensive or go on the offensive. It's more effective to coach how they can do the task more efficiently in the future so they learn from — versus lose face over — their errors.

A sales manager named Glenn didn't agree with this. "I'm in charge of training our new hires. I thought it was my job to correct their mistakes. How are they supposed to learn if I don't point out what they're doing wrong?"

I said, "Please change that perception. It's your job to teach them how to do things *correctly* instead of belaboring (and imprinting) what they did *incorrectly*."

Let's return to the metaphor of tennis for a moment. Telling people "You should stop hitting off your back foot" actually perpetuates them hitting off their back foot. Telling a player "You should stop going for risky shots" actually keeps that thought top of mind, and they'll keep going for risky shots.

Be a coach (not a critic) by suggesting, "Step *into* the ball," and "Keep the ball *in* the court." It helps to say this *out loud* to verbally reinforce the preferred behavior.

If a supervisor offers the comment "You should stop putting so much information on your slides. And you went through them so fast that no one could read them," the employee might resent the one-sided feedback that didn't mention the hours that went into developing that deck.

The employee will be more receptive if the supervisor says, "I can see you poured a lot of time and effort into preparing that presentation. Thank you. And in the future, could you please keep your deck to ten slides, with each slide having three bullets max and twenty-four-point font, to make it easy for everyone to absorb your excellent information?"

Notice this combination of *complimenting effort* and *coaching results*. Other examples include:

"We appreciate the design of our new website [*effort*], and could you please add a section featuring our company mission statement so stakeholders are familiar with our values [*results*]?"

"Kudos for creating those guest service guidelines for our fundraiser [*effort*], and could you please add our protocol for collecting donations so everyone is clear about that [*results*]?"

See how that works? People can receive your feedback without resentment because they feel that they are getting credit for what they did well instead of being criticized for what they didn't.

We Can't Motivate People to Do Better by Making Them Feel Bad

"Correction does much, but encouragement does more."
— WRITER JOHANN WOLFGANG VON GOETHE

A workshop attendee said, "I wish you'd tell my ESL [English as a second language] instructor this! I moved here from Korea last year and registered for night classes at the local community college. The thing is, anytime I make a mistake, he immediately corrects me in front of everyone. He never notices what I get right, only what I get wrong."

I smiled. "Looks like you agree with the baseball umpire Doug Harvey, who said, 'When I'm right, no one remembers. When I'm wrong, no one forgets.'"

"Exactly. It makes me reluctant to ask questions in class."

She's right. *Proportion of feedback matters.* If we only hear about what we do poorly, we often withdraw. Criticism can crush our spirit and curb our curiosity. We don't want to risk getting humiliated in front of peers, so we remove ourselves from the playing field so we don't risk looking foolish. What's worse is we often know, when corrected, what we "coulda" or "shoulda" done. After-the-fact criticism can feel like a verbal assault.

That's why it's crucial to *reward progress* and turn *reprimands* into *recommendations*:

Reward progress: "I can tell you're studying at home."
Recommendation: "And we will be able to better understand what you're saying if you speak more slowly and pause between each word."

Feel the difference? Sequence is important. Reward people first so they have incentive to keep trying, and then recommend specific ways to get better. When done well, constructive feedback is an offering, not an offense.

Ask for the Type of Feedback You Want to Receive

"No passion in the world is equal to
the passion to alter someone else's draft."
— AUTHOR H. G. WELLS

A woman in a workshop said, "I wish my writing group was attending this session."

"What do you mean?"

"Last month, it was my turn to have my manuscript *critiqued*. They took that word seriously! They didn't have one good thing to say about it. By the end of the night, I was ready to throw it in the trash because they had so thoroughly trashed it. It made me want to give up."

"First, I'm sorry you had that experience," I said to her. "Unless someone has written a book, they have no idea of all the blood, sweat, and tears we pour into trying to produce something that will add value to the world. Now, let's get proactive and figure out how you can get back on the writing horse.

"It sounds like the group needs some guidelines for future meetings so members don't drop out as a result of being editorially eviscerated in front of their peers." Here is what I recommended to her.

- **Ask for the type of feedback you want.** You may say, "Hey, I've spent months on this, and my ego is a little fragile. It is a work in progress. I know it isn't perfect, so please be gentle." Or you can say, "Have at it. I'd rather hear what's missing *now* so I have a chance to clean it up before I turn it in to my publisher."
- **Ask for balanced feedback.** As stated before, the proportion of critique to compliments matters. You might want to say, "I really appreciate you pointing out what you *do* like and what I've done well. That way, you'll be an encouraging wind beneath my writing wings."
- **Ask for suggestions on what *would* work versus feedback simply pointing out what *doesn't*.** Instead of redlining a passage with "This is unrealistic dialogue," the group might share specific ways the dialogue could be more realistic. Instead of saying, "This chapter goes on too long," they could make recommendations as to what they would cut.

This writer got back in touch to say she did share these guidelines with her group, and they agreed to follow them from then on. Several members confessed they'd been on the verge of quitting before their "critique" because they didn't want to put themselves through that.

As you can imagine, these recommendations apply to everyone, not just writers, because *no one* wants to put themselves through that. Next time you're tempted to "alter someone else's draft," ask what *kind* of feedback they'd like so your input is welcome.

There Are Times When "Tough Talk" Is Warranted

"We made too many wrong mistakes."
— MAJOR LEAGUE BASEBALL HALL OF FAMER YOGI BERRA

"This sounds a little too kumbaya to me," a manager I worked with once told me. "What if someone makes an expensive mistake? It seems disingenuous to 'praise their effort.' I don't want to give them a slap on the wrist, because there better not be a next time! They need to understand the financial consequences of their mistake."

I was glad he brought this up. Reiterating how badly someone blew it doesn't undo it. It may be temporarily satisfying to blow off steam; however, it can permanently damage a relationship. That person may never forgive you for humiliating them in front of peers. Plus, anyone watching will tiptoe around you because they don't want this to happen to them.

At the same time, there are occasions when "tough talk" is warranted and necessary. Judy Gray, former chair of the Fairfax County Chamber of Commerce, told me, "If you 'let someone off the hook' for an egregious error, others involved might disrespect the boss for not addressing a serious transgression. Instead of being 'soft,' it might be more appropriate to issue a formal reprimand and put the employee on notice with the consequences if this happened again. I would document it for his personnel file (in case I had to fire him later) and have him sign the statement of what future poor decisions would mean to his continued employment."

If you'd like a step-by-step process for giving "tough feedback," you might want to try this approach created by Erin Weed, founder of the Dig method for leaders to clarify their purpose and message. Erin shared her Head, Heart, Core approach with the Transformational Leadership Council group I'm a part of. To a person, we all had epiphanies that helped us "tell a tough truth" without risking a relationship.

Who is someone you need to give feedback to, and you've been putting it off because you didn't know what to say? Mentally rehearse having the conversation with these steps:

1. **Head and Facts:** Put your hand on your head. State the facts of what happened without using the word *you* (which comes across as accusatory). Use a neutral voice. For example, "That lost file will set us back a week, as we need to reenter the required data."

2. **Heart and Feelings:** Put your hand on your heart. Share how *you* feel, not how *they* should feel. "I feel disappointed we have to redo work we've already done." Avoid saying things like, "*You* should feel ashamed we have to work all weekend to make up for your mistake."

3. **Core and Wants:** Put your hand on your core and state your wishes: "I want to hear how you'll keep this from happening again, and I want us to work together collaboratively to complete this."

Would this help you have a hard conversation you've been dreading? Can you picture someone thanking you for the fair and firm way you handled this? Could this be a mutually beneficial teaching moment for both of you? I hope so!

Are You *Should*-ing Yourself?

"You've been criticizing yourself for years now and it hasn't worked. Try approving of yourself and see what happens."
— SELF-HELP AUTHOR AND PUBLISHER LOUISE HAY

And, yes, this works with self-talk, too. From now on, if you disappoint yourself, instead of going down the castigation/denigration spiral, coach yourself through the experience using the Head, Heart, Core approach. It can help you extract the lesson and move on.

A woman asked, "What if there is no next time? My friend went in for what she thought was an outpatient medical procedure. She had a bad reaction to the anesthesia and died later that day. I can't forgive myself. She had asked me to go with her, and I told her I couldn't. I wouldn't have been able to prevent what happened; at least I would have been with her."

I said, "First, I am so sorry about your friend. I can only imagine what this has been like for you and her family." I paused and gently suggested, "Could you give yourself some grace? Could you use the Head, Heart, Core approach to talk yourself through your feelings, express your remorse, and ask for forgiveness? What might that look like?"

She emailed me later that week to thank me. Here's how she processed this:

1. **Head and Facts:** "You asked me to go with you that day, and I didn't."
2. **Heart and Feelings:** "I feel I let you down and wasn't there when you needed me."
3. **Core and Wants:** "I wish I could go back in time and say 'Of course I'll go with you.' Since I can't, I want to honor our friendship by staying in touch with your kids and continuing to let them know what a special person you were. And I'm starting an annual scholarship in your name to support young women who want to go into your profession."

She said, "At first the words wouldn't come, so I put my hand on my head, heart, and dantien [four inches below the navel] to bring up what I had buried. This doesn't bring my friend back, but at least I'm no longer beating myself up about it."

She's right. *Should*-ing is a verbal put-down. People make mistakes. The question is, when that happens, how can you *suggest*, instead of *should*; be a *coach*, not a *critic*; and *shape* the future, instead of *shame* the past, so the mistake becomes a learning opportunity?

Reminder Card of What to Do
When Someone Makes a Mistake

Imagine you and your start-up cofounder are presenting at a pitch fest. Your partner sleeps through his alarm, arrives late, and forgets to bring the slide deck. You stumble through the pitch.

Words to Lose	Words to Use
Should *"You should have arranged for a wake-up call from the hotel."*	**Suggest** *"At our next pitch fest, let's call each other to make sure we're awake."*
Shame behavior *"I can't believe you slept through your alarm."*	**Shape behavior** *"From now on, both of us will be in by 9 p.m. the night before."*
Criticize what they did wrong *"Why didn't you put a USB drive in your pocket?"*	**Coach how they can do it right** *"In the future, let's both have USB drives in our pockets."*
Make yourself/others feel bad *"You gave us a reputation for being unreliable."*	**Make yourself/others feel better** *"Let's reach out to the investors and ask to set up a ten-minute meeting."*
Provide destructive feedback *"You really blew it big-time. I don't know if I can get over this."*	**Provide constructive feedback** *"We've worked well together up until now. Let's learn the lesson and move forward."*

Chapter 9

— TEASING OR TAUNTING? —

"I'm a social vegan. I avoid meet."

— INTERNET MEME

"I'm a man of a certain size. I fly a lot for business and really bristle when people say things like 'Time to bring out the extender belt.' How can I not be bothered by people's snark?"

If someone says something that gets under your skin, it's important to figure out whether their comment is *innocent* or *intentional*. Sometimes they don't mean to be mean. Their comment is "clueless" in an innocent way. They may not know you're sensitive about this or realize their remark isn't welcome. With these people, it's smart to use *Fun Fu!*

What's Fun Fu? Well, the brilliant Frances Hesselbein, former CEO of Girl Scouts, modeled it. When people found out her background, they often said, "Oh, *Thin Mints!*"

Frances could have taken offense at that. She could have corrected them and explained that Girl Scouts is much more than

Thin Mints. She could have said, "Do you know that Girl Scouts sell more than 200 million boxes — about 800 million dollars' worth — a year? Do you know Girl Scouts have gone on to become executives, company founders, champion athletes, world leaders?" She could have been miffed that they didn't realize how well regarded she is.

But she understood they did not mean to demean. So, she chose to act as an ambassador for her beloved organization and replied with a smile, "Yes, they are very good."

Could You Be Amused Instead of Offended?

*"Perhaps one has to become very old
to learn how to be amused rather than offended."*
— AUTHOR PEARL S. BUCK

Kudos, Frances! What a wonderful example of proactive grace. She realized most people are coming from a "good place" and chose not to put them in their place. Instead of being aggrieved or affronted, she gave an amiable response that validated their affection for their delicious cookies.

In a moment, I'll share ways to discern whether someone's comment could be an awkward attempt to engage you or an intentional dig. For now, here are a few more Fun Fu! responses so you can experience the saving grace of gentle humor.

Could You Handle This with Humor Instead of Harsh Words?

*"It's good to be able to laugh at yourself and the problems
you face in life. Sense of humor can save you."*
— COMEDIAN MARGARET CHO

I was invited to be a guest on Terry Bradshaw's show. Terry, Super Bowl quarterback and popular NFL commentator, pokes fun at himself before anyone else can. If someone gives him grief about his divorces (he's had three), his good-old-boy response is "Mama told me, 'Terry, you married outside the family, you're gonna have problems.'" Terry's easygoing humor makes it hard to give him a hard time, because he doesn't take himself too seriously.

Lan Nguyen Chaplin, PhD (one of fourteen children of Vietnamese refugee parents), was selected by Poets & Quants as one of the world's top fifty undergraduate business professors. When she taught her first MBA class, Dr. Chaplin anticipated that students would be startled to discover a petite woman in her thirties was their professor. So, she was prepared when she walked to the lectern and a student called out, "How long have you been teaching?"

Her Fun Fu! response? "I'm a lot younger than I look."

Grow a Thick Skin So People Can't Get Under Your Skin

"Your humor never fails to abuse me."
— Zazu, in the musical *The Lion King*

If you are on the receiving end of remarks that *are* digs to get under your skin, the question is what to do about it. If what they're targeting isn't going to change, be *proactive* versus *reactive* so people no longer have the power to get your goat. For example, if someone references a friend's hairless head, he smiles and says, "I'm not bald; that's my solar panel."

Proactive doesn't always mean coming up with comebacks. It can help to appeal to people's higher self. Actor Jonah Hill, who has gained and lost more than a hundred pounds during his film career, sent this message to his 3 million followers on Instagram: "I know you mean well, but I kindly ask you to not comment on my body. Good or bad, I want to politely let you know it's not helpful and it doesn't make me feel good. Much respect."

Jonah chose to ask for what he wanted. Did everyone honor his request? Nope. However, he did receive thousands of positive social media shout-outs, which reinforced his decision to ask for support instead of concluding his only option was to continue suffering from the trolls.

Instead of being knocked off balance by unwelcome comments, animal advocate Temple Grandin also has a ready response. I had a chance to meet her at a Houston livestock show and was impressed with how honestly and eloquently she talked about her autism. She says, "*I am different, not less.*" Wisdom in five words. She made this a nonissue for herself by coming to peace with her autism and inviting others along.

Comedian Harry Shearer said, "The reason we become comedians is to have control over why people laugh at us." What an intriguing insight. He is right. Having a repertoire of ready responses means we're no longer relegated to talking on eggshells when people bring up sensitive subjects. It is a proactive way to control the situation instead of being caught off guard.

Laugh and the Whole World Laughs with You (Sometimes)

"When you start to laugh, it doesn't just lighten your load mentally, it actually induces physical changes in your body."
— Mayo Clinic "Healthy Lifestyle" article

There's another reason it's in our best interests to keep a sense of humor — no matter what. The Mayo Clinic team posted an article on their website entitled "Stress Relief from Laughter? It's No Joke." That article shares the benefits of laughing: "It enhances your intake of 'oxygen-rich air' and increases your brain's release of endorphins. It can stimulate circulation and aid muscle relaxation, both of which reduce physical symptoms of stress."

As mentioned before, intentional teasers often target something we're "stressed" about. But what if we stop caring so much what other people think? What if the issue they're targeting is no longer a source of shame for us? Teasers can't embarrass us if we're not sensitive about what they're bringing up. They also can't derail us if we don't listen to them.

That's the advice of arguably the greatest baseball catcher of all time ... Johnny Bench of the Big Red Machine. I got a chance to share a plane ride with him on a short hop from Boston to Nantucket. After we landed and were waiting for our taxis, I had the opportunity to ask him a couple of questions. I told him I was writing this book and asked what he did if a player from another team was trash-talking him or opposing fans in the stands were booing him.

He shrugged and said, "I don't listen to them."

I cocked my head and waited, because it seemed he was ready to say more.

He added, "*If they've got your ears, they've got you.*"

What a wonderful one-sentence summation of why sometimes it's better to not pay any attention at all to teasers or trolls.

Six Options for Dealing with Teasers or Taunters

"I like long walks, especially when they are taken
by people who annoy me."
— PLAYWRIGHT NOËL COWARD

So, what can we do if we're dealing with someone who likes to have a laugh — at our expense? (Other than wishing they'd take a long walk?)

1. **Figure out what the teaser is trying to accomplish.**
   Check their facial expression to see if they're being play-
   ful or punitive. If they have a spiteful gleam in their eye,
   they may be deliberately trying to one-up you. If they
   have a twinkle in their eye, this could be an example of
   adolescent humor. Teasing can be a socially clumsy way
   to get a reaction — any reaction. Ask yourself, *Are they
   trying to engage or abuse?*

2. **Remove the incentive.** Teasers don't pick on people who
   don't rise to their bait. They target people who reward
   them by stammering, blushing, or reacting defensively.
   That's why it's important to desensitize yourself to topics
   you're sensitive about. If you are overweight, are balding,
   have a skin condition, or have an accent, you're going to
   hear about it. It's not fair; it's just the way it is. Anything
   you're embarrassed about is ammunition to an intentional teaser.

   Kudos to the woman who told our group what she
   does if someone tries to put a move on her and she's
   not interested: "I just look at them, smile, and say, 'Five
   brothers!'" Notice, her response isn't hilarious. It doesn't
   need to be. It's her way of letting guys know she's "been
   there, done that, got the T-shirt" and knows how to handle herself.

3. **Give them a dose of their own medicine.** Beating teasers at their own game makes this a losing proposition for
   them. If you have fun with them, it's no longer fun for
   them to make fun of you. One way to turn the tables on
   a teaser is to say, "Look who's talking. This is like the pot
   calling the kettle black, isn't it?" The truth is, teasers like
   dishing it out, and they don't like getting it back. If you
   meet teasers tit for tat, rap for rap, they're not controlling

the situation — you are. There's a great line in the movie *Bridesmaids* when Maya Rudolph's character responds to a snide comment by suggesting the originator of the snarky remark pretend to be happy for her, and then go home and talk behind her back "like a normal person." Snap.

4. **Work the crowd.** Is a teaser playing to an audience? If there are witnesses, the teaser may be trying to heighten their status by taking you down. The key in this situation is to address the *group*, not the teaser: "Buddy's at it again, picking on people half his size." It's no longer Buddy against you; it's you and the group against him. Outnumbered, he'll probably slink away and think twice before taking you on again.

5. **Yawn and roll your eyes in mock exasperation.** Adopting an "I'm so bored with this" posture frustrates teasers because it's the opposite of what they're trying to achieve. You may want to look upward and say resignedly, "Here we go again. Didn't work last time; what makes you think it'll work this time?"

6. **Agree and exaggerate.** Another way to take the fun out of teasing is to agree with someone's taunt and then add your own twist. This "If you can't beat them, join them" approach that Terry Bradshaw uses is a form of verbal martial arts and is a way to *flow* back instead of *fight* back.

Laughability Is Likability

"It has always surprised me how little attention philosophers have paid to humor since it is a more significant process of mind than reason. Reason can only sort out perceptions, but the humor process is involved in changing them."
— CREATIVITY EXPERT EDWARD DE BONO

An excellent example of someone who *changed* perceptions with her strategic sense of humor was Marilynn, who ran for her local school board. Her kids had all attended public schools and been active in clubs and sports. The thing was, she had gotten married when she was eighteen, had her first child when she was nineteen, and never attended college. She was sure this was going to come up in the town hall featuring the candidates.

Sure enough, one of the other candidates said rather pompously, "I think we all agree it's important for our trustees to have academic backgrounds, so they're informed about the issues they'll be deciding. I have an MEd and a PhD from [a famous university]." He turned to her and said, "What's your degree in, Marilynn?"

She smiled and announced to the audience, "I have a 5K degree."

He was puzzled and asked what that was.

She told the group, "*A Five-Kid degree*. My two sons and three daughters all graduated from schools in this district. I am well aware of the issues facing our educational system, and I'm confident of my ability to handle them in a way that serves students, faculty, and school administrators." The audience applauded, and his zinger was transformed into winning votes.

Remember, next time someone tries to tease you, it's an opportunity to change perceptions. If you beat them to the punch(line), you can increase likability and laughability.

Please note: If this person has a pattern of hurtful teasing, especially if they double down and make it *your* fault if you get upset, that is veering into bullying. You'll discover how to deal with manipulative, passive-aggressive digs in chapters 24 and 25.

Reminder Card of What to Do When People Are Teasing or Taunting

Imagine you're in your thirties and single, by choice. You're tired of all the incredulous looks and uninvited comments about your marriage status. What do you do?

Words to Lose	Words to Use
Feel flustered *"That's so out of line. I can't believe she asked that!"*	**Practice Fun Fu!** *"I'm just avoiding my first divorce."*
Push your hot buttons *"If one more person brings this up, I'm going to lose it."*	**Uninstall your hot buttons** *"I like being single, and I'm confident about and comfortable with my choice."*
Choose to be offended *"Who asked for your opinion?!"*	**Choose to be amused** *"I think, therefore I'm single."*
Feel ashamed/embarrassed *"Maybe I am going to end up alone as a bag lady."*	**Feel self-assured and self-accepting** *"Didn't your mama teach you better manners than that?*

Chapter 10

— MAKING FALSE ACCUSATIONS? —

"A lie can run round the world before truth has got its boots on."

– AUTHOR TERRY PRATCHETT

"A woman at work is telling lies about me. She's claiming I got my promotion because I have a relationship with my boss. She's bad-mouthing me to anyone and everyone who will listen. I'm afraid this will ruin my reputation. I told a few friends about it, and they just shrugged and said, 'That's Madison. It's just how she rolls.'"

I can only imagine how upsetting it is to have someone spreading rumors about you. In this case, it's important to talk to Madison directly about this instead of hoping this will "go away." Approach her in private, and bring a colleague so you have a witness to the conversation.

Say, "Madison, it's come to my attention you are spreading rumors that I got my promotion because I have a relationship with my boss. You know that's unfounded, untrue, and a complete fabrication. Do you also know this is slander and you can be held accountable for violating our company's anti-harassment policy? This is your one and only warning to cease and desist."

You may want your colleague to record the conversation so you have proof that you have talked to Madison about what's happening and asked her to stop. If Madison persists, take your recording to the HR director or your supervisor so they have evidence that you've tried to resolve this and can take the appropriate action.

You may be wondering, "What if someone isn't telling lies about me, they're just making accusations that are offensive or unwelcome?"

In that case, you might want to follow Amy Poehler's example: She was once called "bossy." Instead of taking umbrage, she reframed that accusation by saying, "I just love bossy women. I could be around them all day. To me, *bossy* is not a pejorative term at all. It means somebody's passionate and engaged and ambitious and doesn't mind leading."

What a classic case of how to deflect an accusation with verbal Jujitsu.

It reminds me of the time a woman put her hand up in a LeadHership training (the title of the leadership program I offer for females in the workplace) and asked, "Why are women so catty to each other?"

I had heard this before and decided it was time to *Amy Poehler* it: "Can we all agree to never ask or answer that question again? Every time we do, we reinforce that unflattering stereotype. Instead, let's change the conversation to how we *do* want to be perceived instead of how we *don't*.

"Maybe we can say, 'You know what I've found? Women are

real champions of each other. In fact, I wouldn't have this job if it wasn't for ...' and reference a woman who's mentored us. Or say, 'I believe just the opposite. I believe women go out of their way to support each other. For example ...'"

Notice that, if someone makes a negative accusation, you don't want to *deny* it, or you'll end up *debating* it. For example, if someone says, "You don't care about your customers," and you come back with "We do, too, care about our customers," now you're arguing with your customer about whether you care about your customers.

If someone says, "You never listen to me," and you insist, "That's not true!" you've just, in a weird way, proved their point.

If someone accuses you of turning everything into a fight, and you protest, "I do *not* turn everything into a fight," you just did.

So, what do you say if someone makes an untrue, unfair, un-kind accusation? Ask, "*What makes you think that?*"

The customer who says you don't care may reply, "The only time I ever hear from you is when you want to sell me something." Now you can say, "I'm glad you brought this to my attention," and promise to call more frequently just to check in without trying to make a sale.

The person claiming you don't listen may say, "You're texting on your phone and not even looking at me." Now, you can put the phone down and give them your full attention.

The person accusing you of fighting may say, "You raise your voice and cut me off before I have a chance to finish," and you can promise to keep your voice level and listen.

Asking what they mean surfaces the subtext and reveals the *real issue* so you can address the underlying concern instead of reacting to their attack.

Use *Your* Words, Not Theirs

"I didn't lose the gold. I won the silver."
— OLYMPIC FIGURE SKATER MICHELLE KWAN

Has someone made an unfair or unkind accusation against you, and you told everyone except the person who said it? That doesn't help. If you're not saying anything to people who are calling you names, they'll assume it must not bother you, because you're not saying anything.

If someone insults us and we "turn the other cheek," we *teach* them it's OK. We're showing them we won't hold them account-able. We may think we're avoiding ugliness. Unfortunately, we're permitting and perpetuating it.

You have a voice. Use it. The good news is, there are diplo-matic ways to speak up if people are putting you down. Here's a sample scenario.

Imagine someone tries to get a rise out of you by saying some-thing like, "Now, don't get mad." Whatever you do, *resist the urge to say*, "I am *not* mad." That means you took their bait. Instead, say, *"What do you mean?"* Those four words put the conversa-tional ball back in their court and give them an opportunity to explain their remark.

They might have a genuine reason for what they said: "Well, you're clenching your fists." Now, do a pattern interrupt by re-sponding with *your* words, not theirs: "You're right, I care deeply about this issue. Let's both take a deep breath so we can discuss this calmly."

Get Your Story Straight

"You get to decide how the story ends."
— AUTHOR BRENÉ BROWN

You may not get to decide how the story starts, but you can decide, as Brené points out, how it ends. If someone has dissed you, you may initially have decided to say nothing, as you felt it wasn't your place to let this person know they were out of line. Please recognize, it *is* your place to set the record straight. It is your responsibility to hold people accountable for what they say to you. If you don't speak up, their story stands, and you don't want to take that chance.

Remember that people can't walk all over you unless you lie down. If someone is telling an inaccurate story about you, these tips can help you stand up for yourself instead of taking it lying down.

1. **Decide if it's better to address this in public or in private — now or later.** Calling someone out in front of others can cause them to lose face. They will resent you — even if what you're saying is true. They may feel a compulsion to escalate matters in an effort to put you down so they're back "on top." Or, they may feel a need to put you down if they feel you're threatening their stature or position, especially if they're higher in the corporate structure. Most of the time, it's better to say, "Let's talk about this privately," so they feel no need to "show off" or "save face" because others are watching.

2. **Ask, don't counter-accuse.** If this accusation is egregious and you believe it's better to address this now instead of wait, you might want to take the person aside and ask, "Do you realize what you said is illegal and against company policy?" If this person is senior to you, you might

point out, "Did you know someone could file a grievance against you for saying something so inappropriate?" Eggshells are warranted here. If you perceive that this person is not open to this feedback and might view this as insubordination, it may be wiser to document this and speak to someone who's in a position to hold the person accountable.

Be sure to avoid inflammatory words like *sexist*, *racist*, *bigoted*, and *misogynistic*. Even if what you're saying has merit, those words come across as judgmental accusations, and now you're both making counterproductive counterclaims.

If a colleague is carrying on, it may be better to interrupt with "*Enough*. Let's remain professional, please." Then redirect the conversation. Nature abhors a vacuum (and I'm not too fond of them either). If you just say, "That's offensive," and stop talking, it leaves a verbal vacuum and they may feel the need to retaliate with "Who are you to tell me what to do?!"

3. **Don't repeat negative accusations or you'll reinforce them.** As stated before, denials backfire. If someone says, "You're so rigid," and you try to refute that with "I am not rigid," now you *are*. Instead, ask, "*What makes you say that?*" If they have a legitimate reason for their remark, even if you don't agree with it, at least you know what's really going on. They may say, "I wanted to discuss my climate-change project at today's meeting, and you said there wasn't time." Aahh, now you can say, "Thanks for reminding me. Let's add that topic to next week's meeting, which has open space on the agenda."

4. **Repeat what they said as a question and emphasize the offensive word.** "Really? All women are *catty*?" Repeating

an overstatement can be a gentle way to indicate what was said was an exaggeration. Say, "Wait. Back up. You said *all millennials* are entitled and can't be trusted?" People will often back down from over-the-top generalizations when they're asked to be more specific.

5. **Change the conversation to what you *do* want to be known for.** If someone accuses you of having unconscious bias and you react with "I do *not* have unconscious bias," you are arguing their point. Instead, say something like "I am glad you're bringing up the importance of diversity. I agree it's important, and we are updating our hiring practices so everyone has equal opportunities, which is why we've appointed Denise to be our new DEI officer this week." Go on record with what you do believe instead of denying a false claim and unintentionally giving it more traction. Whatever you do, don't respond in your head. That helps no one.

What If the False Accusation Is Gossip?

"The better we feel about ourselves, the fewer times we have to knock someone down to feel tall."
— AUTHOR COLETTE

A woman in a public workshop in Hawaii said she had a coworker who loved to, as they say in the islands, *talk stink*. "I don't take lunch in the employee cafeteria anymore because she's always there bad-mouthing someone. What can I do to get her to show some aloha?"

"First, good for you for not wanting to take part in the snark." I suggested several ways she could respond next time someone tries to draw her into the bad-mouthing, including:

- Say, "She's always been nice to me," and then change the subject: "Let's talk about something else."
- Say, "I don't know him personally" or "I don't know the details of the situation," and then add, "Let's give him the benefit of the doubt."
- When someone tries to hook you into their gossip with "Did you hear what so-and-so said?!" just say, "I don't find that productive," and move on. Don't take their bait.
- If someone is spreading rumors about you, reach out. Use their name: "Tiffany, if you have something to say about me, say it to my face," or "If you have problems with me, Tiffany, have the courage to talk *to* me instead of *about* me."

As the saying goes, people who gossip about others will someday gossip about you. Be the pattern interrupt who refuses to go along with the crowd. If pressed, you might even want to use a line from Hollywood producer Samuel Goldwyn, who said, "Include me out."

Or try entrepreneur Maureen Giles Birdsall's response if someone is snarky. She smiles and says, "I think your inside voice slipped out." She says that one line is usually enough for someone to realize what they said was not welcome and they take it somewhere else.

Create a Team Policy about Disparaging Others

"To speak ill of others is a dishonest way of praising ourselves."
— HISTORIAN AND AUTHOR WILL DURANT

Civility expert Christine Porath reported in an eye-opening *Harvard Business Review* article that it's important to "weed out toxic people before they join your organization."

One way to do that is to ask specific questions like "What would your former employer say about you — positive or negative?" and "When was a time you had to deal with stress or conflict at work?" to see if they disparage people they worked with at previous jobs.

Disparage is defined as "to describe someone or something as unimportant, weak, bad; to deprecate, degrade, lower in rank or reputation."

Disparaging — which includes bad-mouthing and making false accusations — is poisonous because it creates a culture of disrespect and distrust. If you are a leader (whether you own a business, manage a team project, or chair a committee), it's crucial to get ahead of this destructive behavior by addressing it in your orientations, meetings, and organizational manual.

When my son Andrew founded a nonprofit, Dreams for Kids–DC, he created a set of expectations about acceptable and unacceptable behavior. Rule 1 was "No gossip or snark. If you have issues with someone's performance, take it to them. No bad-mouthing. Ever. If you talk negatively about a customer or coworker, people will no longer trust you, because they'll think, *If you talk behind their back, you'll talk behind mine.*"

One of Andrew's interns reached out several years later to say, "Dreams for Kids–DC was my first job out of college, so I thought every organization had a behavioral manual. Wrong! In my current job, everyone bad-mouths everyone. I'll always be grateful to you for setting standards for behavior and instilling in me a personal policy around gossip. I just don't do it — and that's thanks to your clarity that it's a nonnegotiable nonstarter."

Does your company address gossip in its hiring interviews, team meetings, and employee handbook? If not, you might want to check out Dana Wilkie's excellent article "Workplace Gossip:

What Crosses the Line?" in the SHRM (Society of Human Resource Management) blog (cited in the notes section).

Create a Personal Policy about Gossip, Snark, and Bad-Mouthing

*"The real art of conversation is not only to say
the right thing in the right place, but to leave unsaid
the wrong thing at the tempting moment."*
— WRITER LADY DOROTHY NEVILL

You've probably noticed that a through line for this book is how to say the right thing at the right time. Equally important, as Lady Dorothy Nevill points out, is "to leave unsaid the wrong thing at the tempting moment."

This is easier to do if we have a "No disparaging" policy so we're not pulled off course when others are doing it. I got clarity on this while attending a National Speakers Association meeting where they honored Norman Vincent Peale, who had died the month before. NSA's founder, who'd known Peale personally, said, "He never had a bad word to say about anyone."

I thought, *That's quite a eulogy.* Peale, the author of the seminal book *The Power of Positive Thinking*, said, "If you want things to be different, perhaps the answer is to become different yourself." I decided then and there that I'd never say a bad word about anyone.

As former first lady Eleanor Roosevelt said, "Great minds discuss ideas, average minds discuss events, small minds discuss people." I decided I would speak and write about uplifting ideas. I would also speak and write about "rising tide" events. The only time I would speak about people was to elevate them, celebrate them, or connect them.

If You're Tempted to Gossip or Snark, T.H.I.N.K. First

T — is it True?
H — is it Helpful?
I — is it Inspiring?
N — is it Necessary?
K — is it Kind?

— **POSTER IN MANY SCHOOL CLASSROOMS**
(ORIGINATOR UNKNOWN)

I was moved to add this section to the book following a Thursday Night Football game. In the last minute, instead of going for an almost guaranteed field goal that would have put points on the board, Super Bowl MVP quarterback Tom Brady threw a risky pass that sailed over his receiver's head. The camera showed Brady holding up four fingers, mouthing a confused "Fourth down?" as the game ended without his team having a chance to run another play.

The Twitterverse exploded with snark. Fans had a field day piling on vicious "What a stupid mistake," "You suck," "You're too old — you should have retired" comments, and worse. Here's the thing. Could any of those fans play NFL football at the level Brady's played for years? Did they stop to empathize before they dumped on him (and his family)?

Hopefully, next time we're tempted to unload on someone, even if everyone else is, we choose to T.H.I.N.K. before we speak (as suggested above) and ask ourselves these questions:

- Could I have done any better? (Could I play pro ball at this level?)

- Is there context I'm not taking into account? (For example, Brady has made thousands of miraculous plays over the years. This was one mistake.)
- Would I say this to this person's face or to someone who cares about them? (Is this a form of "anonymous" bullying, and I'm doing it because there's no risk?)
- Will this undo what happened? (If not, it serves no good purpose.)
- Am I trying to make myself feel tall by making this person small? (Am I putting this person down so I can be "on top" and feel superior?)
- Have I ever made a mistake I regret? (If so, could I give this person some grace and choose to commiserate with them instead of have contempt for them?)

The world doesn't need more snark — it needs more compassion.

Snark can become a habit, a bad habit. The good news is, compassion can also become a habit. May these tips help you hold others accountable if they make a false accusation about you, and may they help you hold yourself accountable for not doing this to others.

Reminder Card of What to Do
If People Are Making Accusations

Imagine your company's president has resigned under "suspicious circumstances." You go into the employee lunchroom and everyone's buzzing about it. A colleague turns to you and says, "I heard that sexual-harassment charges were filed against him. What have you heard?"

Words to Lose	Words to Use
Deny/defend an accusation *"Really? I hadn't heard he was charged with sexual harassment."*	**Redirect an accusation** *"What makes you say that?"*
Refute an unfair, unkind claim *"Are you sure he retired under suspicious circumstances?"*	**Redirect an unfair, unkind claim** *"So, who is taking over as president of the company?"*
Speak without thinking *"If what they're saying is true, I hope they throw him in jail."*	**T.H.I.N.K. before speaking** *"Let's give him the benefit of the doubt until the facts come out."*
Gossip, snark, bad-mouth *"I always felt there was something off about him."*	**Adopt a "No gossip, snark, bad-mouthing" policy** *"I don't have anything to say about this. Include me out."*

Chapter 11

— SAD OR UNHAPPY? —

"Empathy is the opposite of spiritual meanness.
It's the capacity to understand that someone else's pain
is as meaningful as your own."

— AUTHOR BARBARA KINGSOLVER

"My daughter just broke up with her boyfriend, and she's miserable. I tried to console her and said everyone's been through a breakup and she'll get over this, and she got mad at me. I don't understand — I was just trying to help."

This is probably one of the biggest lessons of my life, and I'm still learning it. When we care about someone and they're unhappy, our first urge is to try to make them feel better. At that moment they don't want to feel better. They want to feel heard. They don't want our advice; they want our ears. They don't want to hear about the time this happened to us. They want to express how they feel without being told how they ought to feel or how others have felt.

A mom told me, "This contradicts every instinct I have as a mother, but I know it's true."

"What do you mean?"

"My daughter got braces and felt incredibly self-conscious about them. She wailed, 'Everyone at school is going to laugh at me.'

"With the best of intentions, I told her, 'They're not going to laugh at you. They probably won't even notice you're wearing braces.'

"She cried, 'I hate them. I look like a nerd.'

"What did I do? I tried to console her: 'You're going to be glad you got these when you have nice, straight teeth for the rest of your life.'

"She stormed off, saying, 'You never listen to me.' My heart was in the right place, except I should have realized she didn't want advice; she wanted empathy."

Use a Feedback Loop So People Feel Understood

"It is a luxury to be understood."

— POET, ESSAYIST, AND PHILOSOPHER RALPH WALDO EMERSON

Has this ever happened to you? Did you try to comfort someone who was unhappy and get rebuffed? What we don't realize is that well-intentioned phrases such as *It can't be that bad* and *Come on, look on the bright side* don't encourage people who are sad — they invalidate them. Attempts to cheer people up, like saying, "You can't expect to do it perfectly the first time," or "You'll feel better tomorrow," actually shut them down.

Next time someone is sad, use the *Feedback Loop* — that is, paraphrasing what they shared so they feel heard — to talk them *through* their troubles instead of trying to talk them *out of* them. Echoing what someone's said encourages them to go deeper.

For example, if a child says, "I don't have any friends," it doesn't help to say, "Surely you have at least one friend." It *does* help to say, "You feel like you don't have any friends?"

They may say, "Yeah, I hate going to lunch because I don't have anyone to sit with."

Resist the temptation to try to fix this. Just restate what they said as a question: "So, you don't have anyone to sit with at lunch?"

"Yeah, if you're not a member of the in crowd, it's like you don't exist."

You may think, *But I'm not helping.* Yes, yes, you are. You are giving this person exactly what they need, an opportunity to talk about what's going on with them. You're giving them a chance to express what they're feeling. The word *express* is defined as "to get out," and they are getting their feelings off their chest and out of their system so they're not so alone with them.

Don't Just *Say* You Care, *Show* You Care

"The simple act of caring is heroic."
— ACTOR EDWARD ALBERT

The beauty of the Feedback Loop is that it is a way to *show* you care, not just *say* you care.

- **You keep the focus on them.** If you're doing most of the talking, you're dominating the discussion, not facilitating it. My mom used to say, "Whoever does the most talking has the most fun." When someone is sad, the goal is for you to talk 20 percent of the time and for them to talk 80 percent of the time. Want a clue as to how to do that? Minimize the use of the word *I*. If you're saying, "Well, I think..." or "I suggest..." or "I remember the time that happened to me," you're shifting the conversation off them and onto you.

- **You're not parroting, you're paraphrasing.** You may think, *Isn't feeding back what they said going to annoy them? Won't they think, That's what I just said?* Actually, it doesn't annoy people to have you reflect what they said. It's verbal confirmation there has been "an exchange of meaning," which is the definition of communication.

- **The goal is for them to say a heartfelt "Yeah!"** It's amazing how universal that one syllable of affirmation is. No matter what language you speak, when you mirror what someone has just said, they almost automatically grunt their agreement. It is the moment of connection. It means, "You get it!" It's one of the reasons people pay to go to a therapist — it's often the only place they can truly talk out their feelings without being judged and told how they should feel or what they should do.

Are You Fixing or Feeling?

"We want people to feel with us more than act for us."
— AUTHOR GEORGE ELIOT

A man gently hit himself on the forehead while I was teaching a seminar and said, "I've got to apologize to my brother."

"What for?" I asked.

"He and his wife have a new baby who rarely sleeps. He called and really needed to vent. He said, 'This is supposed to be the best time of our life, but we're both exhausted.'

"Guess what I said? 'Join the club.' Then I made a joke: 'This is just preparing you for the next eighteen years of your life.' Then I went for the triple whammy and told him our youngest didn't sleep through the night until she was two years old. Not surprisingly, he hung up on me.

"I'm going to call him when I get home from work and apologize. And then I'll say, 'If you want to talk, I promise to zip my lip.'"

When People Say They're *Fine*, They're Usually Not

"Sometimes when I say, 'I'm fine,' I want someone to look me in the eyes and say, 'Tell me the truth.'"
— AUTHOR UNKNOWN

The above internet meme is printed on T-shirts and coffee mugs, along with this one: "The average person tells 4 lies a day, or 1,460 a year, and the most common one is 'I'm fine.'"

Sandra Joseph has a unique perspective on this. She played Christine in *Phantom of the Opera* for ten years on Broadway. We were discussing her TEDx talk and what to call it. She said, "The Phantom hides his self-perceived 'ugliness' behind a mask, thinking no one could possibly love him if they knew the *real* him. Yet, at the end, when he dares to take off his mask, Christine truly sees him and loves him with all his flaws. After all, we all have flaws."

What did Sandra end up calling her talk and her subsequent book? *Unmasking What Matters*.

When someone is sad, they are often afraid to take off the "I'm fine" mask and reveal what's underneath. Yet that is when we grow closer to people. When we share our human condition, we realize what we have in common and rediscover how we're alike. When we give people a chance to put what is inside them into words, there is often a *Eureka!* of connection.

Do They Want Space or Support?

"If you know someone who's depressed,
please resolve never to ask them why. Depression isn't
a straightforward response to a bad situation;
depression just is, like the weather."
— ACTOR AND DIRECTOR STEPHEN FRY

A therapist told me, "Be sure you differentiate between sadness and depression. They're not the same thing."

I asked, "What do you suggest we do if someone is clinically depressed?"

"Ask if they want *space* or *support*."

"What do you mean?" I asked.

"This is just one example. One of my patients is a father who dearly loves his family. When he's depressed, his wife goes above and beyond to cheer him up. She fixes his favorite meal, plays his favorite music, volunteers to watch the kids so he can have a night out with his buddies. What she doesn't understand is that trying to make him feel better makes him feel worse."

"How so?"

"He's ashamed because he can't make his depression go away. He says it's like being colorblind and people are constantly telling him how beautiful and colorful the world is."

"What does help, then?"

"Asking whether he wants space or support. Sometimes he just needs to close the curtains, crawl under the covers, and sleep. Sometimes he'd rather just sit on the couch with her and not talk. What he wants most of all is for her to just be there for him without trying to cheer him up."

Sometimes Helping Doesn't Help

"Never help a child at a task at which he feels he can succeed."
— EDUCATOR MARIA MONTESSORI

Do you have someone in your life who is sad? Have you tried to help them, only to discover they didn't want your help?

Helping can sometimes come across as rescuing. Trying to be helpful can make people feel helpless. If someone we care about is hurting, everything in us wants to go to their aid. That instinct comes from a good place, yet it can have the opposite of the intended impact.

Could you ask this person what they want? Space? Support? Ears? Advice? Just for you to "be there" for them? That may not feel like it's enough. If it's what they want, it *is*.

Words of Comfort, Words of Courage

"You are allowed to feel messed up and inside out. It doesn't mean you're defective. It just means you're human."
— NOVELIST DAVID MITCHELL

With that said, here's another option for what to do if someone's sad. I had the privilege of seeing the movie *Mission: Joy — Finding Happiness in Troubled Times*, featuring Archbishop Desmond Tutu and the Dalai Lama, at the Washington West Film Fest.

Toward the end of the film, Tutu is given a surprise eightieth birthday party at a school. A young Tibetan girl who's been exiled from her country to attend this school stands up and shares how homesick she is. In the middle of saying how much she misses her family, she breaks down in tears and is unable to continue.

Desmond Tutu looks at her with heartfelt compassion and says, "I am so sorry."

The Dalai Lama says (I am paraphrasing, as I didn't take notes in the dark), "Stay strong, focus on how fortunate you are to get this education. It is your chance to serve."

In the moment, the Dalai Lama's response comes across as a bit aloof, abrupt. However, narrator Douglas Abrams puts the two different responses in perspective when he observes that the archbishop gave the young woman words of *comfort*; the Dalai Lama gave her words of *courage*.

Aahh. The pebble dropped for me as soon as he said this. Both types of feedback have their place, don't they?

The young girl felt *acknowledged* by Tutu. She felt *empowered* by the Dalai Lama. If she had only received *support*, she might have stayed stuck in her story, because *rewarded behavior gets repeated*. She might have continued to dwell on her sorrow, spiraled into depression, and gotten more homesick. If, on the other hand, she had only received a *suggestion* on how to reframe this, she might have felt dismissed. She might have even regretted speaking, because she was made to feel weak, *wrong*.

I imagine the Dalai Lama saw that she had already received empathy and opted to offer encouragement to balance the feedback.

Support *and* suggestions. Acknowledgment *and* action. Both have their place, *in the right order*.

The next time someone is unhappy, ask yourself — and them — what they want *most* in that moment. Perhaps what they want most is to know that someone cares enough to take the time to find out how they really feel. They want ears, not advice.

You can gauge that with the Feedback Loop. When they say "Yeah!" or "I feel better just getting that out of my system," you know you've served them.

If it seems this person is stuck in their story, it might be more constructive to be like the Dalai Lama and suggest how they can see it in a different light.

Ask, "Is There Anything You Need?"

"Believe that anything is possible when you have the right people there to support you."
— DANCER MISTY COPELAND

Here is one more option. A friend, Janice, shared how neither she nor her husband Joe are particularly empathetic. They strongly identify with the "pick yourself up by your bootstraps" mentality, which has served them well. Yet, they've learned over time they're not the best supporters of each other when one of them is having a rough day.

Janice told me, "If Joe has a cold, I tell him, 'Man, that stinks. You can still pick up Elena from school, right? And pick up some groceries on your way home?'"

In turn, on days she's not feeling well, Joe acts the same way: "Wow, you went through a lot of Kleenex. It's kind of gross that you left them on the table."

Janice smiled. "Charming, isn't it? After learning from the CliftonStrengths assessment about our low empathy ranking, we trained ourselves. Now, if one of us is not feeling well, the other asks, 'Is there anything you need?' Even if it doesn't come naturally, it's better than what we did before, and we're still married, so I guess it's working."

Please note: If you suspect that someone is more than sad — they're depressed — you can pick up a phone and text a help line. You can find a directory of support organizations at the Everyday Health website (check out the link in the notes section).

Reminder Card of What to Do
When Someone Is Sad

Imagine a friend quit her job to start an online business, and it is not going well. She's barely making enough money to cover bills and is really discouraged and down in the dumps. What do you do?

Words to Lose	Words to Use
Advise her *"You should apply for a loan."*	**Hear her** *"So, you're really discouraged by how the business is going?"*
Come in with reasons *"Well, many small businesses fail the first year."*	**Come in with wishes** *"So, you wish you had more paying clients?"*
Use *I* or *me* *"This happened to me about five years ago."*	**Ask, with *you*** *"What would you like me to do to support you?"*
Correct *"You shouldn't have invested your life savings in this."*	**Comfort and encourage** *"I am so sorry this is not working out the way you hoped. I believe in you. You've got this."*

Chapter 12

— COMPLAINING? —

"There is no waste of time like making explanations."

— FORMER U.K. PRIME MINISTER BENJAMIN DISRAELI

"I manage the front desk of a hotel. It seems like all my team does is handle complaints. Someone doesn't like their room. Their key card doesn't work. Their luggage didn't arrive. We try to help them, but sometimes they won't stop complaining. Help!"

When I lived in Hawaii, I had opportunities to teach on this topic at many of the major hotels. What they all had in common was their front desk was the first point of contact. That meant the staff fielded lots of complaints. Guests had often been in airports and on planes for hours. They were often tired and grumpy. That first interaction had a disproportional impact on whether they were happy with their stay. We emphasized that looking through the guests' eyes and handling complaints quickly and satisfactorily was the key to high ratings and return guests. This is the technique I taught them. Hope you find it useful.

When People Complain, Don't Explain

"To err is human, to forgive, divine."
— POET ALEXANDER POPE

Let's update Pope's quote to "To err is human, to take the AAA Train is divine."

Here's what I mean. If someone complains, "You were supposed to call with an update on my early check-in," and you explain, "I'm sorry, I've been going nonstop," they're likely to say, "But you promised..."

You may try to explain again: "We're short-staffed and 100 percent booked..."

They then may say, "I don't want to hear your excuses. I just want to know when...?!"

See how well-intended explanations fall on uninterested ears? People don't want to know why they didn't get what was promised. They want it fixed. From now on when people complain, don't explain — take the *AAA Train.*

A = Agree: "You're right, Mr. Roberts, I did say I would call with an update."

A = Apologize: "And I'm sorry you ended up waiting."

A = Act: "I just heard from housekeeping, and I'm happy to say your room is ready."

Let's unpack this to see why the AAA Train is so effective.

Agree: When someone complains, ask yourself, *Is what they're saying basically true?* Most people who complain have a legitimate reason for doing so. If so, saying the magic words, *You're right,* acknowledges their point (instead of arguing with it) and makes you allies instead of adversaries.

Apologize: Say, "I'm sorry, *and...*" and then paraphrase what they said. Whatever you do, don't say, "I'm sorry, *but* it's not my fault," because that comes across as a *Sorry, not sorry*. When you summarize their complaint, they feel you heard what they said so they can let it go instead of repeating it again, louder this time.

Act: Instead of dwelling on what went on behind the scenes, focus on what you're going to do now to make this situation better. In the long run, and in the short run, that's what people want... action, not explanations. Explanations extend complaints. The AAA Train ends them.

Replace Reasons with Results

"At the moment of truth, there are either reasons or results."
— AVIATION PIONEER CHUCK YEAGER

After learning about the AAA Train, a young newlywed in one of my training sessions exclaimed, "I wish I'd known this last week!" I asked what happened.

"I forgot my wife's birthday. I've been heads-down on a project and didn't realize what I'd done until she gave me the cold shoulder. I asked what was going on, and she said, 'Nothing,' with that voice that told me *something* was definitely going on. Then it hit me. I told her I was sorry, that I'd been focused on making that deadline and her birthday had slipped off my radar.

"She was not happy. 'If it was really important to you, you would have remembered.'

"'Honey, it is important to me. It's just that this project is due, and I'm way behind.'

"She wasn't having any of it, and now I understand why. I wasn't apologizing; I was explaining. What could I have done instead?"

I told her, "First, thanks for sharing that story. We've probably all had something similar happen. Let's reverse engineer what might have been more helpful, so next time something like that happens to any of us, we can respond more constructively.

"Imagine if you had said, 'You're right, I didn't celebrate you on your birthday, and I'm really sorry. You're the most important person in the world to me, and I wish I had remembered. How can I make this up to you? What can we do this weekend that you'd really enjoy?'"

She said, "That would have worked a lot better. You're right. Explanations come across as excuses. They make people angrier, because they feel we're not being accountable. It is smarter to fast-forward to results instead of dwelling on reasons. From now on, that's what I'll do."

Why Should We Apologize If It's Not Our Fault?

*"The only people you should try to get even with
are the people who are helping you."*
— *SHARK TANK* INVESTOR LORI GREINER

A fellow workshop participant named Dev wasn't too sure about this. "OK, I get why apologizing when we're in the wrong makes sense. But sometimes I'm trying to help people, and they're upset, but I'm not responsible for what happened. Why should I apologize if it's not my fault?"

I smiled. "Have you heard the saying 'We can be right, or we can be happy'?"

Apologizing doesn't mean we're *responsible* for what went wrong. It means we're imagining what it's like for the person who's on the *receiving end* of what went wrong. In a way, whether or not it's our *fault* is immaterial. It is our *responsibility* to empathize with their frustration or inconvenience and do what we can to make it right.

Complainers want someone to understand what they went through. They want someone to say *out loud* that they recognize how awful this must have been. That's when they feel seen and heard. That's when they know we care. Once they get that, they're usually ready to move on. If they don't get the three As, they will keep repeating themselves until they do.

Reveal the Wish Rather Than Reinforcing What's Wrong

"Behind every criticism is a wish."
— RELATIONSHIP EXPERT ESTHER PEREL

Esther Perel's quote is profound. Complaints are criticisms about what's wrong. They can feel like attacks, which result in people going on the defensive or offensive. That gives the original complainer even more to complain about!

It's wiser to envision and articulate what you and the other person *wish* for.

Astronaut Dr. Mae Jemison says, "Never be limited by other people's limited imaginations." Complaining is limited imagination. It is a shortsighted, myopic focus on a problem. It's smarter to envision possibilities.

Want a shortcut to doing this? Simply ask the other person, "What do you wish for?" They will switch from kvetching to articulating what might make it right.

An auto-repair-shop manager committed to trying this, saying, "I can't wait to share this with our repair team. They're on the firing line and often get criticized for things they can't control. For example, people really resent having to bring their car in to get fixed when an automaker issues a recall."

I suggested, "You might want to post the AAA Train reminder card in your employee break room so team members can keep it top of mind. Next time a customer complains, include what you wish for, and what you imagine they might wish for. It has an incredible power to shift negative energy because it's clear you care."

Agree: "You're right, Ms. Camacho. I can only imagine how disappointing it is to have a brand-new car recalled to repair a possible defect. I wish this hadn't happened."

Apologize: "And I'm sorry you had to take time off work to get this fixed."

Act: "I imagine you wish the time this repair takes to be as short as possible. Please know we're going to do everything we can to have this finished in under two hours. Until then, you're welcome to set up shop in our lounge and watch TV or use your computer to get some work done."

When you include what you and the other person wish for, it turns a conflict into a cocreated future that's closer to what you both want.

What If Someone Is Not Right?

*"Most people spend more time and energy
going around problems than in trying to solve them."*
— AUTOMOTIVE PIONEER AND INDUSTRIALIST HENRY FORD

A government employee said, "I still don't understand why we should apologize if we didn't do anything wrong. I work for the county. Yesterday a woman couldn't get her building permit because she didn't have the approved inspection forms. She complained loud and long that she had stood in line for two hours and couldn't believe she'd have to start the process all over again. Why should I apologize? The requirements are posted on our website and on the wall right where she signed in. She should have read them."

I said, "It's not that you *have* to apologize; it's just that it's to your *advantage* to do so. If you tell her, 'Hey, it's not my fault you didn't bring the right form!' she'll take her anger out on you and make your day even more miserable.

"Imagine if you said, 'I understand it's disappointing to discover you don't have the necessary paperwork. Tell you what. We have your filled-out application here. When you come back, please let the guard at the door know you were here today, and we just need to verify your forms. You can be in and out in ten minutes.'"

I asked the county employee, "What would happen if you chose to respond that way?"

He grinned. "She'd probably stop yelling at me."

Exactly.

What If Apologizing Might Open You to Liability?

"Every great mistake has a halfway moment,
a split second when it can be recalled and perhaps remedied."
— AUTHOR PEARL S. BUCK

A paramedic said, "Sam, our supervisor told us we can't apologize when things go wrong because it might open us up to liability."

"Good point. There are exceptions to every rule. Can you think of a recent example where apologizing might have caused legal problems?"

"Yesterday our crew wasn't able to revive a drowning victim, despite working on him for an hour. His wife grabbed me and said, 'You could've saved him if you'd gotten here sooner.' As much as my heart went out to her, there was no way I was going to say, 'You're right.'"

If agreeing could land you in court, take the Express *AA Train*.

Acknowledge: "I can only imagine how painful it is to lose your husband."

Act: "How can we help? Is there a family member we can contact to be here with you?"

Taking the Express AA Train doesn't admit responsibility or accept culpability. Rather, it compassionately acknowledges someone's emotions instead of brushing them aside.

Why Taking the AAA Train Is in Everyone's Best Interests

"A man must be big enough to admit his mistakes, smart enough to profit from them, and strong enough to correct them."
— AUTHOR JOHN C. MAXWELL

I love Maxwell's quote because it captures the essence of this chapter. Taking the AA or AAA Train is a way to be "big enough" to take the high road. We're more interested in *making* it right than acting out of ego and having to *be* right. The A Trains are ways to step up and have the moral strength to correct what happened instead of claiming it wasn't our fault. This servant-leader approach pays off for all involved.

A White House Office of Consumer Affairs report found when you handle complaints proactively, *customers feel more favorably about you than if nothing had gone wrong in the first place.* British entrepreneur Sir Richard Branson said, "A complaint is a chance to turn a customer into a lifelong friend. I say that seriously, not as some press release baloney." Agreed. If we have an opportunity to turn complainers into friends and return customers, why *wouldn't* we do that?

When People Complain Just to Complain

"Sometimes people complain like it's an Olympic sport (for the record, it's not)."
— ENTREPRENEUR IVAN MISNER

A sister writer is a big fan of the Stephanie Plum series by bestselling author Janet Evanovich. She said, "There's a character in Evanovich's books called Shirley the Whiner. Her name tells you all you need to know about her. I have an aunt who's like that. She complains about…everything. Sympathizing with her doesn't make her feel better; it eggs her on. It took me a while to realize she doesn't want help; she wants to vent.

"The thing is, I'm busy. I don't have the bandwidth to listen to her complain. I started avoiding her because it was always a long list of petty grievances. It didn't feel right to shut her out, though, so I decided to do something with her my mom did with us. If my brother and I were griping about something, she would say, 'There's always a reason to complain, and there's always a reason to be grateful. You'll be happier if you choose gratitude.'

"Every time she said that, we'd groan and roll our eyes. But guess what? We stopped complaining! Now, when I'm around my aunt, I mentally give her ten minutes to get things off her chest. If she keeps with the complaints, though, I repeat my mom's mantra and ask, 'What's something you're grateful for?'

"If she keeps grumbling, I say, 'Auntie, my heart goes out to you. And I've got something going on and would love your advice.'"

In his book *The Last Lecture*, Carnegie Mellon professor Randy Pausch shared the life lessons he wanted to pass along to his children. He knew he had terminal cancer and wanted to distill what he had learned into a literary "message in a bottle." In his last lecture at the university, he said, "If you took one-tenth the energy you put into complaining and applied it to solving the problem, you'd be surprised by how well things can work out. Complaining does not work as a strategy. We all have finite time and energy. Any time we spend whining is unlikely to help us achieve our goals. And it won't make us happier."

If you manage a group of people, or are raising a family, you might want to discuss Randy's insight. It can serve as a valuable wake-up call about the futility of complaining. Decide right here, right now, that from now on, you will take the A Trains instead of wasting precious time going back and forth about who did what to whom.

Reminder Card of What to Say — and Not Say — When People Are Complaining

Imagine you're a wedding planner. The big day has arrived for an outdoor wedding, and it's raining. Everyone is distraught. They're complaining and taking it out on you. What do you do?

Words to Lose	Words to Use
Argue *"Don't blame me. I can't control the weather."*	**Agree** *"You're right, this is not what any of us wanted for your big day."*
Explain *"I told you there was a 30 percent chance of this happening."*	**Apologize or acknowledge** *"I can only imagine what a disappointment this is for you."*
Accuse or attack *"Stop taking this out on me. I'm not at fault here."*	**Act** *"We have a contingency plan in place. We're moving everything indoors."*
Open to liability *"No, I won't give a refund even if you sue me."*	**Take the Express AA Train** *"I understand this is not what you hoped for, and let's make this a marvelous day you remember fondly."*

Chapter 13

— NOT COOPERATING? —

"Look, demanding somebody do anything
in this day and age is not going to fly."

— SINGER-SONGWRITER JOHN MAYER

"Why won't my kids obey me? They drag their feet and resist almost everything I say. Sometimes I have to tell them to do something two or three times, and they still don't cooperate. Then I get upset, and things go downhill from there. Help!"

Let's look to an unexpected source to find an answer as to how to motivate people to cooperate. I took our Jack Russell pup (a breed known for their "reign of terrier") to obedience school. At the first session, JR was so excited to see all his new buddies, he started yapping nonstop.

What did I do? I yelled, "Stop barking!" (And yes, I know how ridiculous that was.)

The instructor came over and said, "It doesn't help to yell at a barking dog. He just thinks, *Great, now we're both barking.* You need to model the behavior you want him to follow. You need to speak to him in a low, slow voice."

"How is that going to help? He's so ramped up, he's not even paying attention to me."

"Does he sit on command?"

I said, "Usually."

"Then ask him to sit and reward him the second he does. Catch him doing something *right* instead of catching him doing something *wrong*."

Gee. I thought I was taking JR to doggy school, and instead *I* was receiving a master class in behavior modification and pattern interrupt.

Elicit Cooperation through Behavior Modification

"We may think there is willpower involved,
but more likely, change is due to want power."
— PHYSICIAN AND SENIOR ATHLETE GEORGE A. SHEEHAN

The foundation of behavior modification is to transform our *will*-power into *want* power. One way to do that is to focus on what we want people (or dogs) to *start* doing instead of focusing on what we want them to *stop* doing.

This sounds obvious, yet many of us do just the opposite. For example, I was on my morning walk and passed our neighborhood park, where a mom and her two young sons were playing. The kids started throwing gravel, and she told them to stop.

Guess what happened? They kept throwing gravel.

She then raised her voice: "I said, *stop throwing gravel*!" That didn't work, either.

The next time, she threatened them: "*If you don't stop throwing gravel, we're going to leave!*"

They kept ignoring her. She marched over to the park bench, started collecting their things, and pronounced, "That's it. I've had it. If you're not going to cooperate, we're going home." They started protesting, and she told them, "*Too late!*" and stormed out of the park, with the pair of them trailing behind.

No one got what they wanted. The mom was unhappy. The kids were unhappy. Who knows? She may be a little reluctant to trek to the playground next time because they had a bad experience this time.

What could the mom have said to get better results? She could have:

- used their names to get their attention. Using someone's name is a way to *cause* a *pause*. Most people will stop what they're doing and pay attention when they are addressed by name.
- waited until they looked at her. If people aren't looking, they're not listening. She could have said, "Give me your eyes," which works better than saying, "You better listen to me."
- prefaced her request with "I'm going to say this once." If she just started talking, they'd still be preoccupied and not be paying attention.
- initiated a pattern interrupt by articulating what she wanted them to *start*, instead of *stop*. She could have asked herself, *What do I want them to do?* and then articulated *that* instead of telling them what she *didn't* want them to do.
- made the request as visual and tangible as possible. It helps people cooperate when they can *see* the desired behavior in their mind's eye. She could have said, "I'll count

to three and you need to put the rocks on the ground *now*, and then we're walking over to the slide."

With this more clearly articulated suggestion of what to start (versus her trying to exert her will), her sons probably would have complied, and everyone would have had a good day at the park.

Stop Ordering, Start Asking

"Whether or not we support a decision
depends on whether it's being done to us or by us."
— SAM HORN

Think of a situation where someone's dragging their feet. Have you been telling them what *not* to do, catching them doing something *wrong*, or telling them what they *should* be doing? Those come across as orders. Do you know anyone who likes to be ordered around?

As John Mayer pointed out in the chapter's introductory quote, demanding is not an effective leadership style. If we want people to cooperate willingly (instead of comply reluctantly), it's smart to replace "*You have to*" commands with "*Could you please?*" requests. It's also smart to ask people to *begin* a *desired* behavior instead of to *drop* a *dreaded* behavior.

Imagine you're a store manager. Here are some ways to elicit cooperation.

- Instead of saying, "*You need to* restock the shelves," say, "*Could you please* restock the shelves before you sign out, so the store is ready when we open at 10 a.m. tomorrow?"
- Instead of "*You have to* close out tonight because Joyce needs to leave early," try "*Could you please* close out

tonight because Joyce is leaving early for a doctor's appointment?"

- Instead of "*Don't wait until it's too late* to take inventory," ask, "Will, *could you please* take inventory in between customers so we have it done by the end of the week?"

- Instead of "*I don't want to have to tell you again. Stop* smoking in the employee lounge," say, "*I'll say this once.* If you choose to smoke, please do so outside twenty feet from our building."

These phrases are a combination of courtesy and clarity. Instead of feeling "ordered around," people understand what's expected of them, and they're more motivated to cooperate because they're being treated with the respect we all want, need, and deserve.

You're Not the Boss of Me

"Life is not so short but that there is always time for courtesy."
— POET, ESSAYIST, AND PHILOSOPHER RALPH WALDO EMERSON

A surgeon pushed back: "Not so fast. In the middle of an operation, I don't have time for niceties. I'm not going to *ask* the nurse, 'Could you please pass the scalpel?' That's way too soft. A patient's life is on the line. I tell my team what I need, and they better do it *stat.*"

I said, "I'm glad you brought this up. There are certainly exceptions to the 'ask, don't order' advice. If this is a life-and-death situation, it makes sense that the person in charge give an order and everyone's expected to hop to it. The question is, has giving orders become a habit, and we treat everyone in our life that way?"

He blanched, then admitted, "I've got some apologizing to do.

You're right: giving orders has become such a habit that I go home and treat my wife and kids that way, too."

Military officers, senior executives, and celebrities can get accustomed to ordering people to jump, and the only allowed response is "How high?" However, this can come across as off-putting arrogance. A habit of *telling* people what to do is based on the belief that we are "senior" and know best. Even if that's true, it's not tactful.

Ordering someone around often backfires even if you *are* the boss. People may "do as they're told," while internally they're resenting you because it's an insult to their dignity to be ordered around like a child. When you ask for cooperation instead of giving commands, people are more likely to honor your requests because they *choose* to, not because they're being paid to.

And when you ask people to *start* doing something rather than *stop* doing something, they are more likely to produce the desired behavior instead of the dreaded behavior.

Orders End Affection

"Politeness is the flower of humanity."
— MORALIST AND WRITER JOSEPH JOUBERT

A man in a seminar said he couldn't wait to get home. I asked why, and he said, "I can't wait to talk about this with my wife. This has helped me realize why the romance has gone out of our marriage. We constantly tell each other what to do: '*You need to* take the dog to the vet. *You have to* pick up the dry cleaning on the way home. *You need to* pick up the kids from daycare.'"

He continued, "It's a way of taking each other for granted, isn't it? You've heard the saying 'Familiarity breeds contempt'? Well, ordering others around breeds contempt. After ten years together, there's a lot more orders than affection. 'You were supposed to call the plumber.' 'Stop watching so much football.' I can already see how asking for what we do want — instead of getting upset about what we don't want — will help restore some romance to our relationship."

Visually Articulate What You *Do* Want vs. What You *Don't*

"When I began writing science fiction, one of the things I found lacking in it was visual specificity. It seemed there was a lot of lazy imagining, a lot of shorthand."
— AUTHOR WILLIAM GIBSON

Sci-fi writer William Gibson is onto something. The more visually specific our suggestions are, the more likely it is people will be able to picture it, perform it, and produce it. This is a crucial *mind shift* and *language shift* I hope you remember moving forward.

If you tell someone, "Don't worry," they'll continue to worry.

If you tell someone, "You'd better not be late again," they'll be late again.

If you tell someone, "Stop interrupting me," they'll keep interrupting you.

A key to changing people's behavior is to visually describe the *wanted* behavior, versus the *unwanted* behavior, so they can *picture* it in their mind's eye.

For example:

- Instead of "Don't *worry*," say, "*Trust* that this will work out for the best."
- Instead of "You'd better not be *late* again," say, "Be five minutes *early* for this meeting."
- Instead of "Stop *interrupting* me," say, "Ed, please *let me finish*, and then it's your turn."

Author Esther Hicks says, "What you think and what you get always matches." What you ask for and how constructively you ask for it also often matches.

That's why, if there is a weather delay and a plane needs to return to the terminal, pilots get on the intercom and say, "Thank you for your *patience*. We promise to give an update as soon as we receive one. Until then, please know how much we *appreciate* your *understanding*."

Feel how they're planting positive emotional seeds that produce positive emotions?

Imagine if they said, "Well, I've got some bad news. The tower just told us a thunderstorm is moving into the area, and we have to go back to the gate. I don't know how long this will be. You'll just have to sit and wait."

The first announcement sets a tone for grace. The second announcement sets a tone for grumbling.

If Someone's Not Cooperating, Don't *Take* Control, *Share* Control

"It's coexistence or no existence."
— PHILOSOPHER BERTRAND RUSSELL

There's another way to inspire people to cooperate. Many conflicts are based on a battle for control. If someone is not cooperating, ask yourself, *Is this a battle for control?*

If it is (and it probably is), ask yourself, *Instead of me being in control, and the other person being* out *of control, is there some way we can* share *control?*

Unilateral is defined as "done or undertaken by one person or party." It is also defined as "one-sided." No wonder people resent unilateral decisions. It means they play no role, have no say, are left out of the loop. It means someone's driving the agenda without consulting them. No wonder they drag their feet.

A way to share control is to offer two options, both of which are acceptable to you, and ask, "Which do you prefer?"

For example, if someone asks, "Can I stop by your office later today? I need to update you on our budget," instead of replying, "Can't today, my calendar's packed," say, "Yes, we can connect. I can make it tomorrow at 10 a.m. or at 4 p.m. Which works best for you?"

This approach is especially useful if you're in customer service. If a customer is complaining, part of the reason they're upset is they've "lost control" of the situation. If you say, "We could do this, or we could do this. Which do you prefer?" the customer will be a lot happier because they're back in control and the decision is being made *by*, rather than *for*, them.

This may seem minor yet can make a big difference in determining whether you come across as doing your half to get along or as summarily making decisions without asking for input.

Starting today, if someone is being recalcitrant, ask yourself if you're telling them what *to* do or what *not* to do. Both are orders. If so, it's not too late to *ask*, instead of *order*, and *request*, instead of *reprimand*. Chances are, they'll stop pushing back and start cooperating.

Reminder Card for
When Someone's Not Cooperating

Imagine you're a dance instructor getting ready for a recital. It's a hot summer day, and the kids aren't paying attention or following instructions. You're at the end of your rope. What do you do?

Words to Lose	Words to Use
Lose your cool *"The recital is Saturday, and you're not ready!"*	**Keep your cool** *"Dancers, the recital is Saturday, and I trust you want to be ready."*
Say what you don't want *"Stop checking your phones. They're distracting you."*	**Say what you do want** *"Dancers, give me your eyes, and let's practice this and get it right."*
Command *"You better pay attention or I'm going to lose it."*	**Courteously request** *"Thank you for giving me your full attention for the next half hour."*
Order them to stop *"Stop your side conversations."*	**Ask them to start** *"Start on three and immerse yourself in the music."*

Chapter 14

— MAKING EXCUSES? —

"I've heard every excuse in the book, except a good one."

— FITNESS EXPERT BOB GREENE

"I've got an employee who comes in late. She's always got a good excuse, but enough is enough. What can you do when you're dealing with someone who's never accountable?"

An entrepreneur asked this question during an online training, and it prompted a thought-provoking discussion of why some people don't keep commitments, and what to do about it.

She said, "I own a nail salon. One of our employees is habitually late, but I kept excusing her excuses because she's been here so long. I'm embarrassed to admit I kept giving her a pass until another stylist complained, 'This isn't fair. I'm on time every day. It's not easy, and I do it anyway. Priya blames her kids for why she's late. I have kids, too, and don't use it as an excuse for traipsing in a half hour late every day. I'm starting to wonder why I should be on time when I don't get rewarded, and she doesn't get punished.'"

She had brought up an intriguing issue. Sometimes when

people have a habit of making excuses it's because they've "gotten away with it" up until now. They think, *Why change?*

Who is someone you work with who frequently makes excuses for why they didn't do what they were supposed to? Walk through the "How to Hold People Accountable" process to see if a precedent of unaccountability has been set and discover how you can change it.

How to Hold People Accountable

"Never make excuses. Your friends don't need them and your foes won't believe them."
— BASKETBALL COACH JOHN WOODEN

1. **Consider whether the policy about this behavioral expectation was outlined at the outset.** Was coming to work on time discussed during the hiring interview or employee orientation?
2. **Reflect back on whether this policy has been consistently enforced.** Have you said anything about this at the time it happened or in a one-on-one meeting? Do employees get reprimanded if they arrive late (or has it been discussed and dropped, without consequences)?
3. **If the answer to the above questions is no, recognize that this employee feels *entitled*.** They feel, "Well, if it really bothered you, you'd say something," or "Well, Carla comes in late and nothing happens, so I guess it's OK."
4. **Speak up with a *mea culpa*.** *Mea culpa* means "my fault" in Latin. It's not fair to suddenly hold people accountable for a policy that wasn't outlined or enforced. Take responsibility for not clarifying this as a job expectation that needs to be met.

5. **Give a starting date for a *new* behavioral expectation.** You can't "drop the hammer" with no warning and expect an employee to instantly change their behavior. There may be legitimate adjustments that need to be made — like rideshare arrangements or daycare drop-offs.

6. **Say, "Things are going to be different from now on," and outline consequences.** State what will happen if this behavior expectation is not met — and say, "Don't test me on this. You will be held accountable for it — no excuses, no exceptions."

7. **Do *not* ask, "Do you understand?"** They may nod; however, that doesn't count. Ask, "What is your understanding of our agreement?" so they voice what they'll do differently and acknowledge they're aware of the consequences if they don't comply. If this has been a persistent problem, you may want to ask them to sign a document indicating they've been informed of this and agree to change their behavior.

8. **Schedule a follow-up meeting so this doesn't "disappear."** Get out your calendars and pick a date and time to review this issue so the individual knows you mean what you say and are not going to "look away" and continue to let it slide.

Understand That Habitual Excusers May Play on Your Sympathies

"Rationalization is a process not of perceiving reality, but of attempting to make reality fit one's emotions."
— WRITER AND PHILOSOPHER AYN RAND

Did you have an epiphany as a result of asking those questions about whether a precedent had been set? As Ayn Rand pointed out, excusers are attempting to make reality fit their reasons in the hopes that you'll go along with their rationale.

In fact, people who *habitually* make excuses may try to turn the tables and make you feel guilty for enforcing the rules. Instead of owning their behavior, they try to portray you as unsympathetic. Following the "How to Hold People Accountable" process can help you stay the course even if they're trying to convince you you're a terrible person for doing this.

A friend told me this process helped her husband Matt have an accountability conversation with an employee who had, repeatedly, been caught playing video games on company time. Prior conversations about "the need for professionalism" had gone nowhere with this employee.

Matt laid out the expectations of what needed to change. "I drew a line in the sand. No more video games at work and no more disappearing for hours on end. I couldn't believe it. He kept rationalizing what he'd been doing and saying this was 'no big deal.'"

I told him, "Trevor, it is a big deal. I've outlined our policy, and we'll be holding all employees accountable for following it. Our clients pay us to work on their projects, not to play *Pokémon GO*. You need to state your understanding of our agreement, and that you realize this is a requirement for continued employment with our company."

Excusers Often Try to Make You Feel Sorry for Them

"For any meaningful business transaction, trust — built up over time — is the essential ingredient."
— BUSINESS AUTHOR DORIE CLARK

A workshop participant named Lenora said, "I agree with this, but every time I tell an employee she can't keep making personal calls on the job, she always has some kind of sob story. It's hard to trust her because I never know if she's telling the truth."

Lenora had brought up an important point. People who have an excuse for everything can be hard to trust, because they're masters at manipulation. They may say things like, "You don't understand how hard this is for me," or "But my kid's school called, and I had to answer." Their goal is to somehow make it your fault instead of theirs.

An experienced recruiter named Li confirmed this: "In ten years of hiring people, I've noticed a pattern. Some people consistently speak in positive terms, like 'I was lucky to work at a first-rate company right out of college,' and 'I'm glad I got to report to a boss who really mentored me.' Even when something wasn't 'picture-perfect,' they focus on what they learned: 'There was turnover during the pandemic; however, our team was resilient and picked up the slack.' Those are the job candidates I refer and hire because they have shown their stripes. They adapt even when going through hard times, like acquisitions or economic downturns.

"In contrast, there are job candidates who have a history of toxicity. They play the victim. It's not just one awful company, it's that *every company was awful.* I don't present these candidates to any of my clients. If every company treated them poorly before, it's only a matter of time before they start complaining that their new company is treating them poorly, too."

How will you act on this insight — that a *pattern of excuse making is a predictor?*

When determining whether to get involved with someone personally or professionally, look for the *theme* in how they talk about their previous relationships. If there was something wrong with most of the people they've dealt with before, you're next on their list.

Don't Dodge the Consequences, Do the Consequences

"Sooner or later, everyone sits down to a banquet of consequences."
— NOVELIST ROBERT LOUIS STEVENSON

A friend named Heidi told me, "Sam, my job as a parent is to *not* let my kids get away with excuses. If they do it at home, they'll do it at school, they'll do it in their job, and they'll do it in all their relationships. And that won't go well for them."

"That's wise. So, what do you say if your son or daughter makes an excuse?"

"Well, this just happened. My daughter spilled bright red nail polish all over the kitchen floor. When I saw the mess, I got upset because we have a rule that nail polish stays in the bathroom. My daughter tried to turn it on me: 'Mom, why are you getting so mad? It was an *accident*. I didn't mean to do it. I just forgot.'

"I told her, 'Everyone forgets sometimes. That doesn't change the fact that you broke the rule. Accidents have consequences. Clean it up, then turn over the nail polish. You can have it back next month so you remember to follow the rules.'"

From now on, when someone makes an excuse, remind yourself that you don't do them a favor by looking the other way. You do them a lifelong favor by holding them accountable for their actions … or inactions. If they grumble, "That's a stupid rule," you say, "Nevertheless, it's the rule, and you need to follow it just like everyone else."

Heidi says, "Holding someone accountable *now* helps them be more accountable *in the future*. I contribute to their character every time they do consequences instead of dodge them."

Heidi's right. The sooner someone sits down at the banquet of consequences, the fewer times they'll have to later.

We Don't Help People When We Let Them Off the Hook

*"If you really want to do something, you'll find a way.
If you don't, you'll find an excuse."*
— SELF-HELP EXPERT AND MOTIVATIONAL SPEAKER JIM ROHN

It can be helpful to think of accountability in terms of *integrity*. A shout-out to my son Andrew for prompting this epiphany. My New Year's resolution was to get back in shape. In a show of support, Andrew bought me a gym membership and agreed to meet me there three mornings a week. Like millions of others who've made this pledge, I followed up the first few weeks, then got busy and my good intentions faded away. After a couple of months Andrew called me on it. "Mom, do you want to get in shape or not?"

I'm embarrassed to say, I started giving all the reasons I wasn't getting to the gym. Andrew wasn't buying it. In fact, he actually used a quote to remind me of my original intentions (like mother, like son?!). He said, "You're the one who shared Jim Rohn's quote with me. Mom, are you going to find a way or an excuse?"

Thank you, Andrew, for reminding me that not doing what I said I'd do is a form of lying. If I want to be in integrity, and I do, I need to *keep my word* to myself and get to the gym.

Do I get to the gym every Monday, Wednesday, and Friday? No. Do I get there more often than I did? Yes. The catalyst is reminding myself, *I can have excuses or integrity. Not both.*

As author Laurie Buchanan says, "Whatever you are not changing, you are choosing." Next time someone makes an excuse, you might opt to use the Jim Rohn or Laurie Buchanan quote to remind them that keeping commitments is a way of keeping our word. While they may not like hearing it at the time, they may ultimately thank you for helping them stay in integrity.

Reminder Card of What to Do
If People Are Making Excuses

Imagine you run a doggy daycare center and have hired two students to take the dogs outside for walks twice a day. You discover the teens are going around the corner and texting and scrolling social media instead of walking the dogs.

Words to Lose	Words to Use
Set no expectations *"My bad. I never specified exactly what to do."*	**Establish and enforce expectations** *"Remember in your entry interview, we said the dogs must be walked around the park twice?"*
Be swayed by reasons *"I know it's hot, so you don't have to walk them today."*	**Ask for results** *"You're right, it's hot outside, so please make sure you and the dogs have plenty of water."*
Dodge consequences *"I'm going to let it go this time."*	**Do consequences** *"What is your understanding of our agreement?"*
Continue to defend your decision *"I am not being unreasonably hard on you."*	**Hold them accountable** *"Steve, Sinjin, think about what's best for the pups and for keeping this job."*

Chapter 15

— NOT LISTENING? —

"Listening is not just about being quiet, it's about being present."

— PODCASTER KRISTA TIPPETT

"My boyfriend has his head down looking at his phone all the time and rarely gives me his full attention. He says he's listening, but I can tell he's only hearing half of what I say. I feel like I'm competing with his phone for attention. Help!"

The irony is you *are* competing with his phone for his attention. We'll get into how many people are addicted to their phones and how that is affecting their relationships later in this chapter. For now, I want to share an intriguing insight that's emerged from my interviews with thousands of people around the world.

When we think people aren't listening to us, we're probably not listening to them.

Let's focus on how we can be a better listener; then we'll focus on what to do if someone is not giving us their attention. To put this in perspective, please answer these questions:

- Who is someone who *really* listens to you?
- What do they do that makes them such a good listener?
- How does that person make you feel?
- How do you feel about them?

In the twenty years I've been asking those questions, there's been a surprising trend. Most people can only think of *one* or *two* individuals who *really* listen to them. It's that rare.

Think about it. Many of us know hundreds (thousands?) of people. Yet only one or two really listen to us?! What's that about?

Well, some of us have what Buddhists call a "monkey mind." We've got all this chatter going on in our brain at any given time. Someone's talking to us, but we're thinking, *Look, a squirrel! Did I forget to turn off the stove? What time is Timmy's soccer game?!*

As long as we're distracted by our internal yak-yak-yak, we're really not "there"; we're here, there, and everywhere. We may be standing right next to someone or seeing them through video conferencing; however, we're a million miles away in our mind.

To really listen, we want to temporarily *care* more about their agenda than ours. Here's an example of the meaningful connections that can happen when we listen *carefully*.

To Really Listen, We Must Set Our Agenda Aside

"I have learned a great deal from listening carefully. Most people never listen."
— WRITER ERNEST HEMINGWAY

As I mentioned previously, my son Andrew started a nonprofit called Dreams for Kids in Washington, D.C. (DFK-DC). He and his team were planning a holiday party for kids with special needs to give them the Christmas they might not have otherwise. Andrew was thrilled to get on the calendar of Howard University's Roberta

McLeod-Reeves, the director of the campus center, and was hoping she'd give them approval to use the three-story center for their event.

Three minutes into the meeting, Andrew realized Roberta was being polite as she waited for him to stop talking so she could tell him this wasn't going to happen. Instead of forging ahead, he paused and put himself in her shoes.

He imagined she might be thinking, *You want the center for free?! Do you know we have a waiting list of dozens of groups who want to book it?*

He realized if he didn't stop pitching and start paying attention, he was going to get turned down. He looked around and noticed her office walls were covered with pictures of students who had gone on to become successful business leaders, politicians, and educators. Free information about what mattered to her.

He switched the focus to her and asked, "How did you get into this line of work?"

She told him about her upbringing and how getting an education helped her become the person she wanted to be. She spoke of how satisfying it was to help students get the support and opportunities they deserved. Andrew listened to the pride she took in this positive impact on the lives of these young people.

When she was finished, he said simply (and truthfully), "That's what we want, too."

She gave him a long look, smiled, got out her calendar, and said, "OK, Andrew, what was that date again?"

Look, Lean, Lift, Level

"If I have made any valuable discoveries, it has been owing more to patient attention than to any other talent."
— MATHEMATICIAN AND PHYSICIST SIR ISAAC NEWTON

Andrew did not listen as a manipulative *tactic*. He simply realized he was one of thousands who wanted something from Roberta. What he was saying was going in one ear and out the other because she had heard it many times before. When he stopped talking and took the time to *care* about what was important to her, *that* was when they *connected*.

Want to know the rest of that story? Howard University has cohosted *ten* DFK-DC Holiday for Hope parties. Hundreds of families have filled the campus center dancing, singing, playing, celebrating, and being celebrated. And who's been there, witnessing the happy kids and smiling at what they created together? Andrew, Glenda Fu Smith (the current director of DFK-DC), and Roberta McLeod-Reeves.

The bottom line? If we want people to pay attention to us, we must first be *patient* and pay attention to them. And the way to do that is to "give 'em 'L" — *Look, Lean, Lift, Level.*

L — **Look the other person in the eyes.** M. Scott Peck says, "You cannot truly listen to anyone and do anything else at the same time." Our attention is where our eyes are. If our eyes are moving around or focused elsewhere, people will think we're distracted and will either shut down or get loud to get our full attention. They won't believe we're focused on them until we look at their face. (Please note: in some cultures, it's not appropriate to look people in the eye.)

L — **Lean toward them.** If you're working on your computer or fidgeting with your phone, people will conclude you're only half listening. In fact, Sherry Turkle, author of *Reclaiming Conversation* and *Alone Together*, said, "Even a phone facedown on a table indicates your priorities are elsewhere." That's why it's so important to put your phone away or to turn away from your computer when someone's trying to talk to you. These body movements say, "That can wait. *You* are more important." *Facing* people fully indicates, physically and psychologically, that this person is your top priority. Furthermore, when you *lean toward* someone, you are literally and figuratively reaching out to them. Your "edge of your seat" posture indicates you really want to hear what they have to say.

L — **Lift your eyebrows.** If your face is slack, your interest will be slack. Even if you're tired, the mere act of lifting your eyebrows animates your face and eliminates lethargy. Try this right now. Raise your eyebrows. Don't you feel more energized? You will both *appear* more intrigued and *feel* more intrigued. It's a win for you and for whoever's talking.

L — **Level.** No matter how empathetic you are, if you are tall and the other person is small, or you're standing and they're sitting, it feels like you're towering over them. They'll never believe you see things from their point of view because you're not *at* their point of view. Only when you are at face level will they truly believe you're seeing things eye to eye.

When you have a lot on your plate, it takes discipline to give your undivided attention. One time at dinner, I could tell my son Tom was distracted. I said, "Tom, are you listening to me?" He said, "Sure, Mom, you have my *undevoted* attention."

Want a test to see if you're giving someone your undevoted attention? Just ask, *Am I really listening, or am I waiting for my turn to talk?* Pianist Alfred Brendel says, "The word *listen* contains the same letters as the word *silent*." It can help to give yourself a time frame so you know this is finite, not forever. Say to yourself, *Yes, I have a lot going on, and this person matters to me. I will Look, Lean, Lift, and Level and make them the most important thing in my world for the next ten minutes.*

Am I Really Listening, or Am I Waiting for My Turn to Talk?

"Oh, I'm sorry, did the middle of my sentence
interrupt the beginning of yours?"
— PINTEREST MEME

A woman who was in charge of the annual company picnic said she was grateful for this suggestion to "give 'em '*L*" because it kept her from making an embarrassing mistake.

Martha told me she had scheduled a video conference to get updates from her planning committee. The day of the call, she started getting emails from people saying they didn't have their status reports ready. She couldn't believe how irresponsible they were being and was ready to read them the riot act.

Then the food-and-beverage chair apologized and explained that the week before, her daughter had gotten hit by a pitch during her softball game, was rushed to the hospital for surgery, and was still recovering. The logistics chair was dealing with long Covid and admitted that some days he was so exhausted he could hardly get out of bed. One by one, they each described some extraordinary circumstances that had taken priority over their reports.

Martha said, "I was so glad I listened instead of barging ahead and reprimanding them."

If you're thinking, *I understand it's important to put everything else on hold and give someone my complete concentration. I just don't have the bandwidth to do that right now*, then ask for a sun check (Hawaiian for rain check). If possible, make eye contact with the person so they know you're sincere and say, "I really want to hear what's going on with you, and right now I'm focused on this project deadline. Can we please set aside time next week to connect?"

People will understand you have other obligations. What they won't understand (or forgive you for) is being perpetually too busy to give them the time of day.

Who is overdue for some listening from you? Who is someone who has received more than their share of "Not now. Catch you later. Keep it short"? When will you see this person next? Can you promise yourself right now you will get on their level, look them in the eye, and say, "Hey, we've been like two ships passing in the night. Do you have a few minutes now — or later today — to get caught up?"

Writer Alice D. Miller said, "Listening means taking a vigorous human interest in what is being told us. You can listen like a blank wall or like a splendid auditorium where every sound comes back fuller and richer."

And when you do connect with this person you care about, lean forward with eyebrows lifted so you're taking a vigorous interest in what they're saying, and use the Feedback Loop (covered in chapter 11) so you're listening to — and echoing — everything they say like a splendid auditorium.

Your Full Presence Is One of the Best Gifts You Can Give Someone

"None of the most powerful tech companies answer to what's best for people, only to what's best for them."
— TECHNOLOGY ETHICIST TRISTAN HARRIS

Let's go back to the situation that started this chapter: the boyfriend who wasn't listening because he was constantly checking his cell. He's not the only one addicted to his phone.

I had the privilege of meeting Tristan Harris, cofounder of the Center for Humane Technology and one of the featured experts in the Netflix documentary *The Social Dilemma*. He is a man on a mission to alert us to how our digital devices are designed to addict us to constant scrolling. According to Tristan, "Technology is causing a set of seemingly disconnected things — shortening of attention spans, polarization, outrage-ification of culture, mass narcissism, election engineering, addiction to technology."

As he says, "The only form of ethical persuasion that exists in the world is when the goals of the persuaders are aligned with the goals of the persuadees." And the goals of most tech companies are *not* aligned with what they call their "users." As a result, "This is overpowering human nature, and this is checkmate on humanity."

So, what can we do about it? How about instituting a "No digital devices at the table" policy? That may sound extreme, but so are these alarming statistics from Trevor Wheelwright on Reviews.org showing how serious this situation is.

- 74% of Americans feel uneasy leaving their phone at home.
- 71% of Americans say they check their phones within the first ten minutes of waking up.
- 53% say that they have never gone longer than twenty-four hours without their cell phone.
- 47% consider themselves "addicted" to their phones.
- 35% use or look at their phone while driving, and 64% use their phone on the toilet.
- 48% say they feel a sense of panic when their cell phone battery goes below 20%.
- 45% say that their phone is their most valuable possession.

You might want to watch Tristan's film with your partner or family members and then discuss what you're going to do as a couple or as a family to prioritize each other over the internet. And what if someone simply won't stop what they're doing to listen? We cover that in our next chapter.

Reminder Card of What to Say When Someone's Not Listening

Imagine you're hosting an international videoconferencing call. It's 9 p.m. your time, and you can hardly keep your eyes open. You notice other people are having a hard time listening, too; plus, most people are off camera, and you suspect they're checking email and attending to other tasks. What do you do?

Words to Lose	Words to Use
My agenda *"It's ridiculous to expect us to focus so late at night."*	**Our agenda** *"Let's agree to give each other our full attention for the next fifteen minutes."*
Lecture *"You need to put things aside, and listen up."*	**Look, Lean, Lift, Level** *"Let's turn cameras on so we can connect face-to-face."*
Preoccupied, undevoted attention *"I have to get up at six tomorrow, and I'm already exhausted."*	**Present, undivided attention** *"I will give people my eyes and ears and full focus."*
Digital devices out *"Ping. Let me see what that notification was about."*	**Digital devices away** *"Folks, we'll wrap up at 9:15. For now, can we agree to put our phones away?"*

Chapter 16

— TALKING NONSTOP? —

"One reason some people are long-winded is
because they're trying to impress their
conversational counterpart with how smart they are."

— PSYCHIATRIST AND SELF-HELP AUTHOR MARK GOULSTON

"One of our engineers is brilliant, but he doesn't know when to stop talking. People run in the other direction when they see him coming because they know he'll talk their ear off. He's up for a promotion but won't get it unless he learns how to stop droning on and on. Can you help?"

This was an email I received from a large tech firm asking if I would work with Rick (not his real name). I agreed, and Rick came to work with me for a day at my home office. An hour into our session, I understood why Rick was all over the map. He had no map. He was verbally undisciplined and said whatever came to mind without asking himself if it was on point or on purpose, and whether people wanted or needed to hear it.

I knew that as an engineer, he respected numbers, so I

suggested he apply metrics to his interactions. "Think about it. Twitter is 280 characters. Messages won't send if they're longer.

"From now on, give yourself a metric — a measurable accountability — for every communication. In fact, you might want to put an old-fashioned egg timer on your desk as a reminder to never speak for more than three minutes at a time."

He frowned. "But what if what I have to say takes longer than that?"

"Then interrupt yourself and ask, 'Any questions?' or 'Want more details?' or 'What do you think?' That will give people a chance to say what's on their mind so you're creating a two-way conversation instead of a one-sided monologue."

Just then, thunder started rumbling in the distance, and my Jack Russell, who was terrified of storms, started panting and pacing back and forth. I asked Rick, "Can we take a quick break while I put a ThunderShirt on my dog?"

"What's a ThunderShirt?" he asked.

"It's a wrap you put on dogs that calms them down because they feel contained instead of having crazy energy that's all over the place. It's kind of like swaddling a baby," I told him.

Rick started laughing. "Sam, that's what you're doing. You're putting a ThunderShirt on how I talk so I'm not all over the place and driving people crazy."

"Bingo. You've heard of Parkinson's Law — work expands to fill the time allowed for it? Same with talking. In the absence of a time limit, we can be tempted to talk on and on. Next time you're tempted to talk on and on, you might want to hold up that egg timer and let everyone know they (and you) can only speak for up to three minutes at a time. Or, set the timer on your phone to sound a friendly chime (not an annoying alarm) to indicate 'Time's up. Next.' This can help people 'leave out the parts people skip,' as author Elmore Leonard used to say."

End Verbal Sprawl

"When forced to work within a strict framework,
the imagination is taxed to its utmost
and will produce its richest ideas.
Given total freedom, the work is likely to sprawl."
— POET T. S. ELIOT

You've heard of urban sprawl? Saying whatever comes to mind is *verbal* sprawl. The longer we talk, the less impressed and the more irritated people become.

From now on, put a ThunderShirt on what you say. Talk for a minute, or two, or three... and then put a sock in it.

And if you're thinking, *Sam, I'm not the problem; it's the customers or coworkers I deal with who won't put a sock in it*, try these *Tactful Termination* steps.

How to End a Discussion When You Need to Move On

"His misfortune in conversation is this:
he goes on without knowing how he is to get off."
— WRITER SAMUEL JOHNSON

We've discussed the important role active listening plays in creating a climate of cooperation. What can we do if people take advantage of our good nature and simply won't stop talking? What if someone's one-sided, long-winded remarks are causing a conflict?

It's time to do a pattern interrupt. If someone is obviously holding you hostage via verbal sprawl, use the following Tactful Termination steps to reestablish a more equitable exchange.

Seven Steps to Tactfully Terminate Monologues

*"Half the world is composed of people who have
something to say and can't, and the other half
who have nothing to say and keep on saying it."*

— POET ROBERT FROST

1. Determine if the needs being met are out of balance. If someone's been talking nonstop for twenty minutes, their needs are being met. How about *your* needs? How about the needs of the other customers waiting to talk to you? How about the needs of the other employees who are also in the meeting? What about the emails that aren't getting answered because this one individual is monopolizing your time?

You can see that the scale of needs is unbalanced. Picture the scales of justice in your mind's eye. The two plates, balanced, one on each side, are usually held by Lady Justice (or Justitia, the Roman goddess). They symbolize giving fair, objective consideration to all evidence, without showing bias one way or the other.

One of the most important things I've learned is that the success of any relationship depends on whether we're keeping the "scale of needs" in balance.

Imagine the other person has one plate. You have one plate. If the other person is talking, talking, talking (or doing all the deciding), and you're not having a chance to comment or contribute, that scale of needs is out of tilt. Their needs are being met, yours aren't.

In this case, it's not selfish to interrupt and diplomatically bring this monologue to a close — it's smart. It is your right and responsibility to bring the scale of needs back in balance so both people's needs are being met instead of just those of one person who is monopolizing and monologuing.

Here's the thing: many of us have been taught it's impolite to interrupt. Please update that perception. If someone won't stop talking on their own, and if other people's needs are being trampled on, it's not rude to interrupt, it's right.

2. Interrupt by saying their name. Do not send subtle signals in the hopes this person will take a hint. Tapping your foot in exasperation or glancing pointedly at your phone won't get through. Nonstop talkers roll right over polite hints. If they had ISA, they probably wouldn't be talking nonstop in the first place. And if you just start talking over them, they'll probably get annoyed and talk louder. When people hear their name, they pause, which gives you a chance to get your verbal foot in the door.

3. Summarize what they said. If you just grab the conversational ball back, they'll be affronted because it seems like the only reason you cut them off is so you can talk. If you paraphrase what they said, they'll feel heard and know that you get the gist of what they're trying to get across.

4. Wrap up with "As soon as…" or "I wish…" If there's action to be taken, say, "*As soon as* we hang up, I'm going to get in touch with our distribution center and bring this to their attention." Letting this person know what you'll do *right after* the conversation is over motivates them to let you go so you can resolve this issue, sooner rather than later.

If they're going on and on because they like to hear themselves talk, or because they're truly upset and appreciate your sympathetic ear, segue into "*I wish*": "José, *I wish* I had more time to go into this, and I have a staff training right now. Can you please confirm your email and I'll get back with an update after I investigate further?" Using the words *I wish* softens the fact that you're curtailing the conversation.

5. Finish with finality and a friendly phrase. Friendly phrases such as "*I appreciate* you bringing this to my attention" and "*I look forward* to reconnecting tomorrow" offset any perception of abruptness. Make sure your voice ends with warm, downward inflection. If you wrap up with a tentative "OK?" you just threw the conversational ball right back in their court. They'll probably pick it up and run with it again. Warm language such as "*I'm glad* we had a chance to clear this up," or "I'm going to pass along your suggestion to our HR director," prevents them from feeling they were coldly cut off.

6. Use body language to diplomatically disengage. If the other person simply won't stop talking, it's time to be more assertive. Stand up from your chair or take a few steps backward to tangibly say, "This discussion is over." You are, literally and figuratively, distancing yourself and doing a physical pattern interrupt. Be sure to maintain eye contact so they don't feel you're turning your back on them. Say something like "Good to see you again," so they don't feel you're just walking away. Reference your next obligation: "That training's going to start in five minutes. I better grab my notes so I can get there on time," so they don't feel abandoned.

7. Give a heads-up of your hard stop. Give advance notice of how much time you (or the group) have left. Use language like "Tara, heads-up that I've got a client call on the hour so we have ten minutes left to clarify next steps." If you're leading a group call, you can use these same techniques to keep the needs in balance. If someone is derailing the agenda by talking more than their fair share, say, "Francesco, we have twenty minutes left and three items left on our agenda; let's move on."

Two Words to Keep Yourself — and Others — from Going On and On

"Do you know what we need? A 12-step group for nonstop talkers.
We're going to call it On and On Anon."
— COMEDIAN PAULA POUNDSTONE

Kwame said, "I can see where Tactful Termination works in business, but what if the nonstop talker is a parent? My mom calls every Sunday to 'check in.' She'd stay on the phone for hours if I let her. I know she's lonely, but I've got a life."

If someone close to you has a penchant for going on and on, it's time to look at the scale of needs in the context of your overall relationship. For example, you may choose to listen to your mom because you love her, and it's your gift to her. You think of everything she's done for you, and this is something you can do for her.

And you're right, there are limits. If she wants to talk for hours every time she calls, you may start resenting her or stop taking her calls. That's not a win for anyone.

A friend named Sandra said her then-college-age son did her a favor by having an honest conversation with her about this. "My son called and said, 'Hey, I need Elo's number. Do you still have it on the fridge?' I checked, I did, I gave it to him. He was about to sign off, but we hadn't talked for a while, so I asked, 'Did you see that Duke basketball game with Coach K?'

"He said, 'Yeah, it was great,' and was about to hang up again. I asked another question: 'How'd you do on that big test you were studying for?'

"He said, 'I got a B,' and then he said something that stopped me in my tracks: '*Mom, you're never the first one to end the conversation.*'

"Ouch. I explained that I asked those questions to let him know I listen to what he tells me, and follow up because I want him to know I care and what matters to him matters to me. I told him, 'It's a way to connect.'

"'Mom, we *did* connect. I asked for Elo's number, you gave it to me. We're good.'

"That's how I learned two of the most valuable words when dealing with millennials. *Got it.* I realized I equated *talking for a long time* with *connecting.* In his mind, if we talk at all, we've connected. Now, when he calls with a question or an update, I often respond with 'Got it,' and then I'm the first one to end the conversation. Guess who calls more often?"

Could the nonstop talker in your personal life equate connection with T-I-M-E? If so, you might want to use Erin Weed's Head, Heart, Core approach (covered in chapter 8) to have an honest conversation so you keep the scale of needs in balance and you keep taking their calls.

Does the Nonstop Talker See Love as T-I-M-E?

"Children spell love as T-I-M-E."
— MOTIVATIONAL SPEAKER ZIG ZIGLAR

Tamika said, "I'm going to use this technique with my friend."

I asked, "What's going on?"

"She's going through a divorce, and it's all she ever talks about. My heart goes out to her, but enough is enough. The last couple of times she wanted to go to dinner, I told her I was busy because I just don't have the bandwidth to hear all the nasty things her ex has done to her."

I suggested, "It's called *proactive* grace, not *passive* grace, for a reason. Promise you'll use Erin Weed's Head, Heart, Core approach to address this instead of avoid her."

1. **Head and Facts:** "Maura, our conversations the past three months have centered on your divorce, the court battle, and what your ex-husband has done or said."
2. **Heart and Feelings:** "My heart is going out to you. I can only imagine how painful it is to be going through this, because it's so unfair and undeserved."
3. **Core and Wants:** "And can we please switch the topic? I want to bring you up to date on what's going on in my life and see if we can book a massage for us to de-stress."

"Your friend may initially be a bit taken aback; however, you're doing her a favor. If she dwells on this with you, she probably dwells on it with others. And those other people may not have the courage to bring this to her attention; they'll just start avoiding her. You are giving her an ISA perspective and a chance to create more equitable relationships, which is to her advantage."

Reminder Card for When Someone Won't Stop Talking

Imagine you work at a customer call center. You get downrated if you talk too long. On the other hand, if you cut customers off and they report you for being rude, you get downrated for that, too.

Words to Lose	Words to Use
Passively let them monologue *"She won't let me get a word in edgewise."*	**Try Tactful Termination** *"I need to proactively resolve this and move on to the next customer."*
Wait while they talk ad infinitum *"Wow, she hasn't taken a breath."*	**Say their name** *"Mrs. Walker, I'm glad you've brought this to my attention, and…"*
Stay silent *"She doesn't want an answer, she wants an audience."*	**Interrupt with "As soon as…"** *"Mrs. Walker, as soon as we hang up, I'm going to contact our account manager and…"*
Allow them to vent *"She still hasn't taken a breath."*	**Picture the scale of needs** *"I've let her talk for ten minutes. It's my turn."*

Chapter 17

— PRESSURING ME? —

"Stop trying to make people happy. You're not chocolate."

— COFFEE-MUG SLOGAN

"I'm active in my community, and people are often asking (expecting?) me to chair committees and events. I believe it's important to give back, but I'm getting burned-out. How can I say no when people have a worthy cause or project and they're begging me to help out?"

As the saying goes, "If you want something done, give it to the busiest person." If this is you, let's figure out how you can serve other people's priorities *in balance* with your own.

Here are some questions to answer: "*Why* are you saying yes to so many causes or projects? Are you a people pleaser? Do you have a pattern of taking care of everyone else but not yourself? Are you filling your calendar to feel needed? Is your motto 'Is everyone happy?'"

Let's dive into why we sometimes take on too many commitments, and then explore several ways to say no clearly, firmly, and diplomatically if that's what we decide to do.

Do You Feel You Have Agency?

"We are better than we think, and not quite what we want to be."
— POET NIKKI GIOVANNI

Having agency is feeling like you have the ability to influence what happens and can affect your future. How often do you feel you have agency in your life? Or do you more often feel that what happens to you and in your life is out of your control?

When deciding whether you *will* or *will not* do something, it's important to understand the multiple meanings of *will*. *Merriam-Webster Collegiate Dictionary* defines the noun form of *will* as:

- the power of control over one's own actions or emotions.
- a choice or determination of one having authority or power.

Keep that in mind when someone is pressuring you to do something. Will you give in to *their* will or exert *your* will? Ideally, there is a way to do both. Here's how.

Are You a Pleaser or an Appeaser?

"How I like to be liked, and what I do to be liked."
— ESSAYIST CHARLES LAMB

Do you have a history of being a pleaser and an appeaser? If so, in the pressure of the moment, you may cave to people because you want their approval. However, that can lead to a life you don't like, filled with individuals you'd rather not be with.

So, why do we do this?

Pleasers often come from unhappy homes in which they received limited support or love. They thought being obedient and agreeable was the way to get their parents' attention, so they did their best to be the good little boy or girl. Even as adults, they continue to try to ingratiate themselves to others to get the acceptance they never received as kids.

Pleasers are often approval junkies. If someone doesn't like them, they quickly self-examine to see if they did something "wrong." Then they adapt themselves to get back in the other person's good graces. If someone is upset with them, they try to make it right to "keep the peace," at any price. Unfortunately, the price is often giving in and going along and sacrificing their own wants, needs, and rights. They frequently minimize their own opinions with comments like "It doesn't matter" and "I don't mind" when it does matter and they do mind.

They are the quintessential "No, you go first" personality types. As a result, many pleasers feel put-upon by family members, coworkers, acquaintances, and even strangers, as they don't want to risk alienating anyone. So, they say "yes" instead of "no," even when they don't want to be in charge of that fundraising drive or head up the bake sale, again.

As you can imagine, this takes a toll. Outwardly, pleasers can appear to have it all together. Internally, they can feel taken advantage of. Not that they'll complain about it. They wouldn't dare risk alienating public affection. Only to themselves will they admit they're burned-out. Their heart is often broken, because it seems everyone takes their generosity for granted.

A Pleaser's Motto Is "Is Everybody Happy?"

"The reward for conformity is that everyone likes you but yourself."
— FEMINIST WRITER RITA MAE BROWN

I interviewed Mike Domitrz, founder of the Center for Respect, about this topic. While in college, Mike received a phone call informing him that his sister had been raped. This was before the #MeToo movement, and there weren't the resources to give her the support she deserved. Mike felt helpless to undo what had happened and decided to do something to prevent this from happening to others. He developed the Date Safe program, which he's delivered around the world. The premise is *Ask first*.

I saw Mike present a program years ago and was impressed with how he engaged everyone in the room. He asked a popular boy and girl to join him on the stage to role-play going on a date and the dynamics that often unfold. One person rushes the "romance," and the other isn't interested or ready.

Mike told me, "The number one underlying issue is that many of us *don't want to 'disappoint' the other person.* Please understand you have a right to disappoint people for the right reasons. If you don't want to do something, you have a voice and a choice to say no."

I asked him, "What if the other person keeps pressuring you?"

Mike said, "Don't give reasons for your no, as people who want to win and who want their way will see those as barriers to overcome.

"This applies whether you're a teen or an adult. If someone wants sex and you say, 'I don't want to. I'm tired,' they'll say, 'Don't worry; you can just lie there, I'll do everything.' If you say, 'I don't know you well enough,' they'll say, 'Don't you trust me?'

"Every reason you come up with, they'll have an answer. The more you try to defend your no, the more they'll pressure you to say yes. The key is to say, '*I said* no *because I said* no.'"

Mike told me a woman approached him after one of his programs and said, "You can't imagine how freeing this is. I always felt it was my wifely duty to keep my husband happy. When you said I have the right to say *no* because I said *no*, that was a revelation."

The next time you're about to say yes when you want to say no — whether it's to something as personal as having sex or something in your professional life, like covering for a coworker who wants to take a long lunch — take a moment to reflect on the following questions.

Criteria to Consider If You're Being Pressured to Say Yes

"Most fears of rejection rest on the desire for approval from other people. Don't base your self-esteem on their opinions."
— BUSINESS AUTHOR HARVEY MACKAY

These questions can help you think things through from all angles before agreeing to something that will take up your mental energy, time, and resources. Ask yourself:

1. *Am I doing this because:*
    - I owe this person a favor and it's a fair exchange?
    - it's a tangible expression of my regard for this person?
    - they deserve what they're asking?
    - I want to honor them or say thank you?
    - it's a present for a special occasion?
    - I know in my heart it's the right thing to do?
    - I'm doing it willingly and without coercion?
    - I want to contribute to this person or their cause in a positive way?
    - it will serve me and give me something I want?
    - it's a reasonable job requirement?

If you're leaning toward saying yes because of the above, *you're agreeing for all the right reasons.*

2. *Or are these my motives for saying yes?*

- I'm trying to buy this person's approval.
- I don't want this person to get mad at me.
- I have a sense of obligation and feel like I should.
- I don't know how to say no.
- I don't want to hurt this person's feelings.
- I'm afraid people will think less of me if I don't go along.
- This person is pressuring me with "everyone else has agreed."
- I'm afraid this person will cause a scene if I don't.
- I habitually agree to do what people ask.
- I don't have the strength, clarity, courage, or energy to say no.

     If you're agreeing for the above reasons, you would be overriding your own P.I.N. (priorities, interests, needs). Know your P.I.N.! It is not in your best interest to give in to what this person wants in this situation. It's in your best interest to say "No, thank you."

If you're wondering how to apply this when you're next asked for a favor, this upcoming section will provide the answer.

How to Objectively Assess Whether to Say Yes or No

"The oldest, shortest words — 'yes' and 'no' — are those which require the most thought."

— ANCIENT PHILOSOPHER PYTHAGORAS

In addition to asking questions like the preceding ones, you can also do a simple exercise. Get a piece of paper and make two columns with a vertical line down the center. Label the top of the left-hand column *Other People's Needs* and the top of the right column *My Needs.*

Think of a situation where you've been asked to do something, and you're on the fence. On the left write all the ways you've supported or served this person or community in the past and all the reasons why giving them what they want will fill their needs. Then, on the right, list all *your* needs (health, sleep, time with family and friends, personal or professional responsibilities, time for activities that energize and educate you).

After reviewing these two columns, you may be able to see whether you've been serving this other person or community at the cost of your own priorities. This can help you realize it's not selfish of you to say "No, thank you" to this request; it's smart.

Now let's cover how you can say no without alienating anyone.

Four Ways to Give a Clear *No*

"The most common way people give up their power is by thinking they don't have any."
— PULITZER PRIZE–WINNING AUTHOR ALICE WALKER

1. **Say no and yes.** Turn down this particular request and suggest an alternative that's more on your terms. Say, "I appreciate your offer and won't be able to serve as chair. I will be glad to advise the new chair about the best practices so they can learn from my previous leadership experience."
2. **Say no and meet their needs through other means.** Let them know that although you can't say yes to the specific

request, you do have ideas on how they can get their needs met. You can say, "I'm not available to lead that committee; however, I'd like to recommend Benicia, who has mentioned her interest to me. She will do a great job." This is a win for everyone: they still get a leader, you get more free time, and Benicia gets the leadership opportunity she was seeking.

3. **Say no graciously and without guilt.** If you've been giving, giving, giving (and even if you haven't), you have the right to say no without feeling bad. It is not your responsibility to rescue others from their dilemma. Perhaps you can say with a smile, "Thank you for your offer. I have promised my family I'm leaving my evenings and weekends free for the rest of the year, and I want to honor my commitment to them."

4. **Use diplomatic words.** Avoid statements like "I know you desperately need my help, but there's *no way* I can lead this committee right now; I'm already overbooked." Rather, exercise more diplomacy: "I understand you need help, and I wish I had some free time to pitch in, and I don't. What I'd like to suggest is ..."

These responses can help you maintain your relationships *and* your boundaries.

What to Do If Someone Is Pressuring You to Say Yes *Now*

"If people don't want the best for you, they are not the best for you."
— TV broadcaster Gayle King

Sometimes people deliberately rush you into a decision because they don't want you to think it through. They don't want the best for you, they want the best for themselves. They're hoping their intensity will carry the day and sway you into agreeing to something you would otherwise say no to.

If that's what's happening, hold your ground by using my friend Judy Gray's response: "If you want an answer right now, the answer is no." You have the right (unless an immediate response is a documented part of your job requirements) to ask for time to decide.

If, right now, you recoil at the thought of responding that way, practice saying it out loud in the privacy of your own home until it flows off your tongue easily. Then, when you need to, you'll be more comfortable saying "If you want an answer right now, the answer is no," and the person will understand you're not being mean; you just mean what you say.

What to Do When People Ask for Free Advice

"The minute you settle for less than you deserve,
you get less than you settled for."
— COLUMNIST MAUREEN DOWD

An experienced consultant shared with me that he often gets put on the spot by others. "I'm at a stage in my career where I'm well known in my industry. A lot of people want to know my 'secrets to success.' Not a day goes by when I don't get a request from someone who wants to take me out for a cup of coffee so they can 'pick' my brain. The thing is, I believe in giving back, so I mentor new entrepreneurs through my professional association. I don't have time to 'chat,' though, with everybody who wants my advice. Any suggestions?"

I told him, "This is an issue almost every successful professional — whether they're a doctor, lawyer, or entrepreneur — deals with. What do you do when people ask for free advice? I recommend you develop a policy so you don't have to reinvent the wheel every time you're asked this. These 'Give back with boundaries' criteria can help you handle this issue proactively and graciously."

- If people call or email with a "quick question" or an invitation to "treat" you to coffee because they want to get your "thoughts," formalize the process by saying, "I've got time available next week. I'd be happy to schedule a complimentary fifteen-minute appointment to discuss this."

  This does several things. It lets them know you're busy, and time with you needs to be scheduled. If you immediately return their call or shoot back a quick email, guess what happens? You have opened Pandora's box and set a precedent of instant, 24-7 access. They're likely to respond with follow-up questions and will feel free to ask for more advice, because you established a dangerous norm of being at their beck and call. They will think nothing of continuing to "pick" your brain because they don't perceive there's anything wrong with asking for quick favors. After all, it worked before.

- When professionals ask for free advice, say, "I consult on this issue, and I'd be happy to answer your question in a complimentary fifteen-minute appointment. At the end of fifteen minutes, if you'd like to continue strategizing, we can discuss my consulting rates and you can decide how you'd like to proceed." This sets clear parameters on how much free time you're willing to give. Plus, this is a win-win. They have an opportunity to tap into your experience, so you are mentoring peers. Yet at the same time, you are honoring your own priorities and your right to be compensated for your hard-won expertise.

- As the conversation nears the fifteen-minute mark, say

(interrupt, if necessary), "Steve, I've enjoyed our conversation, and we have time for one more question. What do you want to focus on?" If they keep talking past the fifteen minutes, interrupt and say, "Steve, I hope this has been helpful. I've got other commitments and need to wrap this up. If you're interested, my business manager will be glad to send you details about my consulting services."

- Start each appointment with "I've been looking forward to talking with you. What would you like to focus on to make the most of our time together?" *No* small talk. When people only have fifteen minutes, they usually don't want to exchange chitchat. Stay focused on their priorities so they feel this time was maximally productive.

- Suggest they record the call. Often when you're sharing advice gleaned from years of experience, you achieve that welcomed state of focused flow in which you say something "just right." If they don't record or write down this "verbal gold" immediately, that perfect language or brilliant insight could be lost. Furthermore, if they record the call, they can listen to it again and pick up things they missed the first time around. It doubles the value of your time together, because it delivers evergreen bottom-line value.

- If someone wants to "talk shop" and you *do* want to support that person, suggest a "walk/talk." I started doing this years ago because I need exercise more than I need a meal. Many of us sit at our desk all day (and night). If someone I respect offers to buy me lunch, I invite them to join me on a walk and suggest they bring their digital device to record our conversation. And, yes, this can work remotely. Tell the person you'll be out walking during the call and suggest they can do the same. Be sure to confine these freebies to a phone call, not a video call, to reduce videoconferencing fatigue.

Another option is to create content-rich resources anyone can access — a blog, informative LinkedIn posts, a newsletter you send to your (free) mailing list, or low-cost ebooks that people can download from your website. *Voilà.* Mentorship problem solved.

So, who is someone pressuring you to do what? How will you take responsibility for knowing your P.I.N. and keeping the needs being met in balance? Ask yourself, *Am I unclear about this? Will I change my mind later?* If the answer is no, then do yourself and others a favor by giving the *no* now, with a firm "Please respect my decision."

Reminder Card of What to Do If Someone's Pressuring You

Imagine you have a brand-new boat. A friend has asked you to let him borrow it for the day to go fishing. You don't really trust him to take care of it, but he's piling on the pressure.

Word to Lose	Words to Use
Give in and go along *"Well, OK, but you better not bring it back dirty and with an empty tank."*	**Give a clear no** *"Tony, my insurance doesn't cover other people using the boat."*
Honor their needs only *"I understand you want to take your dad out fishing, so go ahead and take it."*	**Honor both your needs** *"Tony, you and your dad are welcome to come out fishing with me next weekend."*
Feel pressured to answer now *"Hey, quit giving me a bad time over this. It's my boat."*	**Take your time** *"If you want an answer now, the answer is no."*
Use disrespectful words *"You're being a real jerk by trying to guilt me into this."*	**Use diplomatic words** *"Tony, I understand why you want to borrow the boat, and I'm clear about not loaning it out."*

Chapter 18

— CARRYING A GRUDGE? —

"Life is too short for long-term grudges."

— ENTREPRENEUR ELON MUSK

"I messed up big-time. I forgot to attend an awards ceremony for my sister, and now she won't forgive me. I have apologized many times, and she's just not hearing it. Help!"

How can we regain a trust once it's been betrayed? How can we convince someone we'll be accountable in the future if we've let them down in the past? How do we choose to let go of grudges instead of holding on to them?

Little could I have predicted my young sons would give me a master class in letting go.

One rainy day, six-year-old Andrew got bored and used some crayons to turn our hall wall into a colorful mural. I was not a happy camper. In the midst of letting him know exactly how I felt, he circled his toe on the carpet, looked up, and said tremulously, "*Fresh start?*"

Two words. Anger over.

Another day, I was late picking him and Tom up from school. I wheeled into the driveway and saw them waiting for me. I started apologizing: "I'm so sorry. There was…" These budding Yodas said two profound words, "*Sorry accepted.*" Yes, they were wise beyond their years (and still are).

Fresh Start?

"*To be wronged is nothing, unless you continue to remember it.*"
— ANCIENT PHILOSOPHER CONFUCIUS

Just two phrases, *Fresh start?* and *Sorry accepted*, can help us clear the air, close the books on what went wrong, and move forward — for good. Those words demonstrate the power of having a "code" that verbalizes our intent to *stop* what we're doing that serves no good purpose and to *shift* our behavior to something that does.

Want other examples of verbal pattern interrupts? How about *Do-over* or *Reset*?

Think of a conversation that didn't go well or someone who "wronged" you. Are you both nursing that grudge? Have you gone your separate ways?

Is it worth asking for a "do-over"? Or asking to "hit the reset button"? A colleague told me they actually have a red button with *Reset* on it on their fridge. (I've got to find one of these!) When they're grumpy, they can walk over to the fridge and press the button as a tangible reminder to not take their mood out on those around them. Or, someone can do it for them ☺.

Creating an agreed-upon code word or phrase is a conscious way to name *our* behavior so we become aware of it, get perspective around it, and choose to do things differently.

Perhaps your parents modeled this for you. Carlos, a young

man in one of my programs, told me, "My parents had a word — coupled with *a look* — that meant 'not in front of the kids.' If we started getting on their nerves and they started taking it out on each other, they would say, 'Later,' and that was it. My wife and I do that now, and it helps us put a lid on stuff before it gets out of hand."

That's the point of a code word or phrase. This is ISA — Interpersonal Situational Awareness — in action. Instead of getting swept up and saying something you both wish you hadn't, you can take a moment to mentally step outside the situation and look at it from a thirty-thousand-foot view. That can help you both see that no good will come of going at each other and give you the presence of mind to stop … for now. Hours later you may not even remember why you were upset in the first place.

Do you and your loved ones have a code word that helps bring you to your "senses" in the heat of the moment? If so, what is it? If not, come up with one. It can be a saving grace.

Here's a family who's discovered a rather unusual code word that works for them.

Create a Code Word for Clearing the Air and Cleaning Up Grudges

"The overall purpose of human communication is — our should be — reconciliation."
— PSYCHIATRIST AND AUTHOR M. SCOTT PECK

A friend told me her family uses a code phrase they learned from one of the Holderness Family videos on YouTube. This particular video is called "Our Biggest Fight: The Battle of the Bra," and it has almost a million views.

In it, the couple, Penn and Kim Holderness, tell the story of the night Penn called to suggest they go out for some chicken wings. Kim is not interested — she's in for the night. Her explanation? "My bra is off, and there's *no way* I'm putting it back on." This escalates into an argument where they bring up everything but the kitchen sink: "You're never spontaneous," "We can't afford to go out. We're not on a Kardashian budget," and more.

So, how do they solve this? They remember an analogy their pastor (who's also their marriage counselor) told them: *Stay in Cleveland*. He coined "Stay in Cleveland" because "Cleveland is freezing in winter. Everyone wants to get out of there and go someplace else. Think of Cleveland as an argument. It's tempting to fly somewhere else (and bring up everything under the sun), but you need to stay in Cleveland and resolve the initial issue instead of escaping somewhere else."

In other words, if you get into a fight and someone starts piling on with long-simmering grudges — "You did this to me last year, remember?!" — use the code phrase *Stay in Cleveland*.

Code words and phrases can bring people to their senses, wipe the slate clean, keep you from going off on tangents, and prevent you from saying or doing things you wish you hadn't.

Here's a list of code phrases you can adapt for different situations.

- "Let's agree to disagree on this one."
- "You know what? We're both right."
- "Hey, we're on the same side."
- "Different strokes for different folks."
- "It's six of one, half dozen of another."
- "You say tomato. I say tom-ah-to."
- "To each his own."
- "This is a no-win situation. Let's move on."
- "Next subject, please."
- "Let's call a truce."
- "Let's circle back to this later."

And remember "Fresh start?" and "Do-over" and "Reset."

As to the man who forgot his sister's award ceremony and has apologized many times … he might want to say, "Sis, could we please have a do-over? I wish I could go back in time and be there when you were honored with that award. I know it was important to you, and I am so sorry I wasn't there for you. How can I make this up to you? And if you need some space for a while, I understand. Just know I'm sincerely sorry and hope we can have a fresh start."

Is It Time to Forgive?

"The weak can never forgive.
Forgiveness is the attribute of the strong."
— POLITICIAN AND SOCIAL ACTIVIST MAHATMA GANDHI

Is there someone you were once close to with whom you've parted ways on less-than-loving terms? Have you vowed not to apologize, because it was *their* fault? Has "foolish" pride kept you from approaching that person? Have you thought about calling or emailing them and then decided not to because you couldn't bring yourself to forgive them for what they did?

Be honest: somewhere in your heart, do you assume that someday you'll make up with this person? What if you're robbed of that opportunity, because something happens in the interim, and you never get a chance to patch things up?

English writer Samuel Johnson said, "Keep your friendships in repair." One of the purposes of this book is for us to stop and take the time to think about how important our relationships are and to take responsibility for keeping them in repair now — not someday. Don't wait for some future reunion that may never happen. Ask yourself, *Would I rather save face or save my relationship?*

Pick up the phone and say, "Let's not even go into what happened and why. I just want us to be _____ [sisters/brothers/friends] again. Can we please have a fresh start?"

Is Ghosting a Form of Holding a Grudge?

"How can I miss you if you won't go away?"
— MUSICIANS DAN HICKS AND HIS HOT LICKS

A woman raised her hand in a session and asked, "What can you do if someone isn't talking to you, and you don't know why? I don't know if I offended him, if he just doesn't want to be around me anymore, or what. Is ghosting a form of holding a grudge?"

Interesting question, isn't it?

In the absence of feedback, it's tempting to fill in the blanks. However, as established before, instead of assuming — telling ourselves a story, which can have absolutely nothing to do with what's actually happening — it's better to ask. It's even better to give the "ghoster" the benefit of the doubt until we can get "their" side of the story.

I'm speaking from experience about this. An organization booked me to keynote a national convention, then...radio silence. This was not the norm. I called and emailed a couple of times to confirm details. Nothing. I started feeling a bit "ghosted" and even told myself a story that maybe they had changed their mind and just didn't know how to tell me.

All of a sudden, I received a flurry of emails from the *new* program coordinator, apologizing for the delay. She explained that the previous meeting planner had quit unexpectedly and had left no records of what she'd agreed to. They'd had to reconstruct what she had contracted from scratch. They were 100 percent gracious and were mortified about what happened. I am so glad I hadn't responded with an impatient email. They were "innocent" and deserved grace, not grumpiness.

How about you? Has someone not responded to your recent calls, texts, or emails? Have you reached out and received nothing back?

Could you give them the benefit of the doubt? You don't know their story. You don't know if they're busy, on vacation, dealing with an emergency, or heads-down on another project.

Get in touch (again) and ask if they'd like to proceed, or if for some reason, this relationship is over and they're ready for you to "go away." Knowing is better than guessing.

Don't Let Ghosting Burden You

"Remember: You can't always change the people around you.
But you can change the people you're around."
— PSYCHIATRIST AND SELF-HELP AUTHOR MARK GOULSTON

A twenty-something said, "I'm glad you're bringing up ghosting because it sucks to *not know* what you did wrong. I met a guy at my brother's wedding. We hit it off and spent the next few months seeing each other every chance we got. Then he canceled out of a weekend trip to the beach we'd planned. That was the last I heard from him. He could have at least sent an 'I'm no longer interested' text instead of hanging me out to dry."

You'd think someone would have the courtesy to explain why they've gone off the grid and are no longer around, right? Not so much. A 2020 Hinge survey found that 91 percent of users had been ghosted at least once. And 40 percent said they had ghosted others because they "simply didn't know how to explain their disinterest and felt that disappearing was less hurtful."

If someone is "shunning" you over a period of time, it may be time to "get the memo" and move on. Their lack of response may be their way of saying "I'm just not that into you."

Or, who knows? Maybe they *are* into you, and it scares them because they're still reeling from a bad relationship and aren't ready to jump into another one. The point is, instead of dwelling on this, renting that person space in your head, and allowing them to continue to make you miserable, choose to mentally move on.

Reminder Card for What to Do If ___ Someone's Carrying a Grudge

Imagine your coworker was just given the promotion you deserved. You're senior to him, but he actively lobbied for the job and got it. You feel betrayed and can't forgive him.

Words to Lose	Words to Use
Carry a grudge *"He better not expect any cooperation from me, because he's not getting it."*	**Let go of a grudge** *"I'll talk to my boss about how best to position myself for the next promotion."*
Focus on being wronged *"I can't believe he'd stab me in the back like that."*	**Start fresh** *"I'm going to ask Bruce how we can work together in the best interest of the team."*
Refuse to forgive *"He's going to be sorry he did this to me."*	**Choose to forgive** *"They must have thought he was the best person for the job."*
Continue dwelling on this *"I just lay there in bed thinking of what I wish I'd said or done instead."*	**Employ code words** *"Next. It doesn't help to dwell on the past. I'm moving on."*

Chapter 19

IGNORING RULES ___
OR BOUNDARIES?

"Where there is no law, there is no freedom."

— PHILOSOPHER JOHN LOCKE

"I'm on the board of our homeowner association. A longtime member acts as if this is his own little fiefdom. We have a revolving door of committee members who leave because he's so contentious and turns every meeting into his own little kingdom. Advice?"

I can relate because I've "been there, done that." I was on the board of a private community in Maui. For the first few years, we had our own little "Camelot." Our kids felt safe riding their bikes and Big Wheels to friends' houses. We had parties in the park, neighbors helped out neighbors, and there was a wonderful feeling of friendliness.

Then, at our annual meeting, a homeowner stood up, announced he had gathered all the proxy votes from part-time residents and now had a "majority," and elected himself chair. We all sat there, stunned. None of us were familiar enough with Robert's Rules of Order and parliamentary procedure to even know if what he had just done was legal.

He strode up to the front of the room, told the current chair he was now in control, and rescinded several measures the previous board had approved. Chaos ensued. People walked out in disgust. The former chair started pounding his shoe on the podium calling for order.

The community deteriorated from then on. One individual created such discord that some neighbors no longer talked to each other. I quit the committee, as did just about everyone else, as it was clear the new chair was not open to changing his style.

So, what did I do about it? What did others do about it? We continued to do our best to be the neighbors we wanted to be and to host parties in the park, but this one individual had an enduringly negative influence on our community.

One of the reasons this mutiny happened was because there were no rules in place to prohibit it. In a perfect world, everyone would act honorably. In the real world, that doesn't always happen. This is why it's so important to establish and enforce rules of behavior.

The Importance of Establishing and Enforcing Rules of Behavior

"We learned about honesty and integrity — that the truth matters ... that you don't take shortcuts or play by your own set of rules."
— AUTHOR AND FORMER FIRST LADY MICHELLE OBAMA

Think about it. Why can we drive on a freeway with huge trucks lumbering by in the opposite direction, yet we don't feel at risk?

Why can pedestrians cross a busy street and feel safe (as long as they stay in the crosswalk)?

It's because there are rules of the road everyone agrees to abide by. There are red lights to tell us when to stop. Green lights to tell us when to go. Yellow lights to caution us to slow down. There are rules in sports. There are even rules in war.

Yet many meetings and groups have no rules. Anything goes.

If you want people to cooperate, feel safe, and be productive, it's necessary to have a code of conduct everyone agrees to follow that makes *my* agenda *our* agenda. Here's an example of a volunteer organization with a socially responsible set of rules that may surprise you.

Why Burning Man Rules

"People out here build whole worlds out of nothing,
through cooperating."
— BURNING MAN FOUNDER LARRY HARVEY

What unexpected model of a community has turned their vision and shared values into a code of conduct that everyone agrees to follow? Two words. *Burning Man.*

You may have heard about this eco-friendly "temporary city" created at the end of every summer in Nevada's Black Rock Desert that draws approximately eighty thousand participants from around the world.

One of the many things that makes this gathering special is that it is primarily volunteer created and run. To make sure people behave in alignment with the event's vision, founder Larry Harvey created ten principles to guide everyone's actions. He was clear that it was important to define behavioral expectations. As the organization says of these principles, "They're crafted not as a *dictate* of how people should act, but as a *reflection* of our community's ethos and culture."

Participants abide by the rules and come ready to embody them. Everyone benefits as a result — which is the point. When everyone agrees to play by the rules, it's a win-win.

Caveat. You may have heard about the "wild parties" at Burning Man. They're there. There is also deep connection and daily wonder at what humankind can create when we put our minds (and hearts) to it.

The point is, why do people come back every year to reexperience this one-of-a-kind celebration? Because their rules are clearly communicated and enforced, which gives the gathering an ethos people trust.

Below are excerpts from Larry Harvey's visionary 10 Principles. (Please note: the copy in *italics* is quoted directly from the Burning Man Project website.) I'll also share a bit of how I experienced each of these play out during my time there in 2018. Please be thinking of how you can adapt and apply these principles to your group.

1. **Radical inclusion.** *Anyone may be a part of Burning Man. We welcome and respect the stranger. No prerequisites exist for participation in our community.* Albert Einstein said, "I speak to everyone in the same way, whether he is the garbage man or the president of the university." At Burning Man, this is not idealistic; it is realistic. People don't care what you do in the "real world." Your job, status, income, background, fame, or fortune doesn't matter. You belong. You are welcome. You are treated with respect.

2. **Gifting.** *Burning Man is devoted to acts of gift giving. The value of a gift is unconditional. Gifting does not contemplate*

a return or an exchange for something of equal value. Everyone comes ready to give something meaningful — whether it's a poem (what I brought), a handmade medallion, or a library of donated books you can borrow. This sets up a feeling of generosity where you are focused on giving, not getting.

3. **Decommodification.** *In order to preserve the spirit of gifting, our community seeks to create social environments that are unmediated by commercial sponsorships, transactions, or advertising.* Ah, the joy of unplugging. Not just from digital devices but from commercials, advertisements, brand competition, and ever-present sales pitches. It was so humanizing to be free from that insidious insinuation that buying more stuff is the key to happiness.

4. **Radical self-reliance.** *Burning Man encourages the individual to discover, exercise, and rely on his or her inner resources.* This means thinking ahead and bringing everything you need to survive. People who don't P.L.A.N. ahead (as discussed in chapter 4) and need to be "rescued" are known as "Sparkle Ponies." Don't be a "Sparkle Pony."

5. **Radical self-expression.** *Radical self-expression arises from the unique gifts of the individual.* One of my favorite principles. This can mean retrofitting a 747, hauling it to Black Rock City, reassembling it, and transforming it into a disco plane. This can mean wearing fun costumes, sharing an original poem at Black Rock TEDx, or trying acroyoga in the center tent.

6. **Communal efforts.** *Our community values creative cooperation and collaboration.* Nearly everyone stays in a "camp" of like-minded people who share meal making, chores, and shaded living rooms. This is the best of all

worlds, because you get to explore the "playa," see original art installations, dance nonstop, and go "home" whenever you want or need to.

7. **Civic responsibility.** *We value civil society. Community members ... must also assume responsibility for conducting events in accordance with local, state, and federal laws.* Rangers (many of them longtime Burners) kindly help people in trouble and enforce these codes of conduct.

8. **Leaving no trace.** *Our community respects the environment. We are committed to leaving no physical trace of our activities wherever we gather. We clean up after ourselves and endeavor, whenever possible, to leave such places in a better state than when we found them.* Burners are scrupulous about this. This is the largest leave-no-trace event in the world. They've even coined a term, Matter Out of Place (MOOP), to define anything that is not native to the immediate environment. If you see MOOP (whether it's a plastic bottle or a piece of trash), you pick it up and take it out.

9. **Participation.** *Our community is committed to a radically participatory ethic. Everyone is invited to work. Everyone is invited to play. We make the world real through actions that open the heart.* No cliques. No "cool people" having all the fun while everyone else stands on the sidelines, spectating. You can volunteer at the coffee canteen and meet people from dozens of countries, play with the Burning Man Orchestra, or cycle into the desert at sunrise and gaze in awe as the early-morning rays hit a sixty-foot-tall silver statue of an entwined couple.

10. **Immediacy.** *Immediate experience is, in many ways, the most important touchstone of value in our culture.* Burning

Man is all about "being here, now." You know you'll return to the "default world" in a few days. So, you're crystal clear that this unique experience is to be savored and imprinted.

Does all that sound utopian? Too good to be true? The truth is, not everyone follows all ten principles all the time. Yet, enough people follow them that what could be complete chaos is not. These guidelines serve as guardrails that keep this gathering from going off the rails.

The question is, when will *you* schedule a brainstorming conversation with your group to create rules that keep your meetings and gatherings from going off the rails?

Ground Rules for Running Meetings
That Get to the Point and Stay on Point

"If you had to identify, in one word, the reason why the human race has not achieved, and never will achieve, its full potential, that word would be 'meetings.'"

— HUMORIST DAVE BARRY

Burning Man happens just once a year. If only the same could be said for some of the meetings we're required to attend. Research reported by career expert firm Zippia in January 2022 revealed, "There are around 55 million meetings held each week in the U.S., with surveys showing that 71% of those meetings are considered *unproductive.*"

Yikes. Here are some sample ground rules that can help you run more productive meetings that are a valuable use of people's time and minds.

- **Honor time promises.** "Time is the new money," says Richard Branson. Time is also the new *trust*. Have you ever been in a meeting where the host says, "Not everyone is here yet, so we'll wait for a few minutes." What's that about?! Why are they honoring the people who are late instead of the people who are on time? Say, "I know your time is valuable, so when we say we're going to start at 9 a.m. tomorrow, you can *trust* us to start on time. When we say this is a one-hour meeting, you can *trust* us to wrap up by 10 a.m."

- **Set the tone.** Participants will feel what you feel. If you're not glad to be there, they won't be glad to be there. If this is a virtual meeting, the first words out of your mouth should *not* be "Put yourself on mute." That's like throwing a party, and as soon as people walk in the door, you tell them to "be quiet." What kind of welcome is that? Set a precedent for positivity with "Kudos to you for the progress you've made. I look forward to hearing your updates. Let's jump in. Uri, how about you go first?"

- **Announce and enforce ground rules.** Distribute an agenda with timelines, and stick to it. That can include limiting how long each person can speak. (Perhaps three minutes?) While this may initially feel uncomfortable, it holds people accountable for getting to the point instead of rambling ad infinitum. You might also have a ground rule that people only speak once on a topic until it's clear that everyone who has something to say about that issue has had a chance to contribute. Another ground rule might be there's no name-calling, telling people they're "wrong," or interrupting whoever has the floor.

- **Ask for cameras to be on *at specific times* for virtual meetings.** Online-meeting fatigue is real. It may be unrealistic to require that everyone keep their cameras on all the time. You might want to request they be on in the *first five minutes* of the meeting to create a feel for the human community and then again during Q & A or during the last five minutes of a meeting so people can bond and reconnect before signing off.

Dave Barry and the rest of us might still silently groan when another meeting invite pops up in our inbox. Some things won't change, but at least we can make our meetings less painful and more productive by following these guidelines.

What to Do If People Aren't Following the Rules

*"A woman knows by intuition, or instinct,
what is best for herself."*
— ACTRESS MARILYN MONROE

Even with ground rules established, you still may not feel psychologically or physically safe. That was the case with Elizabeth, an HR director, who had to terminate a 6′7″ individual. He had received counseling and had been given several opportunities to improve his performance, all to no avail. After she gave him his final notice and walked him out with security, he stormed out of the parking lot, tires squealing.

After his firing, *three* separate women, one by one, confided in Elizabeth how relieved they were he was gone. None of these women spoke to each other. None knew he had a pattern of intimidation. None of them reported him, as they didn't want to "cause trouble." Please understand, if someone is consistently breaking rules with you, they're probably breaking rules with others. Who is someone in a position of authority you can report this to?

Or, if you're involved with a group that's toxic and dysfunctional, and there are no rules — or a lot of people are violating the rules, and no one's doing anything about it — advocate for your own physical and psychological safety. I'm not suggesting you just quit your job or relationship. I'm suggesting you ask yourself the ten "Should I Stay, or Should I Go?" questions in chapter 27. They can help you think things through from all angles and make a wise, not rash, move.

Reminder Card for When Someone Is Ignoring the Rules

Imagine you live in an apartment building that has a rec room with a Ping-Pong table. There are clear rules posted about only using it for thirty minutes at a time, yet some teens ignore those rules and hog the table for hours. What do you do?

Words to Lose	Words to Use
Complain about the broken rules "Those kids have no respect for anyone but themselves."	**Affirm and enforce the rules** "Two more minutes, and then it's someone else's turn."
Allow individuals to misbehave "I give up. I've waited an hour, and they're not giving up the table."	**Hold individuals accountable for behavior** "Thank you for handing over the paddles. I have the table for the next half hour."
Feel unsafe and don't speak up "I can't believe that young man just threatened me."	**Speak up about feeling unsafe** "I'm going to the office to report this young man's behavior."
Ignore a feeling of being unsafe "He didn't mean anything by it. It was an empty threat."	**Act on a feeling of being unsafe** "I don't trust this young man. I'm getting myself out of here now."

PART III

MANAGE YOUR EXPECTATIONS, EMOTIONS, AND MINDSET

"Life begins where fear ends."
— MYSTIC OSHO

What Can I Say and Do If I . . .

Chapter 20

FEEL UNSEEN, UNHEARD, OR UNAPPRECIATED?

"Anyone who waits for recognition is criminally naïve."

— U.S. CONGRESSWOMAN BARBARA JORDAN

"I work long hours yet feel invisible in my job. It's worse because I work remotely. I want to be considered for promotions, but my team lead doesn't even know I exist. Help!"

Can you relate to this? If so, you're not alone. A March 2022 article by Study Finds reports that "59% of people say they've never had a boss who 'truly appreciates' their work."

Are you waiting for your boss to notice you and give you the recognition you deserve? You could be waiting a long time. As Barbara Jordan pointed out, thinking it is your supervisor's job to notice and reward your hard work is idealistic, even naive. And it doesn't matter whether you work in an in-person, hybrid, or fully remote environment.

This was the theme of a program I gave for a Fortune 500 company. I interviewed several of the corporation's senior executives to ask for their input on how employees could position themselves better for career advancement.

One said, "Sam, I try to be a champion for my staff members; sometimes they don't help themselves. For example, last year, we opened an office in Paris. A team member had lived in France as a foreign-exchange student and still speaks French fluently. I thought she'd be a real addition, so I threw her hat in the ring.

"When I brought up her name in the meeting where we were selecting staff, no one knew who she was. A colleague finally said, 'Oh, I know who you're talking about now. She's in some of my meetings, but she never says anything.'

"She ended up not getting that job, and it wasn't because she didn't deserve it; it was because those executives hadn't witnessed her adding value and weren't willing to take a risk on someone they couldn't trust to perform well in that demanding job."

I asked, "Did you talk to her about this missed opportunity?"

"I did. I called her into my office, explained what happened, and asked why she wasn't speaking up in meetings. She said, 'I try to, but everyone's jockeying for position. I can't get a word in edgewise. If I do suggest something, no one says anything. A few minutes later, a man will say the same thing, and the group goes, "Great idea!" It's so frustrating, I just gave up.'

"I told her, 'Don't you realize, if you don't contribute at meetings, people conclude you don't *have* anything to contribute? If you're not giving people an opportunity to see your leadership in action, they can't recommend you when it's time to give out promotions.'"

I thanked the executive and promised to cover this in our course so people would know what to do when someone talked over them or took credit for their idea, and how to take responsibility for speaking up in meetings so decision makers witnessed their leadership.

Take Responsibility for Everyone Knowing Your Name

"Where Everybody Knows Your Name"
— THEME SONG FROM THE TV SHOW *CHEERS*

In that LeadHership program, we discussed a variety of ways to be more proactive on our own behalf — instead of being passive and hoping our good work is recognized and rewarded.

If someone interrupts, do not back down. Use the person's name: "Larry, let me finish." If someone takes credit for your idea, take back the floor by saying, "Jerry, I'm glad you found my idea valuable. As mentioned earlier ..." (and then share your vision for how to operationalize the idea).

And in every meeting, introduce something tangibly positive you and your team have achieved. This is not bragging. This is understanding that people are wrapped up in their own agenda, and if you don't bring your contributions to their attention, they will be overlooked.

Say, "Wanted to report that our department has _____." [Fill in the blank: *exceeded our quarterly quota, finished a client project ahead of schedule, doubled projected sales.*]

We also discussed the importance of having an intentional brand around what we want to be known for. I asked group members, "Do decision makers know who you are? If so, what is one word they associate with you? How would they finish this sentence: 'You can always trust [your name] to _____'? Whether it's fair or not, *that's* your reputation and brand, and that's determining your career success — or lack of career success."

Someone pushed back with "I really don't like that word *brand*. I grew up on a ranch. You brand cattle, you don't brand people."

I said, "I understand you don't like that word. Feel free to replace it with *reputation*. When decision makers talk about you when you're not in the room — and they will talk about you when you're not in the room when they're deciding your career future — what do they say?"

If they *don't know* or *don't like* who you are, you have an *accidental* brand, and that means you're hitting your head on your career ceiling. For whatever reason, your contributions and skills are not visible or not valued. When your name comes up, do people say "Who?!" or "She's always late," or "He never takes responsibility," or "He throws people under the bus"?

Please understand: that doesn't mean you're not the one putting out fires, winning over customers, smoothing out kerfuffles, and getting stuff done; it just means they don't know about it. They're busy with their own to-do list, and you're not on it.

An *intentional* brand is when you are clear about what you want to be known for and you've taken responsibility for making sure your work ethic, interpersonal skills, and track record of results are visible and valued. It means that when coworkers, customers, and executives hear your name, they say, "I *love* working with him," or "She always goes above and beyond," or "He always exceeds his sales quotas," or "He's a real mentor to our new hires."

So, think about a project you'd like to head up or an award you'd like to receive. Who is the decision maker? Do they know and like you well enough to go to bat for you?

Strategically Select a Word
for Your Intentional Brand/Reputation

"We are CEOs of our own companies: Me Inc.
To be in business today, our most important job
is to be head marketer for the brand called You."
— LEADERSHIP EXPERT TOM PETERS

Another participant in that LeadHership program said, "Well, I feel like I'm playing reverse *Cheers*, because in my department, no one knows my name. There are literally dozens of us in cubicles pretty much doing the same thing. How am I supposed to get noticed?"

I told her how I had discovered my "brand" while working with tennis champion Rod "Rocket" Laver. (Remember I mentioned him earlier in this book as having taught me why to avoid using the word *should* when a mistake is made.) An unexpected storm had forced us to cancel an exhibition match with Rocket and three top local players on Thanksgiving weekend. We had advertised this event and a lot of people were going to show up, and we had no way of letting them know the match wasn't going to happen.

We held an emergency staff meeting that Rocket started by saying, "Sam, we can always trust you to be resourceful and figure things out. What can we do to make the best of this?"

Wow. That meant a lot to me that he felt that way. Several days later, I asked how he had come to that conclusion. He laughed. "That's what you say in almost every meeting. Something will go wrong, and you'll say, 'Let's get resourceful and figure this out.'"

So, my brand word was *resourceful*. Thanks, Mom and Dad, for instilling this *Stop bellyaching, get busy* mindset of being proactive and taking responsibility for figuring things out and getting things done. If that's what I'm known for, that's fine with me.

What Do You Want to Be Known For?

"Personal branding is all about managing your name — even if you aren't a business owner — in a world of misinformation, disinformation, plus semi-permanent Google Records. Going on a date? Chances are that your 'blind' date has already Googled your name. Going to a job interview? Ditto."
— AUTHOR AND PODCASTER TIM FERRISS

So, how about you? Think of an opportunity coming up where you want to be selected for something — whether it's Rotary Club president or a union leader.

- Do decision makers know who you are? What one word do they associate with you?
- Does that description and reputation/brand support or sabotage your goals?
- If your name came up in a meeting where decisions were being made, what would they say? "You can always trust [your name] to _____."
- What specific skill, characteristic, or leadership trait would you like to be known for? Write out that intentional brand and post it where you see it frequently so it stays in your sight and top of mind.
- How will you act in alignment with that brand — and plant verbal seeds in conversations where you deliver on that — so people come to associate it with you?

Remember, decision makers can't read your mind. If you want to be considered for opportunities, the ball is in your court when it comes to getting seen, heard, and respected so that the next time decisions are being made, your name comes up and everyone jumps on board your bandwagon.

Six Ways to Contribute at Meetings So You're Heard, Seen, and Valued

"It's important to build a personal brand because it's the only thing you're going to have ... it's pretty much the game. You've got to be out there at some level."
— AUTHOR AND PODCASTER GARY VAYNERCHUK

If you're working remotely, meetings take on added importance because they're often the only way (other than emails and phone calls) decision makers come to conclusions about whether they like, respect, and trust you. Here are six ways to demonstrate the value you bring to those you work with.

1. **Contribute at least one *action*-oriented suggestion at every meeting.** Notice, I did not say an opinion, I said an action. Instead of simply sharing what you think or feel, contribute specific steps on how to move a project forward or tangible ways to turn an idea into reality and achieve a company objective by a deadline.

2. **Find solutions, not fault.** Get to be known as someone who can be trusted to *shift* the conversation from reasons to results. When it comes to developing a brand reputation, it's hard to beat being known as someone who's a problem solver, not a problem reporter.

3. **Graciously accept compliments, instead of deflecting them.** If someone praises you, rather than saying "It was nothing," say "Thank you. Your feedback means a lot." Next add a detail, such as "Our goal was to increase revenue by 30 percent, so we identified three high-profile clients, reached out to them, and were pleased to land three new major accounts." Then talk about your next goal or upcoming initiative so people are aware of how you're continuing to add value.

4. **Keep your comments to two minutes or less.** Become known as someone who's *succinct*. By cutting to the chase and getting to the point, people will always listen to you and take your calls because they trust you'll make good use of their time.

5. **If someone interrupts you, speak up instead of retreating or withdrawing.** Look the person in the eye, use their name, and say, "Zola, I welcome your input right after I wrap up my report," or "Al, one more recommendation, and then it's your turn." Then conclude your remarks.

You're not being rude; you're just exercising your right to have your voice heard.

6. **Tower (vs. cower).** If you sit or stand with a slouch, people will doubt your clout. A concave posture connotes weakness. Instead, roll your shoulders up and back. Sit or stand tall to exude a confident-leadership presence. Project your voice so everyone can hear every word. End your sentences with a downward inflection to project authority instead of ending with "uptalk," which comes across as tentative, as if you're seeking approval.

Use Amplification to Be Heard

"I'm speaking."

— U.S. VICE PRESIDENT KAMALA HARRIS

In a 2016 *Washington Post* article, journalist Juliet Eilperin reported how women staffers under then president Barack Obama used a strategy called amplification to make sure all women's voices were being heard. The tactic was simple: when a woman made a key point, other women would repeat it, giving credit to its author. This forced the men in the room to recognize the contribution — and denied them the chance to claim the idea as their own.

Eilperin quotes Communications Director Jennifer Palmieri, who recalls Obama saying, "This is it, you're in the room. This is the Oval Office. You're here for a reason, and I want to know what you think."

Next time you're in a room, remember you're there for a reason. The only way to increase your impact is to share your recommendations so people have an opportunity to be favorably impressed with your acumen. And while you're taking responsibility for making sure your voice is heard, use amplification to make sure others' voices are heard as well.

How to Be Seen When You're Not Even There

"I didn't learn to be quiet when I had an opinion.
The reason they knew who I was is because I told them."
— FORMER XEROX CEO URSULA BURNS

A participant in an Oracle webinar asked, "Sam, I agree with everything you're saying. How can we be seen and heard when we're not even on the same *continent* as our manager and coworkers? I have *so little interaction* with them, I'm not even on their radar screen."

If that's your situation, it's even more important to stop waiting and start initiating. Perhaps you can suggest a weekly fifteen-minute meeting to swap status updates with your boss and/or peers. Make sure the majority of that meeting is about tangible progress and finished projects and good news so the overall impression is you're doing an excellent job.

If you do need to bring up a challenge, use the four most welcome words in business, *What do you think?* Ask for advice and then report back how you acted on this advice.

An attendee told me, "I was on the verge of quitting until you helped me realize I can't blame my manager for not giving me what I want, if I'm not *telling* her what I want."

Have you been thinking of "voting with your feet"? Before you do, take the steps outlined in this chapter. They can help you create an *intentional* brand so your voice is being heard, your leadership is being seen, and your contributions are being appreciated.

What If You Feel Unseen in Your Personal Life?

"You are not unseen, you are just unsung."
— MOM BLOGGER FROM *SEIZING HOPE*

A therapist suggested, "Be sure to mention people who feel unseen in their personal life. I see a lot of siblings in my practice who feel invisible because a family member has special needs, a health challenge, or a terminal illness. Some of them say, 'I know this is sick, but sometimes I wish something was wrong with me so I'd get some attention.'"

Do you know someone who feels overshadowed by a family member who needs round-the-clock care or special considerations? Do they sometimes feel their needs are being sacrificed — even if they understand the circumstances? If so, I hope you'll read — or suggest they read — a heartfelt blog post, "The Unseen-Siblings of Special Needs Kids," by an unnamed mom blogger at *Seizing Hope*. She pours her soul into describing what it's like to deal with this dilemma — from all sides — and I imagine it will resonate with many people.

If you, or someone you know, feel like an "unseen sibling," I hope you'll self-advocate and reach out to someone — whether it's another relative or a counselor — who centers you in your value and helps you know you do matter, you do count, and the world needs you.

Reminder Card of What to Do If You're Not Feeling Heard, Seen, or Appreciated

Imagine you feel there's an "in crowd" clique in your organization. Several members of the executive team went to the same college and play golf together. You never cause problems, so you kind of get ignored. The C-Suite doesn't get to see you in action because you work from home.

Words to Lose	Words to Use
Accidental brand *"I ran into my boss at the store, and he walked right by me."*	**Intentional brand** *"Hello, Joe, we work for the same company. I handle the AT&T account."*
Get cut off and cut out *"That's the third time Walter's interrupted me."*	**Contribute** *"Walter, I have one more suggestion, and then it's your turn."*
No one knows your name *"John, it's Roberta, not Rebecca."*	**Everyone knows your name** *"Roberta here, wanted to share some good news about our AT&T account."*
Get ignored *"Well, another meeting where everyone talked over me."*	**Amplify others** *"Nell, your idea to reach out to the other utilities is brilliant, and…"*

Chapter 21

— FEEL AFRAID TO SPEAK UP? —

"Worrying is like carrying around an umbrella
waiting for it to rain."

— RAPPER AND SONGWRITER WIZ KHALIFA

"I got passed over for a project lead I was promised. I want to talk to my supervisor about it, but I worry he'll think I'm pushy, and I don't want to get on his bad side."

Wiz is right. Worrying is a negative form of storytelling. As humorist Erma Bombeck said, "Worry is like a rocking chair: It gives you something to do, but it doesn't get you anywhere."

In this chapter, you'll discover how to replace worrying (which is a negative form of "mind time") with wishing (which is a positive form of "mind time"). You'll have a chance to evaluate the stories you're telling yourself (for example, *I'm afraid he'll think I'm pushy*), determine whether they're serving or sabotaging you, and understand how to use your "mind time" to tell a more positive and productive story.

Want a powerful example of someone who changed his story — for good? Jim Kwik is considered one of the world's foremost memory experts. He speaks around the world to Fortune 500 companies and has worked with Richard Branson and the *X-Men* cast to "better their brains."

However, he didn't start out as a memory expert. Jim was known as the "boy with the broken brain." He and I are members of an organization I previously mentioned called Transformational Leadership Council that was started by *Chicken Soup for the Soul* coauthor Jack Canfield. One of my fondest memories of that group is the first time I met Jim and he told me his story as we sat on a couch at Whistler ski resort.

Jim found it almost impossible to focus during college. Trying to take tests was so daunting and discouraging that he almost dropped out. He looked for helpful options, couldn't find any, and decided to "learn how to learn." After a lot of practice, he ended up being so good at memory and speed-reading that he was overwhelmed with requests from fellow students begging him to share his system. He decided to offer a free class so he could help a lot of people at once instead of one at a time. The day of the class, he remembers walking across the campus in a state of dread. What if only one or two people showed up? It would be humiliating.

He arrived at the campus building and worked his way through a crowd, wondering why so many were there. He arrived at the door of the classroom, only to discover they were all in line for *his* workshop.

You may know the rest of the story. Jim's YouTube channel has millions of views, and his *New York Times* bestseller *Limitless* was endorsed by Will Smith and brain-disorder specialist Daniel Amen. When I asked Jim the secret to being limitless, he said, "What I have come to find over my years of working with people is that most everyone shrinks their dreams to fit their current reality."

Wow. Being afraid to speak up is the embodiment of limiting and shrinking our dreams to fit our current reality. If you want a new reality, try these steps for speaking up ... even if you're afraid.

Six Steps to Showing Up and Speaking Up... Even If You're Afraid

"Be messy and complicated and afraid and show up anyway."
— Momastery community founder and author
Glennon Doyle

1. **Consider: What's your story?** *Story* is a synonym for *label*. Do you call yourself shy? Introverted? Has someone else given you a label you've bought into? For example, a woman named Pam told me, "I dropped out of college when I got pregnant with twins. My dad was furious with me and told me I had ruined my future and was never going to amount to anything as long as I was a stay-at-home mom. I believed that for the next ten years. When I needed to go back to work, I was embarrassed about my lack of a degree and applied only to entry-level positions because I didn't see myself as 'management material.'"

2. **Determine whether your story is serving you or sabotaging you.** How has that label affected you? Do you have a self-empowering label that has emboldened you to go for what you want? Or do you have a self-defeating label that has held you back from applying for certain jobs, trying new things, meeting certain people? Is it possible the story you've been telling yourself has nothing to do with your real skills, talents, and potential to contribute; it's just something you made up in your head?

3. **Tell yourself a limitless story.** What might happen if you

choose to "Jim Kwik" your life? What experiences might you have if you choose to remove restrictions from your mindset, and if you choose to clarify what you want and go for it instead of putting an unnecessary ceiling on yourself?

4. **Put old stories in the past.** The key to opening yourself to new possibilities is to not allow that limiting story to creep back in. Say to yourself, "I used to _____. And now I _____." Pam updated her story by saying, "*I used to* let what my dad said ten years ago undermine my self-esteem and keep me from applying for jobs I thought I'd be good at. *And now I* use my experience of managing twins and being PTA president at their school and raising $50,000 for an antibullying program as proof of my managerial ability."

5. **Don't revert, retreat, or withdraw — reach out.** Pam also said, "In the past when I would encounter someone with a PhD or MBA, *I used to* immediately put them on a pedestal and see them as smarter and more important than me. I would often shrink in comparison and not speak up. *And now I* seek them out and ask for their input and give them an opportunity to add value. I realize we all have something to contribute and no longer see people positioned on a ladder, with some people higher than me."

6. **Play tall.** Chances are you've read the famous Marianne Williamson quote that includes these lines: "Your playing small does not serve the world.... As we let our own light shine, we unconsciously give other people permission to do the same." Have you thought of things that way? That playing small not only keeps you from sharing your gifts but also sets a dangerous precedent that may keep others

from sharing theirs? Choose to play tall so that others may be inspired by your example and choose to speak up for what they want, too.

The Antidote to Anxiety Is Action

"Action is the antidote to despair."
— ACTIVIST AND SINGER-SONGWRITER JOAN BAEZ

Someone who takes action despite his anxiety is Carson Daly, the host of the megahit TV show *The Voice*. In a 2022 interview with Jenna Ryu of *USA TODAY*, Carson shared that he has GAD (generalized anxiety disorder) and has been dealing with panic attacks for years. He said, "Viewers may see my right hand in my pocket and think I'm being casual. The truth is, in that moment, I'm probably gripping the flesh of my upper thigh because a wave of panic is coming through me, and I want to run off the stage."

Carson has been open about his struggles with anxiety in the hopes that his advocacy will reduce the stigma and help others take comfort in the fact they're not alone so they'll have the courage to address their mental health issues. If you feel that fear, anxiety, or panic attacks are undermining your mental health, please follow Carson's example and reach out for help. Check the Centers for Disease Control and Prevention (CDC) website (see the link in this chapter's notes) for free, confidential resources that can help you or a loved one connect with a skilled, trained mental health professional. As Carson told Jenna Ryu in that *USA TODAY* article, "My moments of panic and hyperventilation still come and go but I'm in a much better place since talking about it openly."

I hope that by deciding to reach out, instead of retreat or withdraw, you find that the same happens for you. Good luck.

Ask Yourself, *What Do I Want?*

*"The great secret of getting what you want from life is to know
what you want and believe you can have it."*
— AUTHOR NORMAN VINCENT PEALE

Peale's quote sounds so simple, so obvious. But is it?

Do *you* know what you want? Can you say it in one sentence? Do you believe you can have it? Or are you letting your fears talk you out of it?

If I'm driving somewhere or working up a sweat on the treadmill, you'll probably find me listening to podcasts. My favorite is the *Rich Roll Podcast*. Rich is a former lawyer turned endurance athlete who interviews best practitioners on a variety of topics ranging from health to activism. I never listen to one of his shows without learning something new.

For example, a favorite guest was Adam Grant, author of *Think Again*. In an episode titled "Argue Like You're Right, Listen Like You're Wrong," Adam said, "We laugh at people who still use Windows 95, yet we cling to opinions we formed in 1995." Busted. He continued with this observation: "Intelligence is traditionally viewed as the ability to think and learn. Yet in a turbulent world, there's another set of cognitive skills that might matter more: the ability to *rethink* and *unlearn*. After all, the purpose of learning isn't to *affirm* our beliefs; it's to *evolve* our beliefs."

Kudos to Rich and Adam for that powerful interview. They're right. To stop being afraid, we need to rethink stories and unlearn approaches that undermine our effectiveness.

Bertice is a wonderful example of someone who rethought a story. She told me, "I've been afraid of my brother my whole life. He's five years older than me and bullied me mercilessly growing up. He was sneaky and didn't do it when my parents were around, so they didn't know how bad it was. He threatened to make me 'pay' if I ever told them, so I didn't. I've lived in fear of him all these years.

"It took a really good therapist to help me see that I was an adult now and needed to rethink our relationship. He had gotten himself in a financial hole and wanted to borrow money. He was really badgering me about it and making me feel like a bad person for not helping him out."

The therapist asked Bertice a simple question: "Do you want to lend him the money?" She realized that the answer was a clear no, but she was considering doing it anyway so he would leave her alone. The therapist then asked, "Why are you even considering giving him money when you don't want to?"

Bertice told her it was because he was relentless and wouldn't give up. Her therapist then said something that opened her eyes to how giving in would open Pandora's box: *Never do once what you don't want to do at all.*" Bertice realized giving in would set a dangerous precedent, and he would be back for more because she'd done it before.

I asked Bertice, "So what did you do?"

"I told him I wouldn't lend him the money, and that was my final answer. He got loud and belligerent and tried to make me feel guilty, but I said, 'This conversation is over.'"

I asked, "And how do you feel now?"

"I wish I had done this *years* ago."

How about you? Is it time for you to overcome a fear, rethink a story, and do things differently? Irish playwright George Bernard Shaw said, "Progress is impossible without change, and those who cannot change their mind cannot change anything."

He's right. When we change our mind, we change our life. What is a label you've given yourself? Have you been talking on eggshells in a relationship because someone has a history of belittling you, so you give them what they want? In what situation have you been afraid to speak up because you just don't have the confidence? Spanx founder Sara Blakely says, "To me, failure became not trying, rather than not succeeding."

In our next chapter, we discuss how to develop confident speaking skills in four high-stakes situations — *networking, interviewing, presenting,* and *negotiating* — so you have the inner resources to ask for what you want. Because if you've got the clarity, belief, and skills, you've got the trifecta and can walk in with a confidence advantage that will give you a competitive edge.

Reminder Card of What to Do If You're Afraid to Speak Up

Imagine you're being encouraged to run for your local city council. A relative is advising against it, saying you don't have a chance against the incumbents, and it will be time and money down the drain. You're afraid to put yourself on the line; however, you believe someone's got to be an advocate for an issue that's near and dear to your heart.

Words to Lose	Words to Use
Feel afraid *"What if I run and come in last? It will be humiliating."*	**Act anyway** *"I won't know if I don't try, and this is important to me."*
Tell a limiting story *"He's right. I don't have any political experience."*	**Tell a limitless story** *"The way to get experience is to run and seek mentors."*
Keep old stories for life *"I don't want to fail."*	**Adopt new stories for a new life** *"I only fail if I don't try."*
Revert, retreat, withdraw *"I think I'll pass until I have more convincing credentials."*	**Reach out** *"I'm going to ask the outgoing council chair if she'll mentor me."*
Play small *"Who am I to run for office? That's ego."*	**Play tall** *"I want to serve, and that means putting myself on the line."*

Chapter 22

FEEL NERVOUS ABOUT
UPCOMING OPPORTUNITIES?

"I get nervous if I don't get nervous. If I'm nervous,
I know I'm going to have a great show."

— SINGER-SONGWRITER BEYONCÉ

"I'm an engineer. Put me in front of a blueprint, and I'm in my element. Put me in front of a group of people, and all of a sudden, I'm tongue-tied. Any suggestions on how to overcome nervousness?"

Let's start by reframing your perception of nervousness. Beyoncé is not the only one who welcomes it. Many champion athletes know that *not* getting nervous is when they need to worry, because it means they won't have the kinetic energy needed to perform their best.

In fact, there's a famous scene in the Academy Award–winning movie *Broadcast News* where a wannabe TV anchor gets his big chance when there's a crisis and the regular anchor is unavailable. He heads to the studio with his producer, who turns to him and says, "Nervous?" He looks at her like she's crazy and says, "No, I'm excited."

Exactly. The question is, "How will you turn nervous energy into excitement that you can channel into peak performance?"

Here's how. In my book *What's Holding You Back?* I share that *anxiety* can be defined in two words. *Not knowing.* If you *don't know* what to say, you'll be anxious and talking on eggshells.

But what if you *do* know what to say? In particular, what if you know what to say in the first two minutes of networking, interviewing, presenting, or negotiating opportunities, so you can walk in poised and prepared to hit it out of the park? I've cherry-picked a favorite best practice of what to say in the first two minutes of each of those situations so you can talk authentically and win everyone's favorable attention and respect.

First, one more story about how to take action when you're nervous, instead of giving in to doubts and fears. Since an engineer asked me this question about how to overcome nerves, I asked my aeronautical-engineer son Tom his advice, and he told me this great story.

A couple of years ago, he decided to try skydiving. He signed up and attended the training, and the big day finally arrived. He was sitting on the tarmac with his group waiting for their plane to land so they could go up. A woman decided to google "skydiving accidents." (Why did she do that?! We'll never know.) She announced to the group, "Did you know there were ten fatal skydiving accidents last year, a rate of 0.28 per 100,000 jumps."

Her pronouncement turned this formerly "ready to go" group into a bunch of nervous Nellies. All of a sudden, they thought, *Why am I risking my life?!* Several people backed out.

But Tom's an engineer. *He did the math.* He calculated that the odds of something going wrong were so low, *he was willing to take the chance and go.*

The next "nervous Nellie" make-or-break moment came at the door of the plane. It's one thing to intellectually know you're going to jump out of a plane; it's another to stare at thousands of feet of nothingness and step out into it. But Tom had already calculated the odds. He had already made an informed decision. He didn't need to second-guess his choice; he was comfortable with it. So he jumped.

That's what I want you to do, right here, right now. I've deliberately included numerous statistics throughout this book, and the research all agrees on one thing: improving your people skills is *the single best thing* you can do to improve your working relationships, effectiveness as a partner and a parent, and ability to advocate for yourself and what matters to you.

So, *do the math. Calculate the odds.* If you have a networking, interviewing, presenting, or negotiating opportunity in your future, *jump in* with these best practices instead of letting doubts and fears hold you back.

Know What to Say in the First Two Minutes of Networking

"When I'm in social situations, I always hold on to my glass.
It makes me feel comfortable and secure,
and I don't have to shake hands."
— LARRY DAVID, *CURB YOUR ENTHUSIASM*

You know what I've found? One of the biggest stumbling blocks to being comfortable in social situations is that people don't know how to introduce themselves. We've been told to perfect our "elevator speech," but who likes listening to a speech?

What if I told you there's a way to introduce yourself that can turn an awkward conversation into an *authentic* conversation? There is, and here it is.

From now on, when someone asks, "What do you do?" never again *tell* them. Telling people what we do (ad nauseam) makes us a bore, snore, or chore.

Here's what to do instead. Years ago, I was on a speaking tour with my sons. We had a night free, so we went downstairs to the hotel lobby and asked the concierge if he had any suggestions. He took one look at Tom and Andrew and said, "You've got to go to D & B's."

We were from Maui and didn't know what he was talking about. "What's that?"

He must have instinctively known that trying to explain it would only confuse us. Instead, he asked a qualifying question, "Have you ever been to Chuck E. Cheese?"

My sons nodded enthusiastically. He said, "*D & B's is like a Chuck E. Cheese for adults.*" Bingo. Ten seconds and we knew exactly what it was and wanted to go there. (They should have put him on commission.)

Why did that work so well? He turned a one-way elevator *speech* (aka monologue) into a two-way elevator *connection* (aka dialogue). Here's how you can do the same.

I was speaking in Dublin, Ireland, at a Young Presidents' Organization event. A tech executive approached me before my session and said, "I'm an introvert. I go to conferences like this all the time, but I often hide in my hotel room because I'm so uncomfortable with small talk. Plus, my job is complicated. I can never explain it in a way that people understand it. It's so awkward, I'd rather just avoid receptions and hallway chat."

From there, we brainstormed how he could introduce himself in a way that would lead to meaningful conversations and connection. "What are the *end results* of what you do that we can see, smell, taste, and touch?" I asked.

He offered a technical response about credit cards, online

purchases, and financial software. The lightbulb went off in my mind. "Do you make the software that makes it safe for us to buy stuff online?"

He lit up. "Yes! That's exactly what I do."

"That's good ... but don't *tell* people that."

He looked at me, puzzled. "Why not?"

"Because if you *tell* people, 'I make the software that makes it safe for you to buy things online,' they'll go, 'Oh,' and that'll be the end of the conversation. You don't want to *close* the conversation; you want to *create* a conversation."

"What do I do instead?"

"*Ask*, 'Have you, a friend, or a family member ever bought anything online?' They will surely reply with a yes. You've now established that they've *experienced* what you do or know someone who has.

"Now, confirm your connection by linking what you do to *what they just said*: 'Well, our company makes the software that makes online purchases safe.'

"Their eyes will probably light up, and their eyebrows will probably go up. Both are signs of an intrigued connection. People now *relate* to you and what you do. They have a relevant hook on which to hang a conversation and are more likely to want to continue the conversation. All in sixty seconds and all because you engaged and related to them."

Moved by this conversation, he told me, "I can't wait to get home after this conference. I can finally tell my eight-year-old son what I do in a way he understands."

That's the power of turning an elevator *speech* into an elevator *connection*.

How about you? What do you say when asked, "What do you do?" Does your response cause scrunched-up eyebrows (a sure sign of confusion)? If so, you're closing a door on a potential friendship and losing opportunities for yourself, your organization, and your cause.

Why not schedule a brainstorming session with your group to craft *two-way* introductions that open doors and engage people in win-win conversations? If you get good at introducing yourself, you will have the confidence to go anywhere, anytime, and meet anyone, because you know you have the ability to turn strangers into friends.

Know What to Say in the First Two Minutes of an Interview

"You never get a second chance to make a last impression."
— SAM HORN

Are you preparing for an important interview — whether for a job, a contract, or a new account? Follow this advice from Elon Musk. Here's the backstory. In 2011, I found out Musk was scheduled to speak at the National Press Club, near my home. I called my son Tom, who was working at Mission Control at NASA's Johnson Space Center, and said, "Tom, if I have a chance to ask Elon Musk a question, what should it be?"

He said, "I work on the International Space Station, so my job's safe, but friends who worked on the shuttle were laid off. Some are applying to SpaceX. Ask Elon his advice on how to ace that interview."

I did get to ask that question, and Musk gave a brilliant one-sentence response. He said, "Don't tell me about the positions you've held; tell me about the problems you've solved."

Boom! That's how you win the respect of decision makers. *Not* by giving a listicle of previous positions that look like everyone else's. Rather, by saying, "I had an opportunity to review your website, your mission, and the job description. If you'd like, I can give real-world examples of where I've solved problems that may be relevant to you and your organization."

Know What to Say in the First Two Minutes of a Presentation

"I read a thing that actually says that speaking in front of a crowd
is considered the number one fear of the average person.
I found that amazing — number two was death!
This means to the average person if you have to be at a funeral,
you would rather be in the casket than doing the eulogy."
— COMEDIAN JERRY SEINFELD

How about you? Are you comfortable speaking in public? Or can you relate to Jerry's account?

Would you like to give yourself a confidence boost and competitive edge by pleasantly surprising people with an intriguing first two minutes that has them at hello? If so, here's how.

I had the privilege of being the pitch coach for Springboard Enterprises, which has helped female entrepreneurs raise more than $26 billion in funding for their businesses. During one of my workshops for them, Kathleen Callender of PharmaJet told me, "I've got good news, and I've got bad news."

"What's the good news?"

"I have an opportunity to pitch to a room full of investors at the Paley Center in New York City."

"That *is* good news. What's the bad news?"

"I'm presenting at 2:30, and I only have ten minutes. You can't say anything in ten minutes!"

I told her, "Actually, Kathleen, you don't have ten minutes. Audience members will have heard *sixteen* other presentations. You have sixty seconds to prove you're worth listening to."

This is the sixty-second opening we crafted that helped

Kathleen win funding and be selected by *BusinessWeek* as one of their 2011 Most Promising Social Entrepreneurs:

"Did you know there are 1.8 billion inoculations given every year?

"Did you know up to a third of those are given with reused needles?

"Did you know we're spreading and perpetuating the very diseases we're trying to prevent?

"Imagine if there were a painless, one-use needle for a fraction of the current cost.

"You don't have to imagine it; we've created it."

Are your eyebrows up? Do you want to know more? That means Kathleen just got her business idea in your mental door.

Let's put this in perspective. Before we crafted this opening, Kathleen was starting her pitch by explaining that PharmaJet was a "medical delivery device for subcutaneous inoculations."

A *what*?! People were confused, and that's not good news because confused people don't say yes. If you want to win people's favorable attention, use these three steps.

1. Start with Three "Did You Know?" Questions

What startling statistics can you introduce about the problem you're solving, the issue you're addressing, or the need you're meeting that will cause people to think, *Really?! I didn't know it was that big, that bad, that urgent, that much*?

What is a sudden shift in a trend, a dramatic increase in scope, a game-changing pivot in cost, demographics, or logistics that would surprise people and create curiosity?

Are you wondering, *Where do I find these startling statistics?*

GTS. Google That Stuff. Just put into a search "What are surprising statistics about _____ [your topic]?" On your screen will come recent facts that get *your* eyebrows up. And if they get your eyebrows up, they'll probably get your stakeholders' eyebrows up.

2. Use the Word Imagine *So People Picture Your Point*

The word *Imagine* pulls people out of their preoccupation, because they are *seeing* what you're *saying*. They're envisioning your offering as if they've already said *yes* to it.

Now link the word *Imagine* to three benefits of what you're proposing. What did Kathleen's decision makers care about? Painful inoculations. So we turned that into "painless." We turned reused needles into "one-use." Most decision makers care about money, so we pointed out her invention was a "fraction of the current cost." In a world of INFObesity, we distilled her ROI into a succinct "Who wouldn't want that?!" sentence.

3. Say, "You Don't Have to Imagine It; We've Created It"

Introduce evidence and precedents to show your solution isn't pie-in-the-sky or speculative; it's a done deal, and you (and your team) are ready to deliver it.

Reference a benchmark that shows where this has been done before successfully. Provide a testimonial from a respected industry leader who will vouch for your results.

This opening has helped hundreds of my clients win support (and funding) for their start-up, project, or cause. Why does it work so well? Because the quickest way to engage smart, skeptical people is to introduce something they don't know — but would like to know. They now know more than they did a moment ago.

By opening with questions instead of "telling people what you're going to tell them," you instantly engage them, and they listen because they want to, not because they have to.

General Electric executive Jack Welch said, "If you don't have a competitive edge, don't compete." Know what I've discovered after helping entrepreneurs and organizations design winning pitches and presentations for more than twenty years? If you don't have a competitive edge, you *can't* compete.

What you say at the beginning of your talk is a deal maker or a deal breaker. This opening can give you and what you care about an instant advantage. Others will still be telling people what they're going to tell them, and you will have already won the favorable attention of everyone in the virtual or live room.

Know What to Say in the First Two Minutes of a Negotiation

"If you don't ask, the answer's always NO."
— AUTHOR NORA ROBERTS

Nora is right. If we want to be a better negotiator and get a yes to what's important to us, we need to ask. And we need to ask in a way that (ethically) turns a potential *no* into a *yes*.

Here's an example of someone who did that — in under a minute.

Several years ago I attended a Business Innovation Factory event featuring global thought leaders. The most impressive speaker was a surprise. She walked to the center of the stage, waited until everyone was quiet, then leaned into the group with a big smile and said, "I know what you're thinking. *What's a thirteen-year-old going to teach me about innovation?*"

She paused and with a twinkle in her eye said, "We thirteen-year-olds know a thing or two," and then launched into how she had founded a nonprofit called TGIF that turned FOG (fat, oil, and grease) into cash that's donated to low-income families.

The brilliant Cassandra Lin, one of the earliest and youngest biofuel entrepreneurs, had us at hello. Why? *She read our mind.* She anticipated that these seasoned executives might be a bit skeptical that a teenager would have anything to teach them. So, she voiced their objections *first* — and made them moot.

Do you anticipate that the other person in a discussion or

negotiation might reject your request? Here are ways to turn resistance into receptivity.

- **Ask yourself,** *Why will people say "No!"*? **Say it** *first*. Perhaps you're proposing an expensive program and anticipate your boss will have her mental arms crossed thinking, *We don't have any money in our budget for this*. Start with, "*You may be thinking* we don't have any money in our budget for this. If I can have your attention for the next three minutes, I'll point out where we can find that money and how we'll make it back in the first three months and turn it into profits from then on." That'll get her attention.

  Notice I didn't suggest you say, "*I know you're think-ing*" — that's presumptuous. Say, "*I can only imagine you might be thinking*..." to acknowledge (versus ignore) her concerns.

  Remember, if you don't voice people's objections, they won't be listening; they'll be waiting for you to stop talking so they can tell you why this won't work.

- **Bridge with the word** *and* **(not** *but***).** This insight was in-troduced in chapter 6. The word *but* creates an adversar-ial "me against you" tone. Instead of saying "I know this failed before, but..." say, "You're right, this didn't work before, and we've identified what went wrong last time so we can prevent it from happening this time."

- **Take** *less* **time than expected.** Want to favorably impress someone? Start with the magic words "I know you're busy, and..." Then ask for and take a *specific* amount of time that's *shorter* than anticipated. If you say, "I know we have an hour allotted for this meeting, *and* I've distilled my deck into ten minutes," they will be thrilled. No one will ever be angry at you for ending early.

Your Future Is in Your Hands

"Tomorrow is another day, but so was yesterday."
— POET RENE RICARD

Sometime in the next few weeks, you're going to get an opportunity. Perhaps you'll be invited to a business luncheon or social event, have a chance to interview for your dream job, be asked to speak in public, or need to negotiate something important to you.

Jump in! Contrary to the popular adage, good things do *not* come to those who *wait*; good things come to those who *initiate*. Use these best practices to transform nervous energy into confident energy and kick-start a future that's even more fulfilling than you can imagine.

—— ## Reminder Card of What to Do If You're Nervous ——

Imagine you're representing your company at a conference. There will be many VIPs there, and it's intimidating. The butterflies are showing up, and you're considering backing out.

Words to Lose	Words to Use
Do the doubts *"I don't know if I'm up to this. It's scary."*	**Do the math** *"I've calculated the odds and this is a huge opportunity, and I'm taking it."*
Nervous *"What if I meet a bigwig and my mind goes blank?"*	**Excited** *"I'm really looking forward to meeting these industry icons."*
Boring elevator speech *"Uhh, my name is Don, and I work at XYZ."*	**Bonding elevator connection** *"Do you know anyone who yearns to find an inexpensive computer they can trust?"*
Positions held *"I was team lead here, then project manager there."*	**Problems solved** *"We discovered a serious design flaw two weeks before launch and fixed it."*
INFObesity *"It's a platform for automating circuitous systems online."*	**Three "Did you know?" questions** *"Did you know the average computer price has gone down 38 percent this year?"*
Ignore or downplay objections *"Well, yeah, the launch was delayed, but..."*	**Address objections** *"You may be wondering about the launch delay. Glad you brought that up..."*

Chapter 23

— FEEL ANGRY? —

"Anger is one letter short of danger."

— COFFEE MUG

"I let a friend use my lake cottage, for free. I arrived the following weekend and couldn't believe what a mess he left. He didn't
bother to clean up, plus he broke my blender and didn't even
tell me about it. I'm so angry that I'm not sure I'll ever talk to
him again."

First, sorry to hear your friend trashed your cottage. The question
is, what are you going to do moving forward? Hold on to your
anger and get burned twice? As the Buddha is purported to have
said, "Holding on to anger is like grasping a hot coal with the
intent of throwing it at someone else — you're the one who gets
burned."

When someone takes advantage of our kindness and abuses
our generosity, it's important to address it instead of simmering
and seething in silence. Anger is a natural response to our rights

being violated. It's our original warning system letting us know a line's been crossed.

The thing is, some people have been intellectualized out of their anger. Somewhere along the line, they were taught anger is an unenlightened emotion. What I've come to understand is that there are times when it is appropriate — even important — to get angry. There are times it will actually produce more sorrow if we don't speak up.

It Is Appropriate — Even Important — to Get Constructively Angry

"How people treat you is their karma, how you respond is yours."
— SELF-HELP AUTHOR WAYNE DYER

It's time to evolve our beliefs around anger and recognize that we have a right and responsibility to speak up constructively if someone hurts our physical and mental health. It's time to stop apologizing for honest anger and start expressing it responsibly.

I'm not suggesting we go around losing our temper at the slightest provocation. There's a famous scene from the movie *Network* when a fed-up broadcaster yells, "I'm as mad as hell, and I'm not going to take this anymore!" That's a memorable scene, but yelling doesn't solve anything. That outburst may have made him momentarily feel better, but it didn't help his cause because it was *reactive* anger. *Reactive* anger is letting out pent-up fury without considering the consequences and *without* improving the situation. Responsible anger is articulating our emotions after considering the consequences and expressing them in a proactive way that *will* improve the situation.

Are You Acting *Out* Your Emotions
or Acting *On* Your Emotions?

"Anger is meant to be acted on. It is not meant to be acted out."
— AUTHOR JULIA CAMERON

Acting *out* anger often means getting mad in the moment and speaking without thinking. Acting *on* A.N.G.E.R. is a five-act play of thinking before speaking. Here's how it works.

A — **Assess what happened.** Ask yourself, *Why am I upset?* Pinpoint the precise cause so you understand what's making you feel this way. Did someone betray you or break an important promise? Say something mean? Go back to the Head, Heart, Core approach we discussed in chapter 8 and state the facts as objectively as possible so you're articulating the catalyzing event(s).

N — **Nix extreme words.** As stated before, extreme words produce extreme emotions. "All or nothing" words escalate anger. If you say, "You *always* cancel at the last minute," the other person will point out the one exception that disproves your claim.

G — **Give a specific example.** The more precise you are, the more productive you'll be. Instead of "You *never* think of anyone but yourself," identify the particular action you perceive was inappropriate. "You took the car today without asking if I needed it, and I was left stranded."

E — **Express the desired behavior instead of criticizing the dreaded behavior.** Complaining about what they did won't undo it. It's more effective to clarify what you want from now on. Perhaps you can say, "From now on, if you need the car, please ask what my plans are so we can coordinate things." This step helps you bypass any ego needs to go into how inconvenienced you were and how inconsiderate they were.

R — Review to make sure the point got through. Trying to have the last word — "This better not happen again" — creates more conflict, as it's a battle for control. Ask this person to clarify how they'll do things differently in the future so there is a verbal commitment to changed behavior.

How Do You "Normally" Handle Anger?

"You've got to learn to leave the table
when love is no longer being served."
— SINGER NINA SIMONE

What do you do when "love is no longer being served"? Please understand that "turning the other cheek" if someone has a pattern of being hurtful can be silent permission for them to slap that one, too. If someone has violated your trust or trampled your boundaries, expressing A.N.G.E.R. responsibly is an important tool for getting your rights honored.

What I've discovered in my years of teaching how to proactively express anger is that most people normally don't "fly off the handle"; they handle anger the following ways:

- Deny it. ("I am *not* angry!")
- Pretend it doesn't exist. ("It doesn't bother me.")
- Excuse it. ("He didn't mean to be mean.")
- Dismiss it. ("There's no reason to get upset.")
- Dwell on it. ("I can't stop thinking about what she did.")
- Brush it off. ("They're just having a bad day.")
- Stuff it. ("I think I'll eat some ice cream.")
- Sedate it. ("Make that drink a double.")

As a result, anger backs up in their system, where it can end up dominating their thoughts, sapping their strength, and destroying their peace of mind. As German-American theologian Paul Tillich said, "Boredom is rage spread thin."

Hopefully, the five-step process above can help people responsibly express their A.N.G.E.R. so others no longer mistreat them, and they revive the energy that is their life force.

Change Your Anger, Change Your Ending

"You can't go back and change the beginning, but you can start where you are and change the ending."
— WRITER C. S. LEWIS

A property manager pushed back: "Sam, this seems like a very logical way to handle anger. But isn't emotion subjective? How am I supposed to think rationally when someone is cursing at me? Last week, a resident in one of our rental homes lit into me on the phone. Her fire alarm had gone off in the middle of the night and scared her family half to death. The fire department showed up and discovered bugs had gotten into the smoke detector and falsely triggered it. She was yelling at me, and it took everything in me not to yell back."

"Glad you brought this up. Yes, yelling is a logical way to handle anger, which is the point. Yet lashing back in anger serves no good purpose. Our goal is to have the emotional maturity to transform a tempting destructive response into a tactful constructive response."

Although we may not be able to control the thoughts that come to mind (*You have a lot of nerve!*), we can control how long they stay there. We can opt to turn inflamed emotions into informed emotions. We can take the high road and be glad we had the *presence of mind* to respond professionally.

As C. S. Lewis pointed out, we can't change the beginning of what happened, but we can change the ending if we choose to respond with responsible A.N.G.E.R.

Take the High Road

"When they go low, we go high."

— AUTHOR AND FORMER FIRST LADY MICHELLE OBAMA

In a 2018 Time.com article, Raisa Bruner reports that "Michelle Obama's famous phrase has become somewhat of a slogan for how to exercise restraint in the face of frustration." Obama clarified what the slogan means to her: "'Going high' doesn't mean you don't feel the hurt, or you're not entitled to an emotion. It means your response has to reflect the solution. It shouldn't come from a place of vengefulness. Barack and I had to figure that out. Anger may feel good in the moment, but it's not going to move the ball forward."

That is *agency* in action. Encyclopedia.com defines *agency* as "intentionally influencing your own functioning, environments, life circumstances, and destiny." It means you are "self-organizing, self-regulating, and self-reflecting rather than being reactively shaped by environmental forces or driven by concealed inner impulses."

Yes! You have probably noticed by now that *agency* is a river that runs through this book. I believe agency is the core of emotional maturity, and the key to using proactive grace to influence what happens *next* even if we're not responsible for what happened up until *now*.

Comedian and writer Jean Kerr said, "If you can keep your

head when all about you are losing theirs, it's just possible you haven't grasped the situation." Or, perhaps it means you've grasped the situation and realized that losing your head serves no good purpose. You'd rather keep a cool head and go high even if they're going low so you can move the ball (and your life) forward.

How to Intervene If Others Are Angry

"People who fly into a rage always make a bad landing."
— HUMORIST WILL ROGERS

A few years ago I had a chance to teach Tongue Fu! to the Honolulu Police Department. Here are some tips we discussed.

Imagine there's been a car accident. No one was hurt, but both cars were damaged, and the two drivers are getting into it on the side of the road.

1. **Separate the people so they're not in each other's face.** Say, "Sir, you stand here. Ma'am, you stand here." The goal is to get people out of each other's space so they're not in each other's face. This also gives them "distance," which helps them cool off.

2. **Say, "Each of you will get your turn."** Chances are, they've been talking over each other to "get the upper hand." This lets them know they'll both have a chance to say their piece.

3. **Take out a notepad and say, "Start at the beginning and tell me what happened."** Knowing that notes are being taken moves them from *ranting and raving* to *reporting*. They have to think back and reverse engineer what actually happened instead of flinging accusations. They have to slow down — because you can't take everything down if they're talking a mile a minute — which calms them

down. Plus, when they know you're recording this exchange, they're less likely to swear or use slurs that could come back to bite them.

4. **Read back what they said.** Say, "Let me read back what you said to make sure I have it right." When you finish reading their report, they're likely to go "Yeah!" — which, as we discussed in chapter 11, is what people say when they feel heard. They don't have to repeat themselves anymore because they know you've got it down.

A school counselor told me, "Sam, that technique doesn't just work for police officers. Students are often referred to my office because they're 'in trouble.' They're often blaming each other and trying to convince me the other person 'started it.' I give them each three minutes to share their side of the story. If a student interrupts with 'That's a lie. That's not what happened,' I say, 'You'll get your turn,' and then tell the other student how much time they have left. Giving a time limit keeps them from going on and on and focuses the conversation." She smiled and added, "You're right, when I read back what they say, they do say, 'Yeah!'"

A soon-to-be-divorced woman told me, "I used this technique with my abusive ex. Instead of writing things down, though, I would hold up my phone and say, 'Mark, I'm recording this. What did you say again?' He cleaned up his act because he knew his verbal abuse would be reported to my divorce attorney, and that would not go well for him."

So, think of a situation that "made" you angry or a time someone took their anger out on you. How did you handle it? Did you suppress your anger, express it reactively, or express it responsibly? If you had a do-over, what would you do differently?

Please note: If your gut is telling you this person isn't just angry — they are dangerous — please remove yourself from the situation. You'll learn specific steps to take if you feel someone poses a physical risk to you or others in chapter 27.

Reminder Card of What Not to Say — and What to Say — When You're Angry

Let's circle back to the "lake cottage" situation that started this chapter. Here are some options for proactive ways to handle this instead of letting the incident potentially ruin a relationship.

Words to Lose	Words to Use
Act out your anger "I'm so upset with how inconsiderate this was."	**Act on your anger** "I'm going to call him tonight and ask him to make this right."
Suppress your anger "I don't want to lose my friend, so I'll just let this go."	**Responsibly express your A.N.G.E.R.** "I will tell him how I feel so he has a chance to correct this."
Accuse someone of making you angry "You obviously didn't consider our friendship when you trashed my cottage."	**Articulate what made you angry** "I arrived to find the cottage hadn't been cleaned, and the blender was broken."
Tell them what they did wrong "You left everything a mess. This is the last time I do you a favor."	**Request they make it right** "I'd appreciate it if you fixed the blender and had the cottage cleaned."

PART IV

WHAT TO DO IF SOMEONE DOESN'T CARE WHAT'S FAIR

*"Almost every successful person begins with two beliefs:
the future can be better than the present,
and I have the power to make it so."*

— CULTURAL COMMENTATOR DAVID BROOKS

What Can I Say and Do If…

Chapter 24

SOMEONE IS BEING ___ MANIPULATIVE?

"I don't want to be patronizing — that means 'talking down.'"

— ACTRESS WENDY MORGAN

"My mother really knows how to push my hot buttons. After all, as the saying goes, she installed them. She loves to play martyr. Any suggestions on how I get her to stop trying to guilt-trip me?"

I told the woman who asked this question, "Please understand that manipulators will identify and target your emotional Achilles' heel. If you are sensitive about a certain subject, they will hammer away at it because they know they can nail you."

She said, "Well, my lightbulb just went on. Now I know why my mom calls me selfish. I've never wanted to be perceived as selfish, so if I'm not giving her what she wants, she flings that in my face, and I end up caving."

"That's how manipulators work. They not only ferret out your weakness; they often project their weakness on you as well. It is the classic 'pot calling the kettle black' scenario."

"Oh, the puzzle pieces are falling into place. She accuses me of being a bad mother, but she's the one who criticizes everything I do. Nothing I do is ever good enough for her."

I asked, "Want a way to break this cycle? Here's the question: Do *other people* regard you as selfish?"

"Just the opposite. Friends say I'm one of the most caring people they know."

"Exactly. See, the goal of a manipulator is to make you question yourself. They want to undermine your confidence so you are susceptible to their manipulation. If *several people* give you feedback about something, it's worth examining for merit, even if you don't agree with it. However, if someone's feedback flies in the face of how most people feel about you, it is truer of *them* than it is of *you*."

"Oohh, that's deep. I do see now that she's projecting her character flaws on me."

"Right. So, let's focus on how you can call her on her behavior so she no longer has the power to make you feel bad."

If you can relate to this situation, you may want to have a conversation with your mom where you say, "Mom, in the past, you've called me hurtful names, and that's over. From now on, things are going to be different. No name-calling, ever. I won't call you names. You won't call me names. If either one of us does, the conversation's over."

Then keep your promise. If she starts in with "You know what's wrong with you? You're a selfish brat...," say, "Mom, we have an agreement. Is there something you want to say without name-calling?"

If there is, great. If she plays martyr — "How can you accuse me of this?! This isn't good for my heart" — say, "Mom, I love you, and let's talk tomorrow with a fresh start," and then leave the room. Yes, even if you're in a restaurant or at a family gathering. If you're on the phone, say, "Mom, you're welcome to call back this weekend when you're ready to keep our agreement."

As I said before, you're not being mean, you just mean what you say. And what you're saying is "We will treat each other with respect, and I will hold us both accountable for that."

Don't Give Manipulators Access

"I am thankful the most important key in history was invented. It's not the key to your house, your car, your boat, or your safety deposit box.... It's the key to order, sanity and peace of mind. The key is 'Delete.'"
— COMEDIAN ELAYNE BOOSLER

There's a well-known parable about the danger of continuing to give toxic people access.

An alligator was about to cross the river when a scorpion passing by asked for a ride. The alligator said, "You've got to be kidding. Why would I give you a ride? You'll sting me."

The scorpion said, "Why would I do that? I want to get across the river as much as you do."

"No way," the alligator insisted. "I can't trust you."

The scorpion reassured him, "Look, if I sting you, we will both drown. Why would I do a stupid thing like that?"

The alligator admitted that was true and reluctantly agreed: "OK, go ahead, get on."

The scorpion climbed on the alligator, who crawled into the river. Sure enough, halfway across, the scorpion stung him. Shocked, the alligator said, "Why did you sting me? Now we're both gonna die."

The scorpion gargled out, "I am a scorpion. That's what I do."

You've heard the adage "A tiger doesn't change its stripes"? Well, manipulators don't change their stripes or their stings. The only way to stop them from drowning you is to stop giving them rides on your mental back. This chapter offers a few ways to do that.

Is Their Motive to Make You Feel Guilty?

"My mother was a travel agent for guilt trips."
— TV ACTRESS MELISSA RIVERS

Mae, a woman who attended one of my programs, told me, "I wish I'd taken this workshop years ago. My brother is bipolar. When he is taking his meds and in his 'depressive' phase, he's OK. When he's in his manic phase, he goes into hyper-attack mode.

"I'm a Realtor, so I'm showing houses many evenings and weekends. I'm good at what I do professionally but don't have that same level of confidence about my parenting. My brother knows I'm sensitive about this and purposely targets it.

"After one particularly vicious phone call in which he told me my kids hated me, my sister took my face in her hands and said, 'Look me in the eyes. Remember what I am about to tell you: his behavior is medical, it is not your fault, and there's nothing you can do to make him better.'

"My sister had expressed what I felt but was never able to put into words. I'd always believed that if I could just come up with the 'right' way to say things, he'd finally realize how awful he was to me and he'd apologize. My sister convinced me he was not going to change, and I had to stop giving him the power to devastate me."

Mae added, "My sister suggested I picture a plastic bubble

around me and then see his attacks as verbal arrows bouncing harmlessly off. That works, most of the time. Sometimes, though, if I'm not vigilant, I let him get to me. He sent an email not long ago that carried on about how I should stick to real estate and leave the parenting to someone who knew what they were doing. My sister called while I was crying and asked what happened. She listened and then said something that stopped me in my tracks: '*Sis, why did you read the email?* You know what he's like.'

"Good question. Why had I read the email when I knew he was in a manic phase? I had given the scorpion a ride on my back...again."

Learn the Lesson

"I told the doctor I broke my leg in two places.
He told me, 'Stop going to those places.'"
— COMEDIAN HENNY YOUNGMAN

Why do we do this to ourselves? One reason is that we simply can't comprehend how human beings can knowingly, intentionally be cruel, especially when they're aware they're hurting someone they used to love — or are supposed to love.

It's time to stop going to those places — and people — who have consistently hurt us.

You do not have to tolerate verbal abuse. Let individuals who have done this in the past know that in the future, you will hang up the phone or stop reading the email at the first sign of verbal abuse. Let that person know you will screen-capture cyberbullying texts and social media messages and keep voicemails and emails so you have documentation of their behavior.

What If Verbal Abuse Takes Place in Public?

*"Tolerance is admirable. When dealing with verbal abuse,
intolerance is even more admirable."*
— SAM HORN

I had an opportunity to interview Angela Tennison, a certified Tongue Fu! trainer, who was senior manager of the White House Executive Residence for President Barack Obama and his family. I said to Angela, "I can only imagine you've encountered some challenging circumstances. Can you think of a time someone got out of line and what you did about it?"

She immediately brought up a situation where someone had heckled the president in the East Room. She said her phone "blew up" with messages from friends saying, "Are you on duty?" She wasn't, and they said, "We thought not, because if you'd been there, you would have done something!"

I asked her, "What would you have done?"

"I would have gone over to the heckler and said, 'There is a time and place for this — and this is not the time or place for this.'"

Perfect! "What if he ignored you and kept heckling the president?"

"Then I would have asked security to escort him out. He was invited into *our house*. It was disrespectful for him to behave that way, and I would not have allowed it."

You may be thinking, *Good for her, but I don't have security to escort someone out if they're heckling me or verbally abusing me.* Then escort yourself out. Do not give verbal abusers a bully pulpit. If they will not listen to reason and if they are set on harming you or others, it's time to be elsewhere. Here are some other phrases to try if someone is heckling or being verbally abusive.

- "I'm sure I didn't hear you right. Please rephrase that."
- "Take that language somewhere else."

- "You might want to reconsider that. This is being witnessed and recorded."
- "Excuse you. We don't talk like that in my home [in my office]."
- "We don't use words like that. Try again."
- "Shame on you. Say what you have to say, this time with respect."
- "I'm recording this. Do you want to repeat that?"

This reminds me of the time I caught an airport taxi, and the driver discovered it was only going to be for a short ride to a nearby hotel. He launched into a tirade, using every swear word in the book. I knew why he was upset. He had probably waited hours and was hoping for a hundred-dollar ride, not a ten-dollar ride. My heart goes out to cabdrivers, who often work twelve to fourteen hours a day to make a living. I usually compensate for short rides with big tips, but not when a driver's yelling at me.

I took a pen and piece of paper out of my purse, peered at his license on his dashboard, and asked very politely, "Excuse me, how do you spell your name, please?" It was quiet the rest of the trip. When we got to the hotel, he jumped out, came around, opened my door, and said, "Please don't report me."

Sometimes all we have to do to incentivize someone to clean up their act is to ask how to spell their name. They don't want a record of their behavior, and they'll cease and desist.

How to Handle Someone Who Is Being Passive-Aggressive

"You despise me, don't you?"
"Well, if I gave you any thought, I probably would."
— Guillermo Ugarte and Rick Blaine, played by
Peter Lorre and Humphrey Bogart, *Casablanca*

One leader who attended a seminar said, "The person I'm dealing with at work is sneakier than this. She doesn't come right out and say something mean, but she still manages to get her digs in."

I asked, "What does she do?"

"Well, I take time off work sometimes to take my kids to doctor appointments. She'll say things like, 'Must be nice having kids to always have a built-in excuse to leave work early.'"

I told her, "Yep, that meets the American Psychological Association's definition of *passive-aggressiveness*. It's 'behavior that is seemingly innocuous, accidental, or neutral but that indirectly displays an unconscious aggressive motive.'"

The key word there is *indirectly*. Instead of coming right out with how they feel, passive-aggressive people make what I call "wolf in sheep's clothing" remarks. Wolf-in-sheep's-clothing remarks are designed to make you uncomfortable, but you're not sure why. The words themselves may seem harmless, but there's an insinuation underneath meant to insult you. You sense dissonance but can't quite pinpoint it. You know what I mean:

- "You should wear stripes more often. They're so slimming."
- "Thanks for the great birthday party." (And you didn't give them one.)
- "I don't mean to be rude..." (When it's clear that's exactly what they mean to be.)
- "I hate to say this, but..." (Doublespeak for "I actually love saying this.")

Passive-aggressive people are emotional hit-and-run drivers. They hit below the emotional belt and then say, "Who, me?" So, how can we respond to manipulators, instead of talking on eggshells around them?

- **Ask, *What's their hidden agenda?*** What do they hope you'll pick up on that they don't have the courage to convey directly? What do they want you to feel bad about?

- **Ask,** *Where do I sense duplicity?* Do they have incongruent body language? Are they trying to appear nonchalant, but they've got a *gotcha* gleam in their eye? Are they saying something "syrupy sweet," but it feels dissonant and disingenuous?
- **Make the covert overt.** Bring their strategy out into the open: "You're not trying to rush me into a decision, are you?" or "Walter, don't put me in the middle of this." They will often deny they're doing this and may even counter-accuse you of "overreacting" or "making this up." Understand that throwing mud on you is their way of keeping it off them.
- **Don't get drawn into their drama.** Be like the Cheshire Cat, who keeps his cool no matter what. The "should wear stripes more often" barb will only sting if you're sensitive about your weight. If you see that a manipulator is trying to make you feel bad about any extra pounds, just smile and say, "Thanks, I like this outfit, too." To the woman at work, say, "You're right, I am lucky to have kids," and leave it at that.
- **Own the kernel of truth.** If what they're saying is partially true, accept responsibility for that part and act on it. Instead of apologizing profusely for forgetting to throw a birthday party, or firing back, "Hey, I'm not a mind reader. If you wanted a birthday party, you should have said something," simply ask, "Vera, would you like a birthday party? If so, who would you like to invite, and when and where shall we have it?"

The way to deal with people who are passive-aggressive (and not succumb to the temptation to snark back) is to hold them accountable for truth telling. If something feels sneaky, look the person in their eyes, use their name, and ask, "George, what are you trying to say?"

They may demur and try to pass it off as "nothing." Don't let it slide.

Reporter Vikram Murthi points out, in a 2016 IndieWire post, that Helen Mirren did an excellent job of this in a TV interview early in her career. Host Michael Parkinson asked several sly questions about whether it was hard for her to be taken seriously because of her ... *equipment* ... and gestured toward her chest.

She wasn't about to let him get way with that. She said, "You mean my fingers?"

He balked a bit and then persisted, "No, your *physical attributes.*"

She responded, "Because serious actresses can't have big bosoms, is that what you mean?" Kudos to her for not allowing his sexist remarks to go unchallenged.

Is there someone in your life who tries to get away with snide remarks? Call them on it. "Oh, guilt. Guilt doesn't work with me. What else you got?" Or, "Don't beat around the bush. Tell me how you really feel so I don't have to read between the lines."

They may feign innocence, but when you name a tactic, you neutralize that tactic.

What If Someone Is Gaslighting You?

"Gaslighting causes us to doubt our own memories, perceptions, and judgments. It throws us psychologically off balance. It's like being in the Twilight Zone."
— AUTHOR DANA ARCURI

One of the most insidious types of manipulation is gaslighting. If you've ever experienced this, or witnessed it happening to someone, you know this Machiavellian tactic is designed to turn you upside down and inside out so you no longer know what's up.

You may know the backstory of this term. It's based on a 1938 play by Patrick Hamilton, *Gas Light*, in which a manipulative husband drives his wife to madness by causing her to question her sanity at every turn.

Because that's what gaslighters do. They deliberately erode your sense of reality by creating a twisted "funhouse" of verbal smoke and mirrors — lies and distortions to invalidate, confuse, and exhaust you.

A career counselor told me, "I've got a story for your section on gaslighting. My college roommate married (seemingly) the perfect man. He was incredibly handsome, took her on surprise getaways, bought her expensive gifts. Soon after their wedding, though, she became suspicious he was having affairs. The thing is, every time she brought it up, he turned on her and said he *couldn't believe* she was accusing him of such a thing. He was *deeply wounded* she would even think he was capable of cheating on her. He made such a big deal of how *offended* he was she could doubt his love that she would back down." He finally agreed to go to therapy with her but was so charming and convincing to the counselor that her friend concluded she must be wrong.

"This went on for *years*, until one day his phone pinged and she picked it up. There was a 'tell-all' text confirming what she'd suspected all along: he was having an affair. Even when she confronted him with the proof in her hands, he tried to wiggle out of it."

The career counselor continued: "I think one of the reasons my former college roommate was so vulnerable to this was that it was incomprehensible to her that someone who claimed to love her could knowingly, intentionally deceive her, all the while insinuating she was 'crazy.'"

Pay Attention to Your "Suspicions"

"I'm not superstitious, but I am a ... little stitious."
— MICHAEL SCOTT, PLAYED BY STEVE CARELL, *THE OFFICE*

If you're unsure if what you're experiencing is gaslighting, but your "suspicions" are telling you this person is manipulating you, here are some telltale phrases gaslighters like to use:

- "There you go again, making stuff up."
- "Wow, you've got an overactive imagination."
- "Do you know how deluded you are?"
- "You're just jealous."
- "You're overreacting. That never happened."
- "Don't be so dramatic."
- "Boy, you're really paranoid."

Notice the above attacks are designed to put you on the defensive. Remember chapter 10, which discussed how to respond if people are making false accusations? *Do not* repeat their negative words. Saying "I'm not being *paranoid*" reinforces and rewards their accusation.

Remember, their mind games are intended to knock you off balance so you're confused and flustered. Their goal is to get the attention *off* them and *on* you. They do this by verbally assaulting so you're busy refuting what they said instead of focusing on what they did.

Instead of reacting emotionally — "I am *not* making stuff up!" — say low and slow, "Adam, the evidence is right there on the phone," or "Susan, take responsibility for what you did."

What to Do If You're Living in Fear

*"Too many of us are not living our dreams
because we are living our fears."*
— AUTHOR LES BROWN

Please understand, manipulators *want* you to live in fear so you don't pursue your dreams. They want to keep you small to keep you in their thrall. They want to cause you to question yourself so you don't have the courage to question them. Their goal is to keep you walking and talking on eggshells so you're afraid of them and don't have the confidence to challenge them.

As you can imagine, we can't begin to do justice to this complex subject in one chapter. If you know someone who is dealing with a manipulator, I highly recommend the work of Shahida Arabi, MA. She's a summa cum laude graduate of Columbia University, and her book *Becoming the Narcissist's Nightmare* has more than three thousand five-star reviews on Amazon. Readers from around the globe thank her for explaining what they've experienced in language that resonates, and for giving step-by-step advice on how to extricate yourself from toxic relationships.

Hopefully, this chapter has helped you *see the strategy* behind manipulation so you're not susceptible to it. And hopefully, it's provided responses that can help you name a manipulator's game (because it *is* a game to them), so they can no longer have the power to hurt you. In our next chapter, you'll discover more ways to deal with people who don't care what's fair.

Reminder Card of What to Do If Someone's Manipulating You

Imagine your brother-in-law is in financial trouble, again. This is the third time he's come to you asking to "borrow" money. He promises to pay it back, but you know you'll never see it again.

Words to Lose	Words to Use
Give in to pressure *"I do make a lot of money, so I better not be stingy."*	**Proactive action** *"Myles, I understand you want money, and I no longer lend money to family members."*
Get driven crazy by the gaslighter *"How can you say I'm selfish when I've lent you money before?"*	**Defuse the gaslighter** *"Myles, that worked last time, it won't work this time."*
Get drawn into the drama *"I do too think of other people than myself."*	**Distance yourself from drama** *"My final answer is no, Myles."*
Tolerate verbal abuse *"I can't believe you would call me those names."*	**Be intolerant of verbal abuse** *"Myles, out of my house, now."*

Chapter 25

— SOMEONE IS BEING A BULLY? —

"You don't have to be the loser kid in high school to be picked on. Bullying and being picked on comes in many forms."

— MUSICIAN LADY GAGA

"I think these win-win techniques work with most people. But I'm dealing with someone who ignores all this. He steamrolls over everyone in his path. We all tiptoe around him so we don't set him off. What if you've tried all these approaches and they don't work?"

Win-win techniques do work with people who *want* to get along with others. Unfortunately, some people don't want *a* win-win, they want *to* win.

If you have the misfortune of working or living with someone who, no matter what you do, continues to make others miserable, you might want to take the upcoming two-minute quiz. It can help you determine if the individual you're dealing with is what I call a "5 percenter."

Bullies Don't Want to Cooperate, They Want to Control

"Please take responsibility for the energy you bring into this space."
— NEUROANATOMIST JILL BOLTE TAYLOR

Please understand, bullies do not take responsibility for the energy they bring into a space. Their goal is to get into *your* space so they can *own* the space. They'll do whatever they have to do to achieve that.

The American Speech-Language-Hearing Association hired me to speak on this topic for their annual conference. What was surprising was how many participants said *it never occurred to them they were dealing with a bully* until they took the two-minute quiz you're about to take.

They said no one ever taught them to recognize the specific patterned characteristics of a bully — so they weren't aware that's what they were dealing with. Plus, they'd been taught to never point fingers at someone else or label others, so they just kept asking themselves, *What have I done wrong? How am I responsible for this? Why am I "attracting" this into my life? How can I be more compassionate?*

Owning our behavior is a beautiful thing but it *backfires* with bullies. Here's why:

95% of people:	5% of people:
are difficult on occasion.	*are difficult on purpose.*
try to fix what's wrong.	*try to make you wrong.*
want to cooperate.	*want to control.*
play by the rules.	*make up their own rules.*

95% of people:	5% of people:
have a conscience.	*don't have a conscience.*
admit fault and are accountable.	*make it everyone else's fault.*
self-reflect and self-correct.	*don't self-reflect or self-correct.*

Does any of this sound familiar? Are you realizing the really challenging person in your life doesn't just do this occasionally — they do it intentionally? Do you realize they have a *penchant* and a *pattern* for controlling, manipulating, and abusing others to get their way?

Quiz: "Are You Dealing with a 5 Percenter?"

Think of someone who consistently makes you feel off balance, confused, wrong, bad, small, or "not enough." Score these questions on a scale of 1 to 5, where 1 = "almost never" and 5 = "almost always."

1. Do you "talk on eggshells" around this person and worry about everything you say because you never know what's going to make them mad?
2. Does this person find fault with everyone *but* themselves? If something goes wrong, do they blame others instead of being accountable, taking responsibility, and doing things differently?
3. Is this person arrogant or a know-it-all? Do they have to be right all the time? Do they act condescending/superior and put others down?
4. Does this person have a Jekyll-and-Hyde personality — they're charming one moment, cruel the next? Do you never know who's going to walk in the door?

5. Does this person like to put people down, but then plays innocent by saying "Just kidding" or "Can't you take a joke?" or "Why are you so sensitive?"

6. Does this person have to be in charge? Do they insist on controlling every situation and attacking anyone who dares to question their judgment, knowledge, authority, or version of events?

7. Does this person play martyr or victim? If they're unhappy, lonely, abandoned, upset, or unappreciated, do they make it *your* fault and try to make you feel sorry, guilty, or responsible?

8. Does this person get you to back down by intimidating you so you're afraid to speak up or stand up for yourself because they will get more intense, loud, violent, or verbally abusive?

9. Does this person indulge in "crazy-making" behavior (for example, deny they said something, or twist things around)? If you protest, do they accuse you of overreacting and being paranoid?

10. Are you happier when you're *not* around this person?

If the challenging person in your life scores 25 or less, you are *not* dealing with a bully. This person may have bad moods or bad days; however, they will usually act in integrity and are open to mutually beneficial solutions. They ultimately can accept input and choose to act in good faith.

If the person you're dealing with scores above 25, you are probably dealing with a bully, or what I call a 5 percenter. Please understand, bullies *want* to run the show and be in charge. They do not self-reflect and self-correct. They will not come to their "senses," apologize, and work to make things right. They will continue to make it *all your fault*, because they don't want to cooperate; they want to control.

Please Understand, Bullies Are Out to Destroy You

*"Sometimes people try to destroy you, precisely because
they recognize your power — not because they don't see it,
but because they do see it and don't want it to exist."*
— author Bell Hooks

It pains me to say this: continuing to be kind to someone who is determined to destroy you is an exercise in futility. In an ideal world, *everyone* would treat you reasonably, rationally, and respectfully as long as that's how you treat them. Fortunately, the *majority* of people do just that, which is why we've spent the majority of this book sharing reasonable, rational, respectful approaches that motivate *most* people to respond in kind.

Five percenters are the exception to that rule. Conscionable techniques that work with most people — active listening, empathizing, cocreating win-win outcomes — will not work with 5 percenters because they want *power*, not *peace*.

Which is why, even though what a 5 percenter is doing is not your fault, it *is* your responsibility to protect yourself, because bullies like things the way they are — with them on top and you on the bottom. You don't have to become a bully — and you don't have to continue to be bullied. You *do* need to change the domination/submission dynamic so bullies know they can no longer "cow" you. Here are several ways to do that.

Protect Your Hula-Hoop of Space

"What you put up with, you end up with."
— rapper and songwriter Wiz Khalifa

Please reread the above quote because it's so powerful. If you are "putting up" with bullying behavior in the naive hope it will "go away," please understand that it will do just the opposite.

For example, I saw an advice column in a newspaper where an eighty-year-old widow had written in asking what to do about a man, married to a good friend, who had started kissing her full on the mouth and letting his hands roam when they met. She had written him a *private* email asking him to stop. He ignored the email and continued his unwanted advances.

She had learned he was doing this to other women and asked the columnist what to do. The widow mentioned she didn't want to be ostracized by the group because she felt lucky they'd kept her in their social circle after her husband had died.

The columnist told her that he respected her desire to handle this *quietly* and without being *blamed*, and suggested she avoid physical contact and just smile and say hello when they met in public. He added that it might feel awkward, but it wouldn't be as noticeable to others as she suspected. *Just smile and say hello.* He advised her to *walk on* when he opened his arms to hug or grope her.

Arghh. Why are we, in this day and age, *still* recommending we handle bullying behavior and unwanted physical contact in "quiet, unnoticeable ways" so we don't get blamed? It's time to start holding aggressors accountable for their inappropriate behavior instead of accommodating it, keeping quiet about it, and hoping it will go away.

A better answer would have been to tell this widow she has the right to keep people out of her *Hula-Hoop of Space*. Stretch your arms out in front of you, to both sides of you, and behind you. That's about three feet of space on all sides of you. This is your Hula-Hoop of Space. You have the right to protect this and *not* let anyone inside it without your permission.

If someone crowds you and violates this boundary, address it in the moment instead of passively accepting it and hoping they won't do it again. Bullies interpret politeness as permission to continue. For aggressors, silence sanctions.

You may be thinking, *What about subways, trains, and planes? We're packed together like sardines on those things. What about conferences, concerts, and sporting events where we're jammed together? There's no way I can enforce my Hula-Hoop of Space in many public settings.* That's true, and when it comes to your private space and people intruding without your permission, you absolutely have the right to tell them to "back up, give me some space."

Tell Bullies to Back Off

"The way to deal with a bully is to take the ball and go home. First time, every time. Where there's no ball, there's no game."
— AUTHOR SETH GODIN

How do you convince bullies to get out of your space? You *tell* them. You don't need to say a lot. In fact, the shorter your command to cease and desist, the better: "Bob, back off," "Deng, stop that," "Earl, enough!" or "Tyra, hands off."

Instead of naively hoping transgressors will leave you alone, you can set a goal to reverse the risk-reward ratio by making their improper behavior *public... when it happens.* Subtle signals *won't work.* Aggressors target nice people because they count on you to be reluctant to "make a scene."

The way bullies test your boundaries is by saying or doing something inappropriate. They will get in your face or invade your space. If you don't call them on it, they continue because *there were no consequences.* They now know you are afraid to rock the boat and won't bring this to the attention of others. They now feel they "own" you and you won't "cause problems" for them. In a way, your silence protects them.

Please understand *you're* not the one causing the problem,

the bully is. They are the one forcing the issue and must be held accountable, because they will not stop unless you make them stop. If someone touches you inappropriately or does something offensive, do *not* continue to be pleasant to them. Do *not* walk on and pretend it didn't happen. That is a form of submission that *rewards* their inappropriate behavior. And rewarded behavior gets repeated.

Do the "You"

"If you're horrible to me, I'm going to write a song about it, and you won't like it."
— SINGER-SONGWRITER TAYLOR SWIFT

If someone has a history of "forcing" themselves on you via unwanted crowding or touching, *preempt it*. As they approach, do not "smile and say hello." Put your hand out (like a traffic cop) to *strong-arm* them and keep them from getting "too close for comfort." Do not use the word *I* — for instance, "I don't want to be kissed." We've been taught to use the word *I* to express our feelings. That's appropriate with people who care what's fair. But bullies only care about what *they* want, not what *you* want. They want to make you uncomfortable because it means they're more likely to get what *they* want. That's why, instead of using the word *I*, which focuses attention on *your* reaction, use their *name* (or the word *you* if you don't know them) to focus the attention where it belongs … on *their* inappropriate behavior. For example, say:

- "Dean, don't even think about it."
- "Steven, take your hand off my shoulder."
- "You, keep your distance."

Please understand, being nice to bullies does not persuade them to be nice to you. They count on your niceness as you try to "keep the peace." If there's anything I've learned in twenty years of teaching how to deal with bullies, it's this ... *what we accept, we teach.*

I do not know you; however, I'm guessing you did not initiate this situation and you wish it weren't happening. It is not your fault; it *is* your *responsibility*, because abusers will not stop as long as they feel they're "getting away with it" and no one is holding them accountable for it.

By all means, continue to be respectful to people who are respectful to you. Continue to use *I* with people who have a conscience. However, if someone has a *pattern* of violating your boundaries, it is not "mean" to hold them accountable; it just means you will protect your space and speak up if someone tries to take advantage of you.

Remember, *I* replies like "I don't think that's fair" and "I don't like that kind of language" are absolutely an appropriate way to communicate with 95 percenters. They backfire with 5 percenters, who *want* you to be hurt and offended. Telling bullies that you don't like what they're doing doesn't motivate them to change. Rather, it motivates them to think, *Good! This is working.*

Tower Instead of Cower

"Art, like morality, consists of drawing the line somewhere."
— WRITER G. K. CHESTERTON

When I was on the media tour for my book *Take the Bully by the Horns*, a radio disc jockey shared a "success story" following our in-studio interview. This DJ, who had been in a wheelchair most of his adult life, told me about a scary experience he'd had while firing an employee. "He was leaning over me, shaking his fist in my face. Instead of backing down, I looked him in the eye and said, 'We'll have this conversation as soon as you sit down in that chair.'

"I was surprised, but he sat down. If I had said, 'I don't like being yelled at,' he would have probably shouted back, 'Tough! I don't like being fired,' and kept letting me have it."

This DJ was right. Saying "I don't like being yelled at" wouldn't have given this employee incentive to *stop*; it would have given him incentive to *continue*.

Have you ever noticed that bullies like to berate others when they're standing and the other person is seated? They are trying to keep you small by looming over you and being tall.

This DJ must have instinctively known that. Since he wasn't able to stand up, it was important for him to "level the playing field" so the employee wasn't "looking down" at him, and he wasn't "looking up" to the employee. That one-up, one-down dynamic would have fueled the employee's feeling of dominance and superiority.

If you're at your desk and a bully starts in on you, *stand up*. Standing up on your own two feet is a physical and psychological pattern interrupt. It "draws the line" and is a way of saying, "I'm not taking this sitting down." If, for whatever reason, that's not an option, then say, "As soon as you sit down, we can have this discussion."

What If the Person Being Bullied Is a Child?

"School is ... two parts ABCs to fifty parts Where Do I Stand in the Great Pecking Order of Humankind?"
— AUTHOR BARBARA KINGSOLVER

One woman who attended my program on bullying said, "It's not me who's being bullied. It's my eight-year-old daughter Amy. She dreads going to school because there's a pack of mean girls who pick on her. I've told her to avoid them and they'll leave her alone, but they're relentless."

I told the attendee, "First, my heart is going out to both of you. Second, please don't suggest she avoid bullies, because that unintentionally reinforces *learned helplessness*, where she continues to live in fear of them."

I asked, "Do you have a dog or cat at home?"

She was puzzled. "Both, but what's that got to do with anything?"

I asked, "Who rules the roost?"

She laughed. "The cat! Which is ironic, as our Doberman pinscher weighs eighty pounds and our cat weighs about eight pounds, but she's the one in charge."

"I bet your cat has a 'Don't even think about it' stance that shows your Dobie who's boss?"

"Yes, but how does that help Amy?"

"Use that example to teach her that dogs don't bother cats who know who they are. Instead of running — which signals fear to bullies — she's going to learn how to *lean into* girls who pick on her. This shows she will not back down, and they'll probably back off."

"Well, that sounds good, but where does she get the confidence to do that?"

"Enroll her in martial arts. She'll learn to exude a physical confidence that sends a nonverbal message that says, *I can take care of myself.* Instead of having a *Please don't pick on me* posture, she'll learn how to tower, not cower.

"Something else you can do is to ask Amy what the 'mean girls' say, and then to *practice* responses so she's no longer caught off guard. She practices soccer; she can practice standing *tall* instead of getting *small*. Instead of flinching, she can practice sighing, 'Is this what you have to do to feel good about yourself?' and walking away with shoulders back, head high, and a relaxed posture that says, *Whatever you're trying to do ain't working.*"

Be an Upstander and Remember There Is Strength in Numbers

"Just one habitually offensive employee critically positioned in an organization can cost millions in lost employees, lost customers, and lost productivity."
— AUTHORS CHRISTINE PORATH AND CHRISTINE PEARSON

A beauty-salon worker told the following story: "We have a stylist who makes life hell for the rest of us. The thing is, she is sugary sweet to the owner, so he doesn't know she's hell on heels behind closed doors. Almost everyone else has left because they can't stand her. I'd quit if I could, but I need the income and don't want to start from scratch somewhere else. Help!"

I told her, "I don't know if it helps, but I've heard a version of this story hundreds of times. It's shocking the disproportionate amount of damage one bully can do. As you pointed out, she isn't just doing this to you; she's doing it to everyone she perceives as 'lower on the ladder.'"

My colleague Barbara Coloroso was one of the first to identify that bullying is actually a triad of bully, bullied, and bystander. Many bystanders don't speak up because they don't want the bully to turn on them. This allows bullies to continue to wreak havoc. That's why it's so important to be an *upstander* instead of a *bystander.*

"But how do I do that? Like I said, I don't want to jeopardize my job."

"Make a bottom-line business case showing how this *one*

toxic employee is costing the salon thousands of dollars of lost revenue, and it's in the owner's long-term best interest to fire her.

"I asked legendary business author Harvey Mackay, 'Of all your lessons learned, what is your single best piece of advice?' He didn't even hesitate; he said, 'It's not the people I've fired who have caused me the most trouble. It's the people I should have fired and didn't.'"

"OK, once again, I agree with you. I just need to know how to go about this."

"Document. Document. Document. Make it about facts, not feelings. Ask previous stylists for their testimony about the Ws (*what* was said, *where, when,* to *whom*?) so you have evidence of her mistreatment. Research what it costs to advertise, interview, hire, train, and onboard new stylists so you have a dollar amount of the financial damage she's caused. Ask other stylists to sign a petition to confirm this isn't just happening to you and it's not an occasional aberration. This is a pattern of egregious behavior that has been undermining the success of the salon for years. Doing this can make it clear to the owner that continuing to 'look the other way' is a bad business decision, so he's inspired to take action."

Inform Yourself and Others about the Unconscionable MO of Bullies

"I stayed because I thought things would get better, or at least not worse."
— AUTHOR ANNA QUINDLEN

I present a lot of "Never Be Bullied Again" programs during October, National Bullying Prevention Month. After hearing heartbreaking stories of how people's mental health was compromised by someone who mistreated them for months (even years!), I realized that *every* month ought to be bullying-prevention month, not just October.

This isn't something we should only focus on one month a year. It is something we need to be constantly alert to, and vigilant about, as it is a *nightmare* for anyone who's subjected to it. In fact, the Workplace Bullying Institute's 2021 U.S. Workplace Bullying Survey estimates that "48.6 million Americans are bullied at work," and it's getting worse, not better.

Which is why I am making my "Never Be Bullied Again" training video available to the public for free from now on. Any group — whether that's a company, professional association, nonprofit, sports league, school, or church organization — can show it to their employees, members, students, and parishioners whenever they want, as often as they want. This is my way of doing my part to provide people with the communication tools to reclaim and re-create the quality of life we all want, need, and deserve. The video comes with a facilitation guide you can use to host discussions after watching it so people can talk about what's happening, receive support, and brainstorm/strategize action steps. You can find the link, as well as some additional antibullying resources, in the notes section.

My hope is these techniques prepare you and your colleagues to protect yourself from 5 percenters who don't play by the rules. I hope they help you stand up and speak up for yourself (and the people you care about) so bullies no longer have the power to run and ruin your life.

In our next chapter, we'll talk about what to do if, no matter what you do, the situation with a toxic person is not getting better.

Reminder Card for What to Do If Someone's Being a Bully

Imagine your sales manager is verbally abusive. He says terrible things to coworkers during in-person and virtual meetings. He gets away with it because he's a rainmaker for the company.

Words to Lose	Words to Use
Avoid and ignore *"I'm just going to lie low and hope he doesn't turn on me."*	**Act with agency** *"If he starts in on me, I will interrupt him instead of suffering in silence."*
I **replies** *"I don't like the way you're talking to me."*	***You*** **replies** *"Tyler, stop. Speak to me with respect."*
Learned helplessness *"If I see him coming down the hall, I'm heading the opposite direction."*	**Learned Hula-Hoop of Space** *"If he gets in my face, I will put my hand up and say, 'Tyler, back off.'"*
Cower *"If I make myself small, maybe he won't notice me."*	**Tower** *"I will stand tall and walk purposefully, with my shoulders back and my head held high."*
Bystander *"He really tore into Bev today and made her cry."*	**Upstander** *"I documented what happened in this and other meetings and will report this."*

Chapter 26

SOMEONE IS MAKING MY LIFE MISERABLE?

"No one can make you feel inferior without your consent."

— U.S. DIPLOMAT ELEANOR ROOSEVELT

"I volunteer at our local food bank. A colleague has a drinking problem and is a real jerk. I've reported his behavior to my supervisor but nothing's changed. What can I do?"

Can you relate to this? Do you work with, for, or around someone who is a jerk?

Hopefully, the techniques covered in this book have given you a variety of ways to take proactive steps to improve the situation. Now, it's time to talk about mindset and about you controlling your mood instead of letting other people hijack your peace of mind.

I often share a PowerPoint slide at the end of "Talking on Eggshells?" workshops with this modified version of Eleanor Roosevelt's quote: "No one can make us mad or miserable without our consent."

One time, a gruff construction boss took exception to this.

He said, "I don't agree with that quote. Do you mean if someone's calling me names, that's not supposed to make me mad?"

A woman stood up and said, "I *do* agree with that quote because I've learned this lesson the hard way. I'm a surgical nurse. I work with a neurosurgeon who is the most abrasive individual I have ever met. He is a brilliant physician, but he has no people skills. A while back I was a fraction of a second late handing him an instrument in surgery. He berated me in front of my peers. It took all my professionalism just to continue with the operation and not walk out.

"As I was driving home, I started rehashing what he had said. The more I thought about how he had humiliated me in front of my peers, the angrier I got. I got home, sat down at the dinner table, and told my husband what happened. I said, '*Oohh*, that doctor makes me mad!'

"My husband had heard this before. He looked at me and said, 'Judy, what time is it?'

"'Seven o'clock.'

"'What time did this happen?'

"'Nine o'clock this morning.'

"'Judy, is it the *doctor* who's making you mad?' With that, he got up and left the table.

"I sat there and I thought about it. I realized it wasn't the *doctor* who was making me mad. The doctor wasn't even in the room! I was the one who'd given him a ride home in my car. I was the one who set him a place at my dinner table. I was the one making us both miserable by dwelling on what he'd done.

"I decided that evening that never again was that man welcome in my home or in my head. When I left the hospital, he was staying there, and never again was I giving him the power to poison my personal life."

Who Do You Give a Home to in Your Head?

*"Nothing ever goes away until it has taught us
what we need to know."*
— BUDDHIST NUN AND AUTHOR PEMA CHÖDRÖN

Who do you give a ride to in your car? Who do you set a place for at your dinner table? Can you promise yourself you're never again going to give that person a home in your head? Can you promise you are no longer going to give that person the power to poison your life?

The class and I gave that nurse a sitting ovation when she shared her sage advice. I added, "I think this is one of the most important lessons we can learn on behalf of our mental health. It'd be really helpful if you told us *how* you don't let that doctor poison your life."

She said, "When my husband and I get home every day, we give each other fifteen minutes to debrief the day and dump out everything that happened — who did what to whom, what bothers us, and so on. After that, we move on to other topics. We have plenty to talk about. Our adult kids. What movie we want to see that weekend. Where we're going to go for vacation. We enjoy our evenings now, because we don't let that doctor dominate our conversation and our life." I now routinely share the nurse's story in my workshops and recommend her "Moan-and-Groan Moratorium.

A man in a different workshop spoke up after hearing the surgical nurse's story. "I also work with a physician who is notorious for verbally abusing his staff. The hospital never did anything about it because he's famous. People fly in from around the country to have him take their case because he's one of the best in his specialties, so he was 'untouchable.'

"My partner and I tried limiting our 'moans and groans' to

fifteen minutes. It helped, but it didn't solve the problem. You had told us we could complain about what we don't like — or create what we would like. So, I mobilized."

Here's what he did that finally motivated hospital executives to take action. Hopefully this helps you motivate decision makers to hold a toxic individual responsible for their behavior instead of allowing them to have a disproportionately negative impact on everyone around them.

1. **Document multiple examples of egregious behavior with the Ws.** Who said what? When? Where? How often? Who witnessed this? Be sure to stay objective so this is not dismissed as "he said, she said" and open to interpretation.

2. **Assemble research showing how this toxic behavior is negatively affecting the bottom line.** To strengthen your case, show how this individual's behavior is causing sick leave, poor ratings, and costly mistakes so it is clear their behavior is both hurting morale and team culture, and affecting the organization's profits.

3. **Gather strength in numbers.** Who will corroborate the pattern of unacceptable behavior? The more people who attest to this, the less it can be dismissed as a "personality conflict."

4. **Schedule an appointment with a decision maker.** Don't casually stop by someone's office to have this serious conversation. If you want your points to be actionable, formalize the process and ask that it be recorded so they are legally responsible for following up on this grievance.

Good news! The hospital leader told me, "I honestly don't know what HR said to the physician. All I know is they said *something*, because he has cleaned up his act."

Former U.S. secretary of state John Foster Dulles said, "The mark of a successful organization isn't whether it has problems; it's whether it has the *same* problems it had last year." Let's adapt Dulles's observation to say, "The mark of a successful *individual* isn't whether we have challenges; it's whether we have the *same* challenges we had last year."

Back to the question at the beginning of this chapter. Who is making you miserable? *How long has this been going on?* It's one thing if the situation is temporary and a result of this person going through a tough time. It's another thing if this is repeated behavior over time.

If you've learned anything in this book, hopefully it's that toxic situations don't get better on their own. If this has been making you miserable for a long time, it's time to ask for help.

Are You "Putting on a Brave Face"?

"Vulnerability doesn't make you weak. It makes you accessible."
— BUSINESS AUTHOR KEITH FERRAZZI

I've learned the importance of fessing up when something is negatively affecting me and confiding in someone instead of trying to be strong and soldier on.

My son had an opportunity to go to the Hoffman Institute, which really digs into how your upbringing has affected you — for better or worse. I asked Andrew if he had any revelations, and he said, "Do you really want to know?" I assured him I did.

He shared that sometimes he felt I wasn't *real* because I always "look on the bright side." He felt I wasn't *authentic* because I rarely talk about what's really going on with me.

Wow, that hurt.

Up until that conversation, I had mistakenly believed that one of my jobs as a parent was to protect him from some of the challenges that were going on in my life. He wanted to know where I had gotten that notion because, in his mind, it kept him from really knowing me.

So we unpacked this. I told him my mom had been in pain with a brain tumor the last decade of her life. Yet when we offered to help, she didn't want to be a "burden" and would often say, "No, thanks." When we asked how she was, she'd "put on a brave face" and say, "Fine."

I think the only time I saw my dad swear was when he hammered his thumb while repairing a pasture fence for my Appaloosa horse Keema. He said, "Damn," and that was it. Otherwise, even when things went wrong, if we asked how he was, he too would say, "Fine."

The lesson my sister, my brother, and I internalized was that the noble thing, the right thing, to do is to never "complain" and to *not* talk about how we feel — even if we're struggling.

It was a humbling experience to realize something I had done with the best of intentions had backfired big-time. At the time, it was demoralizing to find out that, at least in Andrew's eyes, *not* complaining about challenging circumstances had come across as "not being real."

Yet, *our strength taken to an extreme is our Achilles' heel.*

Positivity is a good thing, right? Not when it's taken to an extreme. That becomes *toxic positivity*, which can keep others at arm's length and keep us from being truly seen and heard.

I'm grateful to Andrew for opening my eyes to the fact that it is better to be authentic than to "be strong and soldier on." It is better to talk honestly about everything that's going on instead of "always looking on the bright side. Now I speak my truth to my loved ones, and they speak their truth to me. And my relationships do indeed feel more *real.*

It's a Sign of Strength to Ask for Help

"Sometimes asking for help is just as heroic as giving it."
— ACTOR CHRIS COLFER

Does any of this resonate with you? If you're tiptoeing around someone who's making you miserable, are you being real about how you feel? Or are you keeping a "stiff upper lip" and trying to figure this out all on your own?

The first time I told the story about Andrew in a workshop, a woman told our group that Dr. Susan David's TED talk had prompted a similar epiphany. She said, "Susan lost her father in her teens and spiraled into a depression. The adults around didn't openly grieve, so Susan thought she shouldn't, either. She ended up struggling in silence. One day a teacher, who had noticed her pain, gave an assignment to the class. She handed out little black notebooks and whispered to Susan, '*Write like no one is reading.*'

"That teacher's act of grace gave Susan permission to pour out her soul, and she realized how separated she'd become from herself and others."

Our entire group was hanging on this woman's every word. I asked, "What else did you learn from Susan's TED talk?"

"That as a psychologist, she's found that many people believe emotions are either good or bad. There are, number one, emotions that are 'good,' like happiness, and, number two, emotions that are 'bad,' like unhappiness. If you believe this, then if you're feeling sad, you think that's bad, so now you feel bad about feeling sad. If you're grieving and believe that's not good, you feel guilty for grieving.

"She explained that the key to emotional agility is to understand that emotions are just emotions, not good or bad. And what is important is to acknowledge them and express them instead of ignoring them."

How about you? Do you feel there are good and bad emotions? Do you feel bad when you feel bad? Do you try to hide it or rise above it? From now on, understand that, as Dr. Susan David says, "courage is not the absence of fear but fear walking."

Why not walk yourself over to someone you trust and ask if they have time to talk. And if they do, follow Charles Dickens's advice: "There is nothing so strong or safe in an emergency of life as the simple truth." Tell your truth, the whole truth, and nothing but the truth. It may not set you free, yet it will bring you two closer and you will feel better. You're not being a burden; you're sharing your burden so you're no longer bearing it and carrying it . . . alone.

If You're Miserable, Mobilize

"Hope is the active conviction that despair
will never have the last word."
— POLITICIAN CORY BOOKER

So, what's the point of this chapter? Do not let despair have the last word.

I'll always be thankful to Andrew for that honest conversation that initially brought me up short, yet now has enriched my relationships with just about everyone. Is it time for you to have an honest conversation with someone to bare and share your soul? Keep these options in mind.

- **Feel the feels.** Don't sugarcoat it. Be real about how you feel without trying to put a positive spin on it. Stuffing is for turkeys, not for humans.
- **Clarify the impact of this toxic person or situation.** Exactly how has this affected your health, sleep, self-esteem, performance, and will to live?

- **Go it together instead of going it alone.** Ask people for their ears and their shoulders to cry on. If toxic events are swirling in your brain, it can feel like you're going in circles. Aligning with people who have your back (and front) can create a 1 + 1 = 11 effect.
- **Remember that mood follows movement.** Journalist Sydney J. Harris said, "The time to relax is when you don't have time for it." Same with exercise. Have you ever gone to the gym and been sorry afterward? We almost always feel better after we get up, get out, get moving. Yet when we're miserable, movement is often the first thing to go. We think we don't have the energy, which is the exact sign we ought to put it first instead of putting it off until last.

And if you've tried all this and a stressful situation is still not getting better, we'll address what to do about it in the next chapter.

Reminder Card of What to Do If Someone's Making You Miserable

Imagine your roommate's middle name is Drama. She loves dumping her latest tale of misery on you as soon as you come home. You've tried to be sympathetic and let her know you need your space after a long day at work, but she says, "Who am I supposed to talk to if you won't listen?"

Words to Lose	Words to Use
Deny your "feels" *"She doesn't have any friends. I need to be there for her. I'm making too big a deal of this."*	**Get real about how you feel** *"I dread being in my own home because her misery is making me miserable."*
Go it alone *"Suck it up, buttercup. Deal with it."*	**Get support** *"I'm calling my mom and asking for advice."*
Keep a stiff upper lip *"This isn't world peace."*	**Mobilize** *"I'll listen to her moans and groans for fifteen minutes, and that's it."*
Get depressed *"I don't want to leave my room because I know she'll be there."*	**Get moving** *"I'm going for a run. That always makes me feel better."*

Chapter 27

— SOMEONE WON'T CHANGE? —

*"People are always blaming their circumstances for what they are.
I don't believe in circumstances. The people who get on in this
world are the people who get up and look for the circumstances
they want, and if they can't find them, make them."*

— PLAYWRIGHT GEORGE BERNARD SHAW

"I work in a toxic environment. We've reported our concerns to
our supervisor, yet nothing happens because the company is
struggling to hire replacements. We can't risk losing our pay-
check if we speak up and are labeled troublemakers. Help!"

If you're in similar challenging circumstances, my heart goes out to
you. I can only imagine what it's like to deal with this. In a moment,
I'll share a series of questions that can help you think this through
from all angles so you make a wise, rather than rash, decision.

First, understand there are three things you can do when
you're unhappy. You can:

1. change the other person. (Ha!)
2. change the situation. (May not be an option.)
3. change yourself. (Always an option.)

Note that these three options need to be tried in the *reverse* sequence. Attempting to change other people *first* is an exercise in futility. We may not have the authority or autonomy to change the situation. We *always* have the option to change ourselves. And the good news is, choosing to change how *we* show up can improve the situation and improve how this person treats us.

Yet if you've already tried to improve this situation by voicing your concerns and/or filing a grievance with your union, and nothing's worked, it's time to ask yourself the next set of questions. You might want to copy them and talk through them with a trusted adviser to decide what to do next. These questions aren't guaranteed to help you make a perfect decision. There's no such thing. They can help you strategize your options and reduce the chance of making a hasty decision you regret.

Questions to Ask to Decide "Should I Stay, or Should I Go?"

"Never cut a tree down in the wintertime. Never make
a negative decision in low times. Never make your
most important decisions when you are in your worst moods."
— EVANGELIST ROBERT H. SCHULLER

Schuller's right. Making an important decision when upset is unwise. As the African saying goes, "Only a fool tests the depth of the water with both feet." The following questions are a way to "test the depth of the water" before jumping in with both feet.

1. **What is happening that I don't like?** If you can give more tangible examples of the Ws (*who* said and did *what*, *where*, and *when*), you make this objective instead of subjective. Document what's taken place so this is evidence, not just opinion. What specifically is unfair, unkind, uncomfortable, inappropriate, or inequitable?

2. **Is this person/organization aware that what they're doing — or what's happening — is bothering me?** Is their behavior intentional or innocent? Could this person — or the organizational decision makers — be unaware that what they're doing or saying is disrespectful, out of line, or unwelcome; or are they aware and don't care?

3. **Is this a one-time incident or an ongoing issue?** Could this person/department be going through a particularly challenging time? Is what's happening the exception, not the rule? Is this a pattern and a persistent concern — or is this a temporary aberration that is due to a high-pressure, extraordinary event? Could extenuating circumstances be influencing or causing what they're doing and you're not taking that into account — or is this their norm?

4. **Have I already made reasonable attempts to let this person [my partner, boss, neighbor, fellow committee member] know how I feel?** Have you reported your wants and wishes, not just your complaints? Have they made any effort to improve the situation? Or have they ignored your request, made promises to change and not kept them, or, worse, attacked you for challenging them and bringing this situation up?

5. **How is this person's behavior affecting me?** Are you stressed-out, burned-out, anxious? Are you losing sleep and exhausted or experiencing headaches or stomachaches? Are you unable to focus? How is this undermining your health, quality of life, productivity, and performance? How much time do you spend rehashing what's been said or done?

6. **What will happen if I do nothing and their behavior persists?** Project ahead. Could this get better on its

own, or will it continue to get worse? Are there benefits to waiting for a better time to approach this person? Can you live with yourself if you don't speak up more forcefully than before, or will you regret not acting on behalf of your rights, needs, and priorities?

7. **What do I hope to achieve by addressing this again with them?** What are your wants and wishes? Instead of complaining about what you don't like, how could you request or recommend what you *would* like? When (timing is important), where, and how could you communicate the way you feel so this person is receptive to it? What could improve because you advocated for yourself and helped cocreate a better situation for all involved?

8. **What are the risks and potential negative outcomes of me taking action?** Are you putting your job or income at risk? Could this action result in a separation, divorce, or the end of a relationship? What are the drawbacks of confronting this person? Are you willing to face those consequences? Are there more downsides than upsides to resolving this? Even if opting out would be rocky, is it better than what you're currently experiencing? Are you ready and willing to persevere through those challenges rather than continue to endure the current situation if it stays the same?

9. **Is there any realistic chance this person will change?** Does this person or organization have any incentive to do things differently? Is this "just the way they are," and will they rebuff you, ghost you, or possibly retaliate? Or, even if this is an uncomfortable conversation, could they be glad you envisioned how to have a more mutually rewarding relationship, and will they appreciate you having the courage to initiate this?

10. **Have I discussed this dilemma with people who will be affected by my decision?** Could others have crucial, balancing input that deserves to be considered? Is there an objective third party who could mediate this situation? Have you discussed this with a counselor who could have innovative, workable insights about how to turn this situation around? Could outside input help you see this situation with fresh eyes and come up with different options and a viable, mutually beneficial solution?

Is an Honest Conversation Better Than Voting with Your Feet?

"If you're brave enough to say good-bye,
life will reward you with a new hello."
— NOVELIST PAULO COELHO

Sometimes you don't have to say goodbye to a relationship; you just have to say goodbye to certain elements that aren't working anymore. You can reward yourself with a new hello by initiating a conversation where you explore possible options for a better future.

For example, a friend's daughter, Emily, had been selected as Employee of the Year for her restaurant chain. This was wonderful news, yet it caused a dilemma, as she had just discovered she was pregnant. She was thinking of turning down the award because it didn't feel right to accept it, only to tell management she would be leaving soon.

Thank heaven for career coach Brenda Abdilla, who asked Emily, "Instead of predeciding that quitting is the only way to handle this, could you let your boss know what's happening and ask for ideas? Could you have an honest conversation instead of making a unilateral decision? What about giving them a chance to brainstorm a *next* that serves all involved?"

Emily acted on Brenda's advice, and guess what happened? Her supervisor congratulated her on her pregnancy and said the company valued her so much that they wanted to create a new part-time position so she could continue to work virtually from home. Everyone ended up happy.

Management guru Peter Drucker said, "In every success story, you will find someone who has made a courageous decision." Have the courage to go to bat for what you want instead of resigning yourself to what is.

The question is, is there a way to propose what you would love to happen instead of assuming there's not another option? If it doesn't work out, at least you'll know you gave it your all.

Before Moving On (or Moving In), Consider This

"There is a time for departure even when there's no certain place to go."
— PLAYWRIGHT AND SCREENWRITER TENNESSEE WILLIAMS

Williams's quote may be true in egregious situations where your safety (and that of your loved ones) is at risk. In most situations, though, it is smarter to know *where* you're going and *what* you'll be doing to make sure your *next* is a *trade up*.

For example, a woman met her "match" on OkCupid. She said, "It felt like kismet. We both grew up in small towns, liked the same music, worked in retail, and were fanatical about college softball. We texted and talked almost constantly for three months. When she invited me to come live with her, I didn't even think about it. I just quit my job, gave notice on my apartment, and moved, lock, stock, and barrel, cross-country to be with her.

"Within a week, I knew it was a mistake. What hadn't been apparent communicating online and over the phone was that she had a coke problem. I had been with someone before who was addicted to prescription drugs and knew this was a deal breaker. I wish I'd had your questions *before* I blew up my life. I was so in love; I wasn't thinking clearly."

If you're thinking of leaving a job or partnership — especially if it's toxic — these questions can help you think clearly about the ramifications.

1. **What resources will I need if we part company?** What will it cost in terms of money, time, emotional toll, legal headaches, energy, brainpower, or job status to exit? This is a measurable question. A major decision like quitting a job or relationship is not just an emotional or intellectual decision. It is a financial decision. Determine in terms of dollars what it will cost you so you're prepared. If you don't, you might set events in motion that monetarily devastate you, which is a double whammy.

2. **Is it my job to educate this person as to why I'm leaving? Does someone need to hold them accountable for what's wrong, and I'm that someone?** Should someone else be the messenger? Is there someone who commands more respect or status who could speak up more effectively about this issue? If so, that could increase the likelihood of a favorable outcome. If this information is coming from someone other than you, might this person actually listen and take it on board instead of dismissing it out of hand?

3. **How would leaving affect my loved ones, and what do they suggest I do?** Have you discussed this dilemma with those who will be affected by this decision? Not to worry them but to get their input? Perhaps your family would rather you leave your current job than be exhausted and burned-out, with little time for them. Perhaps your friends have secretly been wanting you to quit for a long time but didn't think you were ready to hear it. If you leave and it backfires, will you regret having initiated this?

4. **Will time heal this wound?** My aunt dearly loved my

uncle and was married to him for almost sixty years. She told me about a time when she was young and pregnant, and he was working seven days a week in his auto shop. She said, "That was a tough seven years." *Seven years?!* Others might have bailed long before that, yet they ended up sharing a rewarding life full of grandchildren and great-grandchildren. Do you want to play the long game? Maybe this is a trying time, but is it worth hanging in there? Could this be one of the downs to be expected on the roller-coaster ride of any relationship — or are you ready to get off this roller-coaster ride once and for all?

5. **Are there penalties or advantages associated with delaying?** People say timing is everything. It may not be everything, but it is certainly something. A woman on one of our virtual calls told our group, "I contracted Covid, which was complicated by a bad case of pneumonia. Thankfully, I recovered and was able to return to work. Within a week of returning, I overheard some male peers complaining about their salary. The thing was, their salary was almost double mine, and we had similar positions. I was so mad that I was going to march into my boss's office and demand this be rectified. A friend asked one question: 'Is this good timing?'

"I realized it was not good timing. I'd been out of the office for two months, and they'd had to scramble to cover my workload. It was more strategic to reestablish my value and initiate a salary discussion in the new year when the decision makers would be more receptive."

So how about you? Do your decision makers have higher priorities right now? Will it be better timing to broach this in a few months? In this case, waiting doesn't mean you are procrastinating. It means you understand the larger circumstances, and it will be advantageous to have this conversation when they'll be open to it.

6. **Is there an objective third party who could bring an impartial perspective?** Could a mediator use their professional skills to facilitate a fair conversation? An impartial third party who acts in the best interest of all involved could ensure everyone gets heard. In a divorce, the court often assigns a guardian ad litem to advocate for the children, instead of favoring one parent over the other. Is there an equivalent third party who can advocate for the greater good in your situation?

I once served as an adviser to two business partners, Denise and Ruth, who were also friends. When they decided to split the business and go their separate ways, Denise reached out to someone she knew, a longtime mediator, and asked for her help in preparing for the negotiation. By paying for an hour or two of the mediator's time, Denise was able to get clarity about what she wanted and how to ask for it, and the two partners were able to quickly come to an amicable parting of ways and remain friends. Even if you don't hire someone to engage during the negotiation, having a separate conversation with an experienced service provider, like a lawyer, coach, or mediator, can go a long way toward ensuring a satisfying outcome.

Is There a Way to Reframe Your Situation?

"You carry the passport to your own happiness."
— FASHION DESIGNER DIANE VON FÜRSTENBERG

That's an intriguing quote from Diane von Fürstenberg, isn't it? What does it mean to you? To me, it means, as Esther Hicks says, "My happiness depends on me, so you're off the hook."

My friend Glenna Salsbury has a wonderful story about this. She was married to Jim, a former linebacker for the Green Bay Packers, who loved being out on the lake. He bought a really big boat for waterskiing that wouldn't fit in their driveway, so he parked it in their backyard.

And there it sat. For months. For years. He ended up not using it for a variety of reasons. Glenna said that every time she walked out in the backyard, there was that darn boat. Every time she looked out the kitchen window, there was that darn boat. Finally, one day she'd had "enough." She got all worked up and pronounced, "Either that boat goes or I go."

Her husband looked at her and asked a simple question: "Glenna, what percentage of our relationship, in your opinion, works?"

She thought about it. "Eighty percent."

"I agree. So, let's focus on the 80 percent that *does* work instead of the 20 percent that *doesn't*. Sound good?"

She agreed... and then went out and bought a *really big rosebush*.

Bada boom. Glenna solved her problem by looking out at beauty (instead of the boat), and she and Jim had many (mostly) happy years together.

How about you? Are you looking at the beauty or the boat? Maybe these questions helped you get clarity that 80 percent of the relationship *doesn't* work and it won't get better, and it's time to move on. Whatever you decide, at least you have mentally tested the water so you can make an informed decision you can live with.

Reminder Card for When Someone (or Something) Won't Change

You're in med school. Your parents, both doctors, always "assumed" you would join the medical profession, too. You don't want to study medicine; you want to be a photographer. But your parents dismiss that as a hobby, not a career. You need to make a decision soon, as you're racking up tuition loans.

Words to Lose	Words to Use
Act rashly *"I'm quitting. I never wanted to do this in the first place."*	**Act wisely** *"I'm going to think this through from all sides so I make an informed decision."*
Walk out *"I'm just not going to class on Monday."*	**Work it out with a series of questions** *"I'm going to copy these questions and talk through them with a career counselor."*
Decide on your own *"I'm embarrassed to talk about this. People will think I'm flaky."*	**Decide with input from others** *"I like her idea to build a photography portfolio for six months so I'm not starting from scratch."*
Vote with your feet *"I don't care about the tuition or college loans. I'm out of here."*	**Test the depth of the water before you leap** *"I need to put a financial plan in place so I can pay off bills and do work I love."*

Chapter 28

I'M WONDERING IF
IT'S WORTH BEING KIND?

*"If you're still looking for that one person
who will change your life, take a look in the mirror."*

— BLOGGER ROMAN PRICE

"I'm struggling. On a daily basis, I have people upset with me
for enforcing policies they don't like and don't agree with. I try
to stay positive, but it's hard when I'm doing the best I can and
people keep taking their frustration out on me. Help!"

This comment is from a principal in Texas whose parents were
both educators. She became one, too, so she could make a difference for students, but most days she's just putting out one fire
after another.

Can you relate? If so, the next story will hopefully serve as
a reminder that we never know who's watching and who will be
influenced by our example of kindness and integrity.

One of our certified Tongue Fu! trainers, Dinny Trinidad, was
an executive with Hawaii's Prince hotels. As part of her community
service, she spoke at local high schools. She was the first from her

family to graduate from college, and she wanted young people to know how important it is to have a dream and get an education.

At one assembly in a high-school gym, she felt she wasn't getting through. Half the kids were on their phones, and the other half were talking, roughhousing, and not paying attention. As she headed out to the parking lot, Dinny came to the conclusion that her message no longer seemed relevant or meaningful to these kids, and this would be her last school talk.

Then she heard someone running up behind her. She turned as a young girl with tears in her eyes tugged at her jacket and asked, "Miss Dinny. Miss Dinny. You think I got a chance?"

Dinny reassured her that, yes, if she worked hard and believed in herself, she did indeed have a chance for a better life.

You might want to think of Dinny's story if you're running on empty and wondering if it's worth it. We never know who's watching. We never know who's feeling the impact of our words. All we know is that we have daily choices to do what we can to make a difference. And it matters.

Kindness Begets Kindness

"Perpetual optimism is a force multiplier."
— GENERAL COLIN POWELL

I recently had a rewarding experience that reinforced my belief that optimism is a force multiplier. Celeste Mergens, founder of Days for Girls International, reached out to let me know she was going to be featured on *Good Morning America* for International Day of the Girl.

I congratulated her, and she asked if we could set up a virtual call to brainstorm how she could leverage this much-welcomed media opportunity for her organization. What I couldn't have predicted is that she was reaching out to me because of something

I said at Maui Writers Conference *twenty years ago* that had changed her approach to dealing with conflict.

Celeste told me she had been invited to a meeting of the head "cutters" in a small Uganda village. In case you're not familiar with this procedure, UNICEF estimates 200 million women in thirty countries have undergone what is called FGM, female genital mutilation, which is performed by "cutters" in different villages around the globe.

When she first received the invitation, Celeste thought, *I want no part of this.* Then she thought, *You can't change behavior if you're not in the room.* So she said yes.

However, she knew that, regardless of how much she disagreed with their tradition, if she *criticized* it, these village chiefs would shut her out and not be open to anything she said. She told me, "I remembered what you said at MWC: 'Instead of making people wrong, ask *What if?* Instead of using the word *but,* use the word *and* so you're acknowledging what people believe instead of arguing with it.' So I asked, '*Why* do you have this tradition?'"

They told her it was a rite of passage. She said, "I understand why this tradition is important to you." Then she asked, "What if you could keep this custom and cut out the cut?"

Celeste told me, "At first they crossed their arms and frowned, yet I continued to calmly *ask questions* instead of *attack their customs.*"

Long story short. Within several months, the number of young girls undergoing this procedure dropped almost 30 percent. All because Celeste asked instead of argued, posed a *What if?* instead of making the tribal leaders wrong, and offered an *and* option instead of a *but* objection.

That is the powerful ripple effect and force-multiplying impact of *proactive grace.* Who knows how many girls have a healthier, happier life because of Celeste's initiative? No wonder she has been honored as among the Women of the Decade by the World Economic Forum.

Aviator Amelia Earhart said, "A single act of kindness throws out roots in all directions, and the roots spring up and make new trees."

Choose to Be a Blue-Caper

"If you're feeling helpless, go help someone."
— NOBEL PEACE PRIZE WINNER AUNG SAN SUU KYI

You may never know when, where, or how your kindness will have an impact on people. Just know that it will. Will these techniques work every time, in every situation, with every person? No. Will they make things better? Yes. And at the end of the day, you'll know you did your part to plant roots of kindness and set in motion a ripple effect of respect. And that's a win for everyone.

I had an opportunity to see Peter Diamandis, founder of XPRIZE, speak at the United Nations. He said, "There are two kinds of people, red-capers and blue-capers. Red-capers are superheroes who fight evil and injustice. Blue-capers are forces for good who elevate the human condition."

I'll admit that I thought, *Well, there are also gray-capers. They don't fight evil and justice, and they're not forces for good. They just complain about everything and don't do anything about it.*

May we all choose to be blue-capers.

Believe in the Possibilities

"When you think you have exhausted all the possibilities, remember this: you haven't."
— INVENTOR THOMAS EDISON

Remember the question at the beginning of this chapter from a school principal? That question came from Rebecca Casas — my daughter-in-law's sister. I want to wrap up this book with her story because she is a walking, talking example of why it's worth being kind.

I had an opportunity to spend a wonderful day at Guadalupe River State Park with the extended Casas family, and she told me about a normal (although there's no such thing as normal) day in the life of a school principal.

Becky's a single mom. She gets up at 4:30 a.m. to go to the gym (!) before coming home to get her three sons ready for school. She's on campus by 7 a.m. and out front, ready to greet the parents and students as they arrive. Some of the parents are not happy about the quarantine and the mask/vaccination policy and let her know about it.

She walks the halls, paying special attention to the kids. Are any of them looking particularly hungry, scared, lonely, sad? She checks in with the school cafeteria staff, the faculty, the administrative team, the bus drivers, and her vice principal. She walks into her office to an email inbox stuffed with hundreds of messages regarding school board meetings, IEP paperwork, curriculum and test requirements, legal and financial documents that need to be approved, field-trip arrangements ... and that's all before 9 a.m.

She told me about a particularly challenging situation. A grandmother had called, again, begging her to please do something about her third-grade grandson with special needs. This young man has a spinal injury and had not been able to go to class because the elevator was broken. The grandmother was exhausted taking care of him all day and night and pleaded with Becky to please, please, do something.

Becky had tried to do something, for weeks. She had called the elevator company numerous times. They were short-staffed, and the school was on a long waiting list. She had talked with the local fire department to see if there was some way they could help.

There wasn't anything they could do. Becky looked at me. "Then I figured out what we could do."

I couldn't wait to hear the answer. "What?"

"We moved his third-grade classroom to the ground floor."

Brilliant! Not so fast. Becky said, "Not everyone was happy with that decision. His teacher was initially upset because she's on the floor with the kindergarten teachers instead of with her peers. But I'm clear, my first responsibility is to the students. It was the right thing to do."

Kindness Is Human Beauty

"Whenever you are creating beauty around you,
you are restoring your own soul."
— Pulitzer Prize–winning author Alice Walker

Kudos to Becky. Even though she was exhausted, she never believed she had exhausted all possibilities. In creating this beautiful solution, she restored her soul and the souls of the people around her who were positively affected by her willingness to continue to give instead of give up.

Are you running on empty? I recall what Viktor Frankl said in *Man's Search for Meaning*: "Everything can be taken from a man but one thing: the last of human freedoms — to choose one's attitude in any given set of circumstances, to choose one's own way."

He's right. Whatever you're facing, you still have the freedom to be the quality of person you want to be — and the quality of person the people around you need you to be. That is your legacy. It is one of the only things you can control. It is in your hands and in your heart.

And it matters.

Reminder Card of What to Do If You're Wondering If Being Kind Is Worth It

Imagine your mother has dementia. You find it painful to see your smart, talented mom in this condition. You wonder if you should keep visiting, as she doesn't even recognize you anymore.

Words to Lose	Words to Use
Helpless *"No matter how hard I try to jog her memory, she doesn't even know who I am."*	**Helpful** *"I am going to brush her hair today. She loves that."*
Give up *"Why visit if she doesn't register my presence?"*	**Keep giving** *"I remember the thousands of hours she poured into raising me. I can do this."*
Cruel world *"She's always been fit and healthy. This is so unfair."*	**Kind world** *"I will continue to be caring and kind. For her and for me."*
Gray-caper *"I wish her doctor had caught it sooner."*	**Blue-caper** *"I'm going to reach out to the families of other dementia patients to form a support group."*
Problem thinker *"It breaks my heart to see her like this."*	**Possibility thinker** *"I'll play her favorite big-band songs today. That may jog some memories."*

Summary and Action Plan

— WHAT'S NEXT? —

"I'm sick of following my dreams. I'm just going to ask them where they're going and hook up with them later."

— COMEDIAN MITCH HEDBERG

So, what are your dreams? Where are you going in your life, career, and relationships? The people skills outlined throughout this book can help take you there.

That is not just *my* opinion. A 2022 *Forbes* article by Caroline Castrillon cited Rohan Rajiv, LinkedIn's director of product management, as saying, "Soft skills have become even more important given the rise of remote work and are growing in importance across industries. In fact, they were featured in 78% of jobs posted globally in 2022. Hard skills can get a recruiter's attention, but soft skills help you land the job."

A 2015 article by Sara Kehaulani Goo on the Pew Research Center website references a study where adults were asked, "Which skills do you think are most important for children to get ahead in the world today?" The answer was clear. Across the board, respondents said "communication skills were most important, followed by reading, math, teamwork, and logic."

Finally, Thomas Oppong wrote an article on the Stanford Center for Compassion and Altruism Research and Education website that claims, "Good social relationships are the most consistent predictor of a happy life."

So, what's that mean for you?

Make what you've learned here a priority in your life.

Comedian Judy Tenuta says, "My parents always told me I wouldn't amount to anything because I procrastinate so much. I told them, '*Just wait.*'"

If you want your life and legacy to amount to something, if you want to be wealthy in what matters, don't wait. Start putting these proactive-grace practices into action — today.

SHOW THE SHIFT SUMMARY
OF *TALKING ON EGGSHELLS*

"Practice what you teach or change your speech."

— MUSICAL ARTIST JAIRUS L. ADAMS

This summary shows how to turn conflict into cooperation by replacing words to lose with words to use. Post this where you can see it (on your refrigerator? by your laptop or desk?) so it can help you practice what you preach *and* change your speech.

Chapter	Situation	Shift from	Shift to
1	Talking on eggshells	Avoid	Assert
2	ISA: Interpersonal Situational Awareness	React to the room	Read/lead the room
3	Proactive grace	Contempt	Compassion
4	P.L.A.N.	Leave it to chance	P.L.A.N. in advance

Chapter	Situation	Shift from	Shift to
5	Rudeness	*Can't because …*	*Can as soon as …*
6	Arguing	*But*	*And*
7	Blaming	Find fault	Find solutions
8	Making mistakes	*Should*	Shape
9	Teasing	Flustered	Fun Fu!
10	Making false accusations	Deny	Redirect
11	Sadness	Advice	Empathy
12	Complaining	Explain	AAA Train
13	Not cooperating	Stop	Start
14	Making excuses	Reasons	Results
15	Not listening	Lecture	Look, Lean, Lift, Level
16	Talking nonstop	Allow to go on and on	Tactful Termination
17	Pressuring	Give in	Give a clear *no*
18	Carrying a grudge	Focus on being wronged	Fresh start
19	Ignoring rules	No rules	Establish and enforce rules
20	Feeling unseen	Accidental brand	Intentional brand
21	Feeling afraid	Limiting story	Limitless story
22	Feeling nervous	Do the doubts	Do the math
23	Feeling angry	Suppress	Express responsibly
24	Manipulation	Drawn into drama	Distanced from drama
25	Bullying	*I* reply	*You* reply

Chapter	Situation	Shift from	Shift to
26	Making life miserable	Go it alone	Go it together
27	Unwillingness to change	Rash move	Wise move
28	Continuing to be kind	Gray-caper	Blue-caper

— ACKNOWLEDGMENTS —

Anyone who has written a book understands why authors often thank a long list of contributors.

Friends, family, and colleagues are the wind beneath our writing wings during the months it takes to complete a manuscript. When our project is finally finished, we want to let them know how much their encouragement and input meant to us.

So heartfelt thanks to the following individuals. I am oh-so-grateful to know you and glad you're in my life.

Cheri Grimm, my sister and longtime business partner, for being exhibit A of proactive grace. I can hardly express what it means to share our life together and work with someone I trust implicitly who is an ongoing resource of support and centered wisdom.

My sons Tom and Andrew, and their families, for becoming my teachers and gifting me with the blessing of what it feels like to be wealthy in what matters.

Georgia Hughes, Editorial Director at New World Library. Who could've predicted all those years ago when swimming at Maui Writers Conference pool parties that we'd have the pleasure and privilege of doing a book together? Thanks to you, and to Managing Editor Kristen Cashman, Publicity Director Monique Muhlenkamp, and the rest of the NWL team for being an advocate for this work and helping to get it out in the world.

Authors always say, "I couldn't have done this without you," and it's true. Heartfelt thanks to Heidi Giusto, Denise Brosseau, Judy Gray, Sherry Cormier, Kendra Wray, and Mary LoVerde Coln for everything you poured into this project and for your 1 + 1 = 11 partnership. Your acumen, different perspectives, rising-tide worldview, and crackerjack editorial suggestions all made this a better book.

Agent Laurie Liss, for representing me all these years and being a champion for my work.

Mahalo to the program participants — and experts I interviewed for this book — for generously sharing your stories and insights. I have included your books, podcasts, TED talks, and websites in the notes section as a way of showing my appreciation for your contributions. I hope people choose to access and benefit from your work on how we can get along better with just about anyone, anytime, anywhere.

— NOTES —

Some of the quotations and ideas that I've mentioned from other thinkers have come from hearing their speeches or podcasts or from personal conversations I've had with them, so no source is provided. For other references, sources are cited here.

Introduction

p. 3   *"Rudeness is on the rise"*: "Rudeness on the Rise," McKinsey Quarterly Five Fifty, McKinsey & Company, 2021, https://www.mckinsey.com /capabilities/people-and-organizational-performance/our-insights /five-fifty-rudeness-on-the-rise.

p. 4   *fight fire with water*: Barry Nalebuff, interview by Guy Kawasaki, *Remarkable People*, podcast, 51:33, August 10, 2022, https://podcasts .apple.com/us/podcast/barry-nalebuff-the-only-negotiation-guide -youll-ever-need/id1483081827?i=1000577215033.

Chapter 1: Why Do We Talk on Eggshells?

p. 14   *a* fixed *mindset or a* growth *mindset*: Carol S. Dweck, *Mindset: The New Psychology of Success* (New York: Ballantine Books, 2007).

Chapter 2: Develop Interpersonal Situational Awareness

p. 20   *A failure to notice what's happening*: Daniel Goleman, "Why Aren't We More Compassionate?" TED: Ideas Worth Spreading, video, 13:01, https://www.ted.com/talks/daniel_goleman_why_aren_t_we_more _compassionate?language=en.

Chapter 3: Set an Example of Proactive Grace

p. 39   *"It's virtually impossible"*: John Gottman, "How Do You Know Whether a Couple Will Divorce?," Gottman Institute, YouTube video, 1:06, May 2, 2018, https://www.youtube.com/watch?v=VUPL9jFj-Jg&list =PL62C8B1A0CoB678C2&index=1.

p. 39   *"Contempt is the most poisonous"*: Ellie Lisitsa, "The Four Horsemen: Contempt," Gottman Institute, accessed January 24, 2023, https://www .gottman.com/blog/the-four-horsemen-contempt.

Chapter 5: Rude?

p. 53   *"anonymity may make it easy"*: Joe Dawson, "Who Is That? The Study of Anonymity and Behavior," Association for Psychological Science *Observer*, March 30, 2018, https://www.psychologicalscience.org /observer/who-is-that-the-study-of-anonymity-and-behavior.

p. 56   *"Rudeness in the workplace"*: University of Florida study, cited in "It's Official: Workplace Rudeness Is Contagious," *ScienceDaily*, July 16, 2015, https://www.sciencedaily.com/releases/2015/07/150716092017.htm.

Chapter 6: Arguing and Disagreeing?

p. 65   *"Why would that be surprising?"*: *CBS Sunday Morning*, "Remembering RBG," YouTube video, 10:52, September 20, 2020, https://www .youtube.com/watch?v=dbEui7DSBCY.

p. 69   *another example of how people from different backgrounds*: "Barack Obama and Bruce Springsteen on Race, Friendship and the Influence of Fathers," interview by Anthony Mason, *CBS Sunday Morning*, October 24, 2021, https://www.cbsnews.com/news/barack-obama-and -bruce-springsteen-on-race-friendship-and-the-influence-of-fathers.

p. 70   *there are basically four types of regrets*: Daniel H. Pink, *The Power of Regret: How Looking Backward Moves Us Forward* (New York: Riverhead Books, 2022).

Chapter 8: Making Mistakes?

p. 91   *try this approach created by Erin Weed*: Erin Weed, originator of Head, Heart, Core approach, www.erinweed.com.

Chapter 9: Teasing or Taunting?

p. 97   *"I'm a lot younger than I look"*: Lan Nguyen Chaplin, "How to Disrupt a System That Was Built to Hold You Back," *Harvard Business Review*, March 8, 2021, https://hbr.org/2021/03/how-to-disrupt-a-system-that -was-built-to-hold-you-back.

p. 98   *"It enhances your intake of 'oxygen-rich air'"*: "Stress Relief from Laughter? It's No Joke," Healthy Lifestyle, Mayo Clinic, July 29, 2021, https://www.mayoclinic.org/healthy-lifestyle/stress-management/in -depth/stress-relief/art-20044456.

Chapter 10: Making False Accusations?

p. 111   *"weed out toxic people before they join your organization"*: Christine Porath, "How to Avoid Hiring a Toxic Employee," *Harvard Business Review*, February 3, 2016, https://hbr.org/2016/02/how-to-avoid -hiring-a-toxic-employee.

p. 112   *check out Dana Wilkie's excellent article*: Dana Wilkie, "Workplace Gossip: What Crosses the Line?" Society of Human Resource Management blog, March 3, 2014, https://blog.shrm.org/workforce/workplace -gossip-what-crosses-the-line.

Chapter 11: Sad or Unhappy?

p. 125   *You can find a directory of support organizations*: Joseph Bennington-Castro, "The Right Resources Can Help You Manage Depression," Everyday Health, September 27, 2021, https://www.everydayhealth.com /depression/guide/resources/.

Chapter 12: Complaining?

p. 136   *"If you took one-tenth the energy"*: Randy Pausch, "Achieving Your Childhood Dreams," lecture, Carnegie Mellon University, September 18, 2007, https://www.youtube.com/watch?v=ji5_MqicxSo.

Chapter 15: Not Listening?

p. 159   *"Even a phone facedown on a table"*: Sherry Turkle, *Reclaiming Conversation: The Power of Talk in a Digital Age* (New York: Penguin Books, 2016).

p. 162   *"Technology is causing a set of seemingly disconnected things"*: Rachel Lerman, "Q&A: Ex-Googler Harris on How Tech 'Downgrades' Humans," *AP News*, August 10, 2019, https://apnews.com/article /technology-business-data-privacy-apple-inc-dea7f32d16364c6093 f19b938370d600.

p. 163   *"The only form of ethical persuasion that exists"*: Nicholas Thompson, "Our Minds Have Been Hijacked by Our Phones. Tristan Harris Wants to Rescue Them," *Wired*, July 26, 2017, https://www.wired.com/story /our-minds-have-been-hijacked-by-our-phones-tristan-harris-wants -to-rescue-them/.

p. 163   *"This is overpowering human nature"*: Tristan Harris in *The Social Dilemma*, Netflix Original Documentary, directed by Jeff Orlowski-Yang, 2020.

p. 163   *these alarming statistics*: Trevor Wheelwright, "Usage Statistics: How Obsessed Are We?," Reviews.org, January 24, 2022, https://www .reviews.org/mobile/cell-phone-addiction.

Chapter 17: Pressuring Me?

p. 178   *I interviewed Mike Domitrz*: See Mike Domitrz, Center for Respect, https://www.centerforrespect.com/about-the-center-for-respect.

Chapter 18: Carrying a Grudge?

p. 191   *Stay in Cleveland*: The Holderness Family, "Our Biggest Fight: The Battle of the Bra," Holderness Family Laughs, YouTube video, 7:17, April 24, 2018, https://www.youtube.com/watch?v=Ruodj3ImLwM.

p. 194   *"simply didn't know how to explain"*: Hinge, "Ghosting," Medium.com, September 3, 2020, https://medium.com/@hingeapp/ghosting-d3248 b07bc5f.

Chapter 19: Ignoring Rules or Boundaries?

p. 200   *excerpts from Larry Harvey's visionary 10 Principles*: Larry Harvey, "The 10 Principles of Burning Man," Burning Man Project, https:// burningman.org/about/10-principles.

p. 203   *"There are around 55 million meetings"*: "28 Incredible Meeting Statistics [2022]: Virtual, Zoom, In-Person Meetings and Productivity," Zippia.com, September 21, 2022, https://www.zippia.com/advice /meeting-statistics.

Chapter 20: Feel Unseen, Unheard, or Unappreciated?

p. 211   *"59% of people say"*: "Survey: 59% of People Have NEVER Had a Boss Who 'Truly Appreciates' Their Work," Workplace News, Study Finds, March 5, 2022, https://studyfinds.org/workers-feel-underappreciated -by-boss.

p. 218   *"This is it, you're in the room"*: Jennifer Palmieri, quoted in Juliet Eilperin, "White House Women Want to Be in the Room Where It Happens," *Washington Post*, September 13, 2016, https://www.washingtonpost .com/news/powerpost/wp/2016/09/13/white-house-women-are-now -in-the-room-where-it-happens.

p. 220   *a heartfelt blog post*: Seizing Hope blog, "The Unseen-Siblings of Special Needs Kids," February 24, 2015, https://seizinghope.com/2015/02/24 /the-unseen-siblings-of-special-needs-kids.

Chapter 21: Feel Afraid to Speak Up?

p. 226   *"Viewers may see my right hand"*: Carson Daly, quoted in Jenna Ryu, "Carson Daly Says He's Suffered from Anxiety, Panic Attacks on 'The Voice,'" *USA TODAY*, May 31, 2022, https://www.usatoday.com/story /life/health-wellness/2022/05/31/carson-daly-today-show-mental -health-series-anxiety-the-voice/9906476002.

p. 226   *free, confidential resources that can help you*: See Centers for Disease Control and Prevention mental health tools and resources: https:// www.cdc.gov/mentalhealth/tools-resources/individuals/index.htm.

p. 227   *"We laugh at people"*: Adam Grant, interviewed by Rich Roll, "Argue Like You're Right, Listen Like You're Wrong," *Rich Roll Podcast*, YouTube video, 1:53:59, February 15, 2021, https://www.youtube.com /watch?v=hQHlvXha4do.

Chapter 23: Feel Angry?

p. 249   *"'Going high' doesn't mean"*: Michelle Obama, quoted in Raisa Bruner, "Michelle Obama Explains What 'Going High' Really Means," *Time*, November 20, 2018, https://time.com/5459984/michelle-obama-go -high.

Chapter 24: Someone Is Being Manipulative?

p. 264 *TV interview early in her career*: Vikram Murthi, "Watch Helen Mirren Take Down Sexist Interviewer Back in 1975," IndieWire, two videos, 7:29 and 7:33, August 23, 2016, https://www.indiewire.com/2016/08 /helen-mirren-sexist-interviewer-1975-michael-parkinson-1201719445.

Chapter 25: Someone Is Being a Bully?

p. 280 *triad of bully, bullied, and bystander*: Barbara Coloroso, *The Bully, the Bullied, and the Bystander: From Preschool to High School — How Parents and Teachers Can Help Break the Cycle, Updated Edition* (New York: HarperCollins Publishers, 2009).

p. 282 *"48.6 million Americans are bullied at work"*: "2021 WBI U.S. Workplace Bullying Survey," Workplace Bullying Institute (WBI), accessed January 24, 2023, https://workplacebullying.org/2021-wbi-survey.

p. 282 *I am making my "Never Be Bullied Again" training video available*: See Sam Horn, "Never Be Bullied Again," YouTube video, 29:35, https:// www.youtube.com/watch?v=5zmgf3qOXMo. For additional antibullying resources, please consult the following sources. Pacer.org, "Pacer's National Bullying Prevention Center," https://www.pacer.org/bullying /info/stats.asp: this website provides an overview of research findings on bullying, numerous free videos, and resources. Stopbullying.gov, https://www.stopbullying.gov: this U.S. government website contains resources and information on bullying, including cyberbullying. National Domestic Violence Hotline, https://www.thehotline.org or 800-799-7233: if you're being bullied at home, use this hotline, which is available 24-7.

Chapter 26: Someone Is Making My Life Miserable?

p. 290 *Susan David's TED talk had prompted*: Susan David, "The Gift and Power of Emotional Courage," TED: Ideas Worth Spreading, video, 16:39, https://www.ted.com/talks/susan_david_the_gift_and_power _of_emotional_courage?language=en.

Summary and Action Plan: What's Next?

p. 312 *"Soft skills have become even more important"*: Rohan Rajiv, quoted in Caroline Castrillon, "Why Soft Skills Are More in Demand Than Ever," *Forbes*, September 18, 2022, https://www.forbes.com/sites/caroline

castrillon/2022/09/18/why-soft-skills-are-more-in-demand-than-ever/?sh=514135515c6f.

p. 312   *"communication skills were most important"*: Sara Kehaulani Goo, "The Skills Americans Say Kids Need to Succeed in Life," Pew Research Center, February 19, 2015, https://www.pewresearch.org/fact-tank/2015 /02/19/skills-for-success.

p. 313   *"Good social relationships are the most consistent predictor"*: Thomas Oppong, "Good Social Relationships Are the Most Consistent Predictor of a Happy Life," Center for Compassion and Altruism Research and Education, Stanford Medicine, October 18, 2019, http://ccare .stanford.edu/press_posts/good-social-relationships-are-the-most -consistent-predictor-of-a-happy-life.

— INDEX —

— ABOUT THE AUTHOR —

Sam Horn is the founder and CEO of the Intrigue Agency and the Tongue Fu!® Training Institute. The Intrigue Agency helps people design and deliver one-of-a-kind presentations, pitches, books, businesses, and brands that scale their impact — for good. The Tongue Fu!® Training Institute offers training workshops and keynotes on Sam's trademarked communication approach, which teaches how to give and get respect at work, at home, online, and in public. Sam also certifies people in her Tongue Fu!®, Talking on Eggshells, and Take the Bully by the Horns methodologies.

Sam is the author of nine books from major publishers, including *Tongue Fu!®*, *POP!*, *What's Holding You Back?*, *Someday Is Not a Day in the Week*, and *Got Your Attention?* Her work has been featured in the *New York Times*, *Forbes*, *Reader's Digest*, and *Harvard Business Review*, and on NBC, CBS, ABC, Fox, and NPR.

Sam has spoken to more than half a million people worldwide and for clients including Boeing, Intel, Capital One, Cisco, Nationwide, Four Seasons Resorts, Accenture, Oracle, National Geographic, and American Bankers Association. She is a popular LinkedIn Learning instructor and has been hired by NASA,

TED Fellows, Entrepreneurs' Organization, and Richard Branson's New Now Leaders to teach their leaders how to speak clearly, concisely, and compellingly.

Sam's books have been published in seventeen languages, and she has spoken internationally in China, Germany, England, Greece, the Netherlands, Ireland, Japan, and Canada.

Sam served as the pitch coach for Springboard Enterprises, which has helped entrepreneurs generate $26 billion in funding/valuation. She has been brought in by TED Fellows, SXSW, and Inc. 500 to teach how to pitch. LinkedIn hired Sam to produce a series on communication that has been used by Amazon, Walmart, and Accenture as part of their employee training. She cofounded the Business Book Festival (held at the *USA TODAY* headquarters) and served as the executive director of the world-renowned Maui Writers Conference for seventeen years.

Want to:

- arrange for Sam to keynote your convention, provide training, or host a book club?
- get certified in these techniques so you can get paid to teach them to your organization's employees or to audiences in public workshops and conferences?
- interview Sam for your publication, podcast, or TV show?
- share a success story of how this book has affected you?
- receive Sam's monthly newsletter?

Contact her and her team at 805-528-4251 or **Sam@SamHorn.com** or via her website, **SamHorn.com**.